Strategic Choices

Supremacy, Survival, or Sayonara

Kenneth I. Primozic
IBM

Edward A. Primozic
IBM

Joe Leben
Leben, Inc.

McGraw-Hill, Inc.

New York   St. Louis   San Francisco   Auckland   Bogotá
Caracas   Hamburg   Lisbon   London   Madrid
Mexico   Milan   Montreal   New Delhi   Paris
San Juan   São Paulo   Singapore
Sydney   Tokyo   Toronto

Library of Congress Cataloging-in-Publication Data

Primozic, Kenneth.
    Strategic choices : supremacy, survival, or sayonara / Kenneth I.
Primozic, Edward A. Primozic, Joe Leben.
        p.   cm.
    Includes index.
    ISBN 0-07-051036-9 :
    1. Strategic planning.   I. Primozic, Edward A.   II. Leben, Joe.
III. Title.
HD30.28.P75   1991
658.4'012—dc20   90-36642
                                                                        CIP

1 2 3 4 5 6 7 8 9 0   DOC/DOC   9 8 7 6 5 4 3 2 1 0

ISBN 0-07-051036-9

*The sponsoring editor for this book was James H. Bessent, Jr., the editing
supervisor was Suzette André, the designer was Naomi Auerbach, and the
production supervisor was Suzanne W. Babeuf. It was set in Baskerville by
McGraw-Hill's Professional & Reference Division composition unit.*

Printed and bound by R. R. Donnelley & Sons Company.

To our parents . . .
who provided the direction and made the
sacrifices.

To our families . . .
who furnished the motivation and gave the
encouragement.

To our friends . . .
who challenged the assumptions and
questioned the ideas.

Thank you for writing this book; we just put it
on paper.

About the Authors

KENNETH and EDWARD PRIMOZIC joined the IBM Corporation in 1965 and 1966, respectively. They work as business development and management consultants both within IBM and externally with IBM's customers. Creators of the innovative management concepts and strategic planning techniques described in this book, they also assist communities and schools in applying these concepts and tools to local economic, educational, and development programs. They are the coauthors of *Linkage Analysis Planning* and contributed to *Labor Force 2000: Corporate America Responds I* and *II*, which were commissioned for the Allstate Forum on Public Issues.

JOE LEBEN is an independent consultant who writes books and develops technical training courses for the information systems industry.

Contents

Appendixes

Foreword

Planning the strategy of a corporation remains the most important activity in business and one of the most difficult to get right. Unfortunately, most books on the subject either get bogged down in the details of process or soar off on the author's pet theme as if one noble idea were all that was needed to invigorate the plans of an enterprise. *Strategic Choices* does neither. It avoids dwelling on the *process* of planning, and it presents not one but many new ideas. Perhaps the book's greatest strength is that it explains how to translate *vision* into an agenda for *action*—the thing that is missing from so many strategic planning exercises. Too often, strategic planning efforts either focus so much energy on documenting the status quo and all its threats and problems that no time remains to plan the future, or they describe the vision of the firm in grand terms with no link to what must be done to reach that exalted state. *Strategic Choices* shows how to avoid both pitfalls.

The authors' overriding message, which is implied in the *make no assumptions,* "linkage analysis planning" methodology described in the book, is that corporate leadership requires a reconsideration of every premise embedded in the strategy of the firm. Some of my business school students have found a bumper sticker that reflects the same view: *Assume nothing!* The authors make a compelling case for such skepticism. Only a fundamental reassessment of the underlying rationale of a corporation's strategy will do. The most significant events in a firm's future cannot be predicted reliably; so companies that prosper in the 1990s and beyond must build enterprises that are surprise-proof as well as ahead of the trends that can be foreseen. Many of today's trends are the result of the rapid creation of information and its dissemination through electronic links among corporations. Interorganizational information systems and the information content of products and services are important themes of the book. They should be, for they will transform the relationships among suppliers, customers, and regulators just as certainly as computers and telecommunications transformed administrative functions in the 1970s and 1980s.

One of the most exciting notions in *Strategic Choices* is a process for linking the firm's vision, strategy, tactics, and implementation plans to gain competitive advantage. This linkage analysis planning technique provides a powerful tool for ensuring that the strength of a corporate vision is actually translated into operational programs and actions. Another extremely useful concept is the use of above-the-line revenue generation activities and below-the-line cost savings as a way to evaluate the projects and agendas generated by strategic thinking.

I hope you enjoy and profit from this excellent addition to the lore of strategic thinking.

Brandt Allen
University of Virginia

Preface

Dynamic and global changes are occurring in today's business, education, and government environments. Our industries, our public institutions, our jobs—the very fabric of our lives—are undergoing drastic change. These changes have been described as chaotic. We are living in a world where technology is reshaping our lives, where globalization of the economy is changing the rules of competition, and where a transition to the Information Age is both opening up and shrinking the world. The populations of the developed countries are aging, and we are facing significant skills shortages. At the same time the populations of the underdeveloped countries are becoming increasingly better educated and more aggressive. In this environment *time*, unless we effectively exploit it, may be one of our most formidable enemies. We must *make no assumptions* about the changes that are occurring.

How can our business, education, and government organizations successfully compete and survive in an increasingly hostile world? What can we do today to regain the initiative and to successfully compete in a world where yesterday's rules do not apply? What are the new management tools that will help us plot a successful course in the future? The realities of the new environment will test every leader in every organization. We must achieve new levels of organizational effectiveness and teamwork in all sectors of the economy if we are to successfully compete and raise our standard of living. It is critical that we clearly understand the changes that are occurring. We must adopt new leadership approaches if our organizations are to survive in tomorrow's world. America's edge has been dulled, and the job of rehoning its steel is in the hands of us all.

Like many other books before it, this book describes the challenges we face. But it goes much further and provides a powerful set of new management tools that have assisted managers in both large and small organizations, in both the private and public sectors, to significantly raise the level of effectiveness of their organizations. These tools can help us to formulate a *strategic vision* for the organization. This vision can help the organization to identify new ways to achieve what Michael Porter and Victor Millar, in a landmark *Harvard Business Review* article, have termed "substantial and sustainable competitive advantage." This book describes visual techniques for *strategic thinking* that can help in evaluating business decisions and in identifying tomorrow's opportunities. It provides a *new set of lenses* for viewing today's environment and the new environments that are emerging. These new lenses aid in visualizing the *linkages* that exist between key elements in the environment of today in order to help choose the investments that the organization must make to remain competitive tomorrow. It provides a *new vocabulary* for effectively communicating the strategic vision and embedding it firmly in the organization's management culture.

Chapter 1 characterizes the environment of the 1990s, describes the major challenges that leaders will face in the new environment, and emphasizes that what is needed to cope with this environment is *strategic thinking* followed by *strategic action*.

The chapters in Part 1 present new ways of thinking that will help in formulating a strategic vision for yourself, for your department or division, and for your enterprise as a whole. In formulating a vision, we must understand the *waves of innovation* through which the organization is passing with respect to the use of technology, determine new ways of exploiting *experience curve strategies,* and identify how the organization can begin to redefine the *power relationships* that exist in the organization's sector of the economy. This leads to an understanding of why we must begin viewing the organization as part of an *extended enterprise* to help visualize how *electronic channels* can provide new ways of operating in the extended enterprise environment.

Part 2 discusses techniques for developing effective strategies for achieving the vision that Part 1 helps to form and articulate. It discusses the *changing roles of management* in today's environment, describes the *new mindsets* that are required for the organization to remain competitive, and shows ways in which the organization can *restructure its channels* for distributing products and services as well as disseminating information and knowledge.

Part 3 presents new methods for doing the planning that is necessary for achieving strategic advantage. These planning methods help in applying the concepts discussed in Parts 1 and 2. They can be used by an individual or by the manager of a department or division in achieving strategic advantage in any area of the organization; however, their greatest impact will be felt if they are used at the highest levels of management to guide the strategic planning for the entire organization. The planning techniques presented in Part 3 provide a proven, effective, and powerful alternative to the cumbersome strategic planning techniques that organizations have used in the past. The new simple, sensible planning techniques described in Part 3 *make no assumptions*. They can be used to aid in *forming a vision, actualizing that vision, and building the new organization* that is required to innovate and be successful in our dynamic and competitive world.

It is our hope that *Strategic Choices* will have a significant impact on your own performance on the job. We also hope that this book will have an impact on restructuring and repositioning organizations in the United States for competing in the 1990s and beyond. Finally, we hope it will contribute in a small way toward reasserting the economic strength of America.

Acknowledgments

This book could not have been written without the generous help of a great many individuals. We would like to give special thanks for the significant assistance provided by Benn Konsynski of Harvard University. Thanks are also due to our many friends at IBM, including Yvon Baley, France; Robert Berland, United States; Brad Lightner, United States; Peter Vamos, Australia; and the executive management team of IBM. We would like to thank our friends in education: Robert Gholson, IBM; Dr. Jean McGrew, Glenbrook School District; Dr. Jose Oliva, Parents and Children Together Organized for Family Learning, New Jersey; Lawrence Williford, Allstate Insurance; and to the many educators in California, Colorado, Indiana, Illinois, Maryland, New Jersey, Utah, West Virginia, and Canada who provided us with assistance. The American Association of School Administrators and Allstate Insurance also helped us in applying linkage analysis techniques to education. Many of the illustrations were developed with the assistance of Image Base of Chicago, Illinois. Finally, we would like to thank Brandt Allen of the University of Virginia for his support and for the excellent Foreword.

Kenneth I. Primozic
Edward A. Primozic
Joe Leben

Innovative Leadership is the ability to . . .

- Formulate a vision for achieving strategic advantage
- Create strategies and plans for adapting and innovating in the changing environment
- Develop tactics for implementing the strategies and plans
- Implement the vision by empowering individuals with the necessary skills

. . . leading to new levels of organizational effectiveness.

1
New Leadership Challenges

Introduction

As the preface to this book has pointed out, the dynamic and challenging environment of the 1990s is creating new exposures as well as new opportunities. The changes that are occurring are having a major impact on the operations, marketing, and distribution strategies of all types of enterprise, in both the private and public sectors. Our challenge in the 1990s will be to develop and continually evolve effective strategies and tactics that individuals and organizations require to *exploit* the changes that are occurring. Many of these changes are technological in nature, and we must understand the capabilities of the new technologies that leading organizations are already employing. The authors are convinced that between the years 1990 and 2000 we will witness a technological revolution the likes of which the world has never seen. The radical changes that are occurring are already restructuring our economy and will require profound changes in the way we manage our organizations. For many, the issue will be either to exploit the new technologies or to *be* exploited by those organizations that do.

A question that we must ask is this: Is our organization a technology leader or a technology follower? Are the strategies that the organization is pursuing proactive with respect to technology or reactive? Strategy involves thinking and deliberate decision making—management consciously thinking about and selecting one course of action over another. But does the organization consciously think about technology when developing strategic plans? The answer to this question may be the same as the answer to the questions we asked at the beginning of this paragraph. The relationship between technology and strategy has tradition-

1

ally been a reactive one, and a company's posture toward technology typically follows from its overall corporate strategy. Typically, no emphasis has been given to the relationship in the opposite direction—on how technology can itself shape the corporate strategy. It is no longer appropriate to develop strategic plans in a vacuum and then try to identify the technology that is required to implement those plans. Thinking about technology must now be an integral part of the strategic planning process. The strategy makers must have a firm grasp of technology—past, present, and future—in order to do a good job of strategic planning.

It is important, however, to note that technology alone will not create strategic advantage. Choosing the targets for the application of technology, developing appropriate strategies, and correctly positioning the organization are all essential steps in using technology effectively. Much has already been written on the use of technology to achieve strategic advantage, and we will provide many examples of what leading organizations have already done. But little has been said or written about how individuals, in organizations like your own, can repeat what these leading organizations have done. In this book, we present tools that you can use to help your organization identify opportunities for achieving strategic advantage.

We begin this introductory chapter by analyzing the business environment as it has existed in the past and as it exists today. We then show how our environment is rapidly changing and examine the transitions that will be needed for success in the 1990s. We then contrast the goals of the traditional business planning techniques that we have used in the past with the requirements for new strategic planning techniques. We then conclude this introductory chapter by presenting a simple planning model that you can use to assess your own position with respect to innovation and your organization's position as well.

Analyzing the Business Environment

Let us begin by looking at the business environment that existed in the United States immediately after World War II. After all, we must know where we have been before we can decide where we want to go. After World War II, the United States began to play an increasingly important role in the world economy. Its greatness in this simpler time was based on:

- Abundant natural resources
- A superior educational system

- A superior manufacturing and agricultural base
- Inexpensive skills
- Inexpensive and abundant energy
- Technical leadership
- Abundant capital
- A superior transportation infrastructure
- A superior communications system

All the preceding were unmatched in the world and in aggregate provided America with overwhelming advantages in the global marketplace. But now let us contrast this environment with the environment in which we find ourselves today. Figure 1-1 illustrates many of the important strategic environmental forces that are at play today in the United States. The following describes some of the ways in which these forces are affecting the U.S. economy:

1. The United States no longer enjoys many of the strategic advantages that it had immediately following World War II.

2. Because we have lost many of our strategic advantages, our competitiveness as an economy has become dramatically diminished.

3. We now live in a global economy in which competition is becoming an increasingly important issue. Of great importance to the competitive environment will be the European Economic Community of 1992 and the changing Eastern Europe. The growing role that Ja-

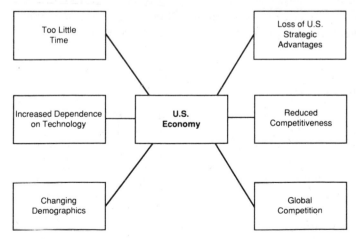

Figure 1-1. Strategic environmental forces having an impact on the U.S. economy.

pan, the Pacific Rim countries, and some South American nations are playing in the global marketplace is also having a significant affect on the ability of U.S. business to effectively compete.

4. Changing demographics is beginning to suggest that we may no longer have an abundance of the skills needed to drive the economy using yesterday's management techniques; the leveraging of our knowledge resources will become increasingly more critical.

5. Technology is playing an increasingly important role in all types of organization as we move toward an knowledge-based economy.

6. Time has become our most critical resource. In the past, we had ample time to react to changes that occurred in the business environment. We now often have little time to react. Technology and the rapid rate of technological innovation is rapidly shrinking both time and distance.

So we now live in an era where classical industry definitions are blurring and powerful interdependencies exist. In essence, the playing fields have all been leveled. We live in an information age, in which 70 percent of the economy is driven by information; therefore technology is playing an ever-expanding role in our lives. The leaders achieve success in this environment only by effectively managing technology; the followers can only respond to the innovations of others. The followers are at risk because a follower's strategy may not be sustainable.

This new environment may be threatening to many, but it can also be advantageous for those who are able to exploit the changes that are occurring. But, whether you choose to view the new environment with apprehension or with anticipation, it is abundantly clear to us, and we hope to make it equally clear to you, that it will no longer be possible for American business to operate in the same manner as we have done in the past.

Lack of Road Maps

A key characteristic of today's environment is that there is a *lack of road maps*. Many have described today's business environment as *chaotic,* as evidenced by books like Tom Peter's *Thriving on Chaos*.[1] Other books, such as *Bottom-Up Marketing,* appear to question the entire role of mission statements, strategy, and long-range plans and seem to advocate placing all responsibility for these activities in the hands of individual line managers.[2] We disagree. Today's business environment may be chaotic, but even within nature's most complex and dynamic systems, we can find order if we look hard enough. The order in today's business environment may be hidden to some, but it exists. A few are already finding a vision of direction in today's environment, and they will be among the winners. A key to creating the new road maps that we need is to find the patterns in what appears to be a chaotic and constantly changing environment and then to exploit these to achieve strategic advantage. The leaders of the 1990s will be the ones who are able to see order within the chaos that others perceive and who know how to use it to write the new rules of competition.

The Elephant and the Blind Men

Many of today's organizations operate in a way reminiscent of the blind men who were asked to describe an elephant. One touched a leg and said, "It's a tree," another the tail, "It's a rope," a third the elephant's side, ... you know the story. In the same manner, many individuals are focusing only on their own small, internal piece of the enterprise, like marketing, R&D, or manufacturing. Individual managers are often unable to clearly articulate the vision, goals, and objectives of the organization as a whole; as a result they do not function as a team.

Organizations today are surrounded by powerful external strategic forces, some of which are shown in the form of clouds surrounding the organization in Figure 1-2. Many individuals in the organization do not even perceive these forces, some of which may be threatening storm clouds. The issue has become threefold in today's environment. First, the entire management team must understand the powerful forces that are emerging that represent both opportunities and threats. Second, individual managers must work together and have a single unified view of the organization. Third, the entire management team must be able to understand and communicate what is required to guide the organization and mobilize it to action. It is clear to us that what is required in the organizations of tomorrow is a new level of *organizational effectiveness.*

Increasing Organizational Effectiveness

Now that we have a better understanding of the environment in which we are operating, we can focus on increasing the level of effectiveness of our organization. To a great degree, organizational effectiveness depends on three factors: exploiting *time* to achieve strategic advantage, making the right *investments,* and setting appropriate business *goals.*

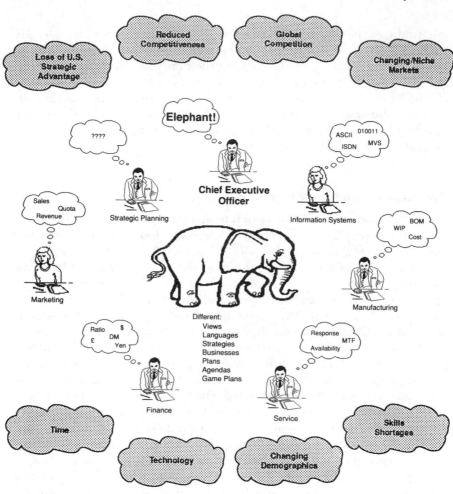

Figure 1-2. Different views of the elephant.

Time as a New Source of Strategic Advantage

Now that the United States no longer enjoys many of the advantages it had in the past, a new source of competitive advantage has emerged—*time*. George Stalk, Jr., in a *Harvard Business Review* article stated:[3]

> **As a strategic weapon, time is the equivalent of money, productivity, quality, even innovation.**

The ways in which leading companies manage time—in production, in new product development, and in sales and distribution—represent one of the most powerful new sources of strategic advantage available today. For example, in manufacturing, the factory accounts for one-third to one-half of the total time associated with getting a product to the market. The sales and distribution functions typically consume as much or more time than manufacturing. Many innovative manufacturers have found that inefficient sales and distribution operations have often undercut the benefits of the flexible manufacturing systems that they have had the foresight to create. In the future, time will be a key factor in the measurement of an organization's long-term success, and much of this book deals with exploiting time to create strategic advantage. A number of elements are required for organizations to exploit time in achieving the new levels of effectiveness that will be necessary in the 1990s. These elements are summarized in Figure 1-3 and are described as follows:

1. *New lenses* that will enable us to clearly perceive the forces that are at work both within the organization itself and in the external environment

2. Simple, effective techniques for *strategic thinking* that we can use to assist in business planning

3. A *strategic vision* that will allow us to visualize opportunities, assumptions, exposures, tradeoffs, priorities, and key survival issues

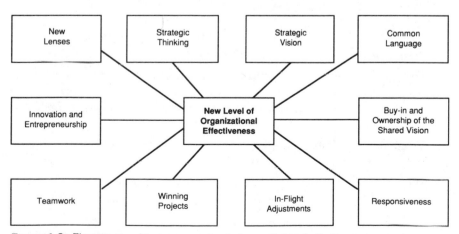

Figure 1-3. Elements in achieving a new level of organizational effectiveness.

4. A *common language* that we can use to communicate information about the new environment within the organization

5. *Buy-in and a sense of ownership of the strategic vision* by the entire management team

6. The ability to be *responsive* to changes that occur both within the organization and in the external environment

7. The ability to recognize the need for and make *in-flight adjustments* to strategic plans

8. New methods for picking the *winning projects* at all levels in the organization, and for pushing the decision-making process further down

9. Newer types of *teamwork* than were required in the past

10. A high level of *innovation and entrepreneurship* in all aspects of the organization

Making the Right Investments

Another key element in achieving organizational effectiveness is the ability to choose the right investments—we must be able to accurately pick the projects that offer the highest payoff. In doing so we must continually redefine what is an acceptable payoff. Yesterday's risk and return analyses are often no longer sufficient. The definitions of an organization's success are constantly changing as markets, conditions, and the rules of the game change. An important job in the new environment is to analyze the business case for potential strategic investments in technology, new markets, and new products and services. In doing this, we must ask the following questions:

1. How much have we been investing in *strategic* opportunities? (*The management team often does not know.*)

2. How do we stack up against the competition in strategic investments, new markets, new channels? (*A difficult question to answer objectively, but the most important question that we can ask in today's environment.*)

3. What impact does technology have on the corporate management process? (*In many enterprises almost none.*)

4. Where in the enterprise should future strategic investments be made? (*It often should not be in the same areas in which investments have been made in the past.*)

5. How are we allocating our strategic resources? (*We often should not*

be simply dividing up available resources among all the business units or trying to play catch up.)

6. What are the important projects and how much will each contribute to corporate growth, profitability, and in some cases survivability? (*These decisions are too important to be made in isolation, by the operational managers traditionally responsible for applications of technology.*)

7. How can the organization exploit both change and time across all functions in the organization? (*As we mentioned earlier, time is an important source of strategic advantage in today's rapidly changing environment.*)

When you finish this book, you will feel differently about your answers to these questions. Good answers to the preceding questions imply a comprehensive plan for future investments. They can help in setting appropriate business goals that can lead to strategic advantage. It is interesting to note that executives in other countries often answer the above questions and, therefore, set business goals, in significantly different ways than managers in the United States.

Business Goals

Management studies have been done in which U.S. executives, Japanese executives, and European executives have been asked to rank their key business goals. Japanese executives tend to rank their goals in this sequence:

1. Revenue
2. Market share
3. Lowest cost
4. Service
5. Profit

Notice that revenue is at the top, but that profit is at the bottom. Japanese executives tend to feel that if the first four goals are met, profit will come automatically. Executives in the United States tend to rank profit much higher initially. However, they often revise their priorities to the above ranking on the second round, *after they see the Japanese results.* Also, U.S. executives often listed *quality* as an important objective; the Japanese did not. When questioned about this, the Japanese executives stated that high quality is a part of their day-to-day habits, and so it did not occur to them even to list it.

Profit is, of course, important. However, it is now becoming clear that the most important goal of business should not be profit alone. James C. Abegglen's and George Stalk Jr.'s article "The Japanese Corporation as Competitor" clearly shows that there is a "winner's competitive cycle" at work in successful businesses in all free market economies.[4] This cycle is very evident in Japan because of that country's rapid growth since World War II. We agree wholeheartedly with the following statement made by Abegglen and Stalk:

> For a company to establish a "winner's competitive cycle" it must grow faster than its competitors. This means that the company must increase its market share so that its volume of business will increase at a higher rate than that of its competitors....Once a superior rate of increase is established, a virtual cycle begins: with increased volume, relative to competitors' volume, comes decreased costs. With decreased costs comes increased profitability and financial strength. More cash is available internally and from external sources to fund growth. This cash is then reinvested in the business in ways that will yield further increases of market share and a replay of the winning cycle.

So to be successful in today's environment, an organization must concentrate on increasing revenue by expanding its markets rather than protecting the markets it already has, even at the expense of short-term profit. This will open up new markets and create new revenue streams that will allow the organization to better target and fund future opportunities. Such a strategy automatically leads to higher profits. As the Japanese have demonstrated, market share becomes a key driving force in today's environment. If the organization is able to gain significant market share, it will then be in a better position to move into other areas and be better able to provide enhanced services to customers. We will have a lot more to say about this in Chapter 8.

We question the wisdom of defensive strategies for an organization that is in a rapidly changing, highly competitive environment. Defensive strategies usually lead to protectionism, loss of customer sensitivity, and dulling of the competitive edge. Such strategies leave an organization open to being exploited by the competition. For example, some key players in the automotive industry in the United States have held back in recent years and have not tried to capture market share; instead, they have tried to defend their tenuous positions. As a result, foreign competition is becoming a major problem for them. The information systems departments in many organizations have also adopted defensive strategies that have led to the "glass house" mentality. This has alienated them from the users they are supposed to serve. The steel industry has responded to foreign competition by attempting to erect barriers to competition using tariffs. We feel strongly that what we need in the United States today are *offensive* strategies that are guided by a clearly articulated *strategic vision*.

Formulating a Strategic Vision

An effective strategic vision is of critical importance to success in today's environment. Executives and managers at all levels must work together to form and clearly articulate a strategic vision. Managers at all levels must then clearly *understand* this vision and must effectively *communicate* it to everyone in the organization. The entire management team must work to ensure that the concept of a strategic vision becomes woven into the very fabric of the organization and becomes an integral part of the management culture. The strategic business vision provides a framework within which the entire enterprise operates. A clear strategic vision allows the enterprise to establish its highest level goals and to formulate the plans necessary to achieve those goals.

Communicating the vision is as important as formulating it. Many a strategic vision has failed to materialize because it was not effectively communicated to those who were required to implement it. It is interesting to note that Roger Smith, who presided over General Motors during a time when GM experienced a drop in the company's share of the U.S. automobile market from about 45 percent in 1981 to about 36 percent in 1988, stated:

> ...I sure wish I'd done a better job of communicating with GM people. I'd do that differently a second time around and make sure they understood and shared my vision for the company. Then they would have known why I was tearing the place up, taking out whole divisions, changing our whole production structure....I never got all this across. ...When I saw that our people didn't understand my vision for GM, I knew I had to go back and get them on board. Today everyone wants in on the vision.[5]

The Changing Focus of Top Management

A vision of one sort or another has always focused the activities of successful senior executives. However, the characteristics of this vision has been changing over the years. (See Figure 1-4.) Each step up in Figure 1-4 also includes the requirements from the previous step, thus making the vision that has been required of a successful executive tougher to achieve with each decade.

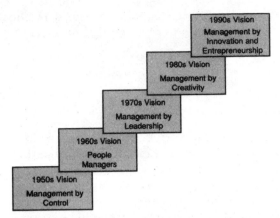

Figure 1-4. Changes in executive vision over time.

- In the 1950s we exited the war years, and the U.S. economy was at that time unchallenged in the world. The management culture of the period led to an executive vision that encompassed *management control systems* for controlling inventory, payroll, costs, and so on.
- In the 1960s we saw people as our most important asset, and the focus was on *people managers.* A vision that espoused *management by objectives* and *performance plans* became prominent.
- In the 1970s the U.S. economy began to be challenged, and the focus of executive vision changed to *charisma* and *leadership.*
- In the 1980s we awoke to discover increased levels of competition and massive trade deficits, and attention of executives changed again to *management by creativity.*

In the 1990s traditional management techniques will not be enough, even when they are combined with charisma and creativity. The vision must now include *innovation* and a *sense of urgency.* Senior executives must identify the strategic opportunities and must then make the *right* things happen *quickly.* In today's environment, a creative idea not implemented, or implemented too late, has little or no value. Technology and world demographics are changing too quickly for us to spend years planning to implement an idea. Management must be willing to take risks and become more entrepreneurial. We must also recognize that time, unless it is effectively exploited, is not necessarily an ally but is often a formidable enemy. Anyone can have an idea. It is timely innovation that counts. In hindsight, what is required becomes obvious; but when doing business planning, it is difficult to differentiate the evolving *strategic* environmental changes from all other forces at work in the environment.

Strategic Thinking

In today's business environment, a lot of people are *thinking*—even doing *strategic* thinking in many cases—and a lot of people are involved in *tactical action*. But not many people are doing what we feel is of critical importance to American business:

> *Strategic thinking* **followed by** *strategic action.*

In *strategic thinking,* we must first seek a clear understanding of the elements and competitive forces at work in the marketplace. We can then make the fullest possible use of brainpower to restructure the environment. *Strategic actions* require that we harness management at all levels in the organization to formulate and execute timely implementation plans. However, the strategic planning techniques we have used in the past may not be the ones we should be using in the future.

Traditional Strategic Planning

The idea of strategic planning is certain to conjure up images in your mind of traditional, tedious long-range planning sessions, in which a group of managers create thick, leather-bound planning documents. It is our contention that the strategic business planning tools and techniques that are used today in American business, when strategic planning is done at all, are mostly out of date and obsolete. Thick planning documents and tedious long-range-planning sessions no longer address the important issues that today's organizations must address. Their results are too detailed, and few people in the organization make use of their findings. We can make the following observations concerning the business planning techniques that organizations use today:

- They were developed for a different era when the business environment was simpler, changed more slowly, and had rules that were more clearly defined.

- They tend to focus on achieving marginal productivity gains instead of totally restructuring existing processes for increased overall effectiveness.

- They are too difficult to use and too time-consuming for executives to effectively employ them.

- They are rule-oriented and tend to stifle creativity and contribution by participants in the planning process.

Many of the management consultants that specialize in turning around organizations that are in trouble have found that a high percentage of the ideas that are required to set things right come from people who are already part of the organization. The ideas were there all along, but the planning process did not find them. After discussing strategic planning with hundreds of executives, we have made the following observation:

> **The thicker the planning document,
> the less likely it will be read.**

If the planning document is not read, it is unlikely that the plans it contains will be implemented. The techniques for strategic thinking described in this book are designed to avoid long, dreary planning sessions and thick, dusty planning documents. Our techniques focus on methods for creating a management culture that encourages strategic thinking and strategic action. They can be used to formulate a strategic vision that can then be communicated to all levels of management.

We can now introduce the *innovation arrow*—our way of structuring the strategic business planning that we feel is necessary if American business is to achieve the kinds of results it must achieve in order to remain competitive.

The Innovation Arrow

Strategic thinking must be a continuous cycle. The cycle begins with formulating a strategic vision for the organization, proceeds through creating strategies that determine how the vision can be used to guide the organization's efforts, continues with developing appropriate tactics to implement the strategic plans, and leads to the implementation and operational steps that all members of the organization must carry out in the day-to-day running of the enterprise. The innovation arrow, shown in Figure 1-5, summarizes these steps. *All* the steps must be carried out if the organization is to achieve strategic advantage and survive in the changing environment of the 1990s. And, what is most important, once an organization gets all the way down the innovation arrow, it is essential that the strategic thinking cycle begin again and be continually repeated. The techniques for strategic thinking described in this book will provide you with a *new vocabulary* that will allow you to better analyze, position, and communicate business considerations and technical issues.

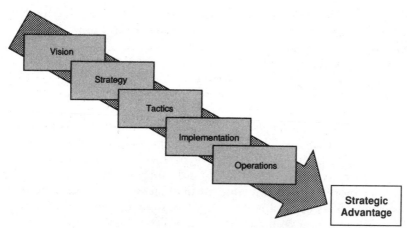

Figure 1-5. The innovation arrow.

The Role of Top Management

Many would assume that it is the job of top management to do the required business planning, and that the role of middle management is to carry out those plans. But we have found that in many organizations the crucial planning tasks have been delegated to a middle management, staff strategic planning or long-range planning department. A key theme of critical importance, which we emphasize again and again, is that this is wrong. *Top management* must drive the strategic business planning process. Only top management fully understands the characteristics of the competitive arena. Business planning is too important to be delegated to middle management.

Although top management involvement is of paramount importance, it is also important for more technically oriented executives to participate in the business planning process. It is only they who fully understand the technical environment. This implies that in your role as a manager, you must focus not only on management expertise but on technical awareness as well. Effective strategic business planning requires the joint skills of top management and technical management to effectively chart the course that the enterprise must follow in exploiting technology to gain strategic advantage. Once the enterprise has a clear strategic vision, technical staff can develop detailed tactical plans that validate the overall business vision and determine the best ways to implement the strategies.

Executive Thought Processes

Elliot Jaques, director of the Institute of Organization and Social Studies at England's Brunel University, has made some useful observations

about the thought processes of executives. These were described by
Walter Kiechel in the *Fortune* article "How Executives Think."[6] According to Jaques, a growing body of research suggests that managerial
minds work differently from everyone else's. At the heart of Jaques's
findings is a concept he calls the *time frame of the individual.* Individuals vary radically in terms of the time periods they can think out, organize, and work through. Most of the population is never capable of
more than a 3-month time span. In the business world, this 3-month
time span may actually be a by-product of the common requirement for
quarterly financial reports. At the top of successful organizations sit
chief executives who can cast their minds forward to encompass the
next 10 or more years. Only one individual out of several million,
Jaques estimates, is ever capable of a 20-year time frame. This ability,
much sought after in executives, is one aspect of the strategic vision we
have been discussing. Appropriate long range planning is a key ingre-
dient to identifying an effective strategic vision. This book presents
techniques that will help in crossing the bridge from 3-month planning
to long-term strategic thinking.

As we have shown, strategic advantage is not achieved in one step, it
happens only by executing *all* the steps in the innovation arrow. The
future belongs to those who can think and act strategically no matter
what their role is in the organization. Communicating and materializing
the vision throughout the organization to achieve strategic advantage is
not easy, but these steps are necessary for the organization to choose the
winning projects and to then be able to quickly implement them.

Right Brain/Left Brain

Time and again, good projects fail to make it all the way down the innovation arrow. This is because we often fail to recognize that implementing all the phases of the innovation arrow involves two fundamentally different types of thought and planning process. An interesting
discussion of the differences between traditional, *systematic planning* activities that largely involve the left hemisphere of the brain and more
innovative *vision formulation* activities that use predominantly the right
hemisphere of the brain can be found in a *Harvard Business Review*
article by Henry Mintzberg. According to Mintzberg:

> If the organization goes the route of systematic planning, I suggest
> that it will probably come up with what can be called a "mainline"
> strategy. In effect, it will do what is generally expected of organiza-
> tions in its situation; where possible, for example, it will copy the es-
> tablished strategies of other organizations. If it is in the automobile

business, for instance, it might use the basic General Motors strategy, as Chrysler and Ford have so repeatedly done.

Alternatively, if the organization wishes to have a creative, integrated strategy, which can be called a "gestalt strategy," such as Volkswagen's one in the 1950s, then I suggest the organization will rely largely on one individual to conceptualize its strategy, to synthesize a "vision" of how the organization will respond to its environment. In other words, scratch an interesting strategy, and you will probably find a single strategy formulator beneath it. Creative, integrated strategies seem to be the products of single brains, perhaps even of single right hemispheres.[7]

A major objective of this book is to provide methods for harnessing and channeling the creative, right-brain activities of individuals and going beyond the traditional systematic planning activities. The planning techniques we discuss allow all levels of management to work together to identify an effective strategic vision that will guide the efforts of the entire management team.

The phases in the innovation arrow can be divided into two parts, each of which uses different types of thought process. Figure 1-6 shows these as the *identify* process and the *define* process.

The Identify Process

In the *identify* process, high-level decisions are required that are often highly intuitive and qualitative—right-brain oriented. Formulating a strategic vision of where the organization should be headed is largely an intuitive, qualitative, right-brain-oriented task. The thought processes

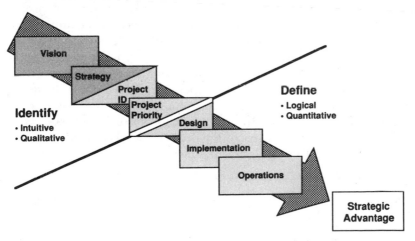

Figure 1-6. The identify and define processes shown on the innovation arrow.

involved in the identify stages involve conducting subjective brainstorming sessions, evaluating market forces, finding and highlighting opportunities, and choosing the winning projects. These are the thought processes that lead to an effective strategic vision.

The Define Process

The *define* process involves operational stages that are logical and quantitative—left-brain oriented. It is at these stages that operational, bottom-up tactical planning and implementation take place. These steps constitute the "systematic planning" that Mintzberg refers to. Most existing strategic planning techniques are logical and left-brain oriented and involve only these systematic planning techniques. Used in isolation, they will generally result only in "mainline" strategies. Although many of these techniques are important to running the organization and formulating business plans, they cannot be effective unless the right-brain thought processes are used first to establish a clear strategic vision.

Bridging the Gap

It is important to realize that there is a *communications gap* between the *identify* thought process and the *define* thought process, shown with the diagonal line in Figure 1-6. In the *identify* process, top management sets project priorities and exits the process; in the *define* process, project implementors enter the picture. When the organization identifies projects that will help the organization achieve strategic advantage, it is important that top management does not simply "throw the project over the transom" to the definers. Before the executives complete the strategic planning process, it is essential that they determine what is important for the success of an identified project and what means can be used to communicate this. In other words, top management must *bridge the gap* between the *identify* part of the planning process and the *define* part. Good communication is required to jump this hurdle. In an environment that is characterized by a proliferation of niche markets, communication throughout all levels of the organization is critical. We must continually ask ourselves the following question:

> **How can we gain a continual recommitment of our employees in addressing the challenges in the new environment?**

Thus far, we have analyzed the business environment in which we find ourselves, we have shown how the environment is rapidly changing, and we have discussed the need for new levels of organizational effectiveness. We then contrasted the traditional strategic planning techniques of the past with the new forms of strategic thinking and strategic action that are required in today's environment. We now conclude this introductory chapter by presenting a simple planning model that you can use to see how you view yourself, and your organization, too, with respect to innovation.

The Innovation/Impact Model

The *Innovation/Impact Model,* shown in Figure 1-7, allows us to position typical patterns of action with respect to two key variables. The first variable, plotted on the vertical axis concerns extraordinary *actions* relating to innovation, creativity, and strategic differentiation. The second variable, plotted on the horizontal axis, concerns the extraordinary *effect* on the environment that these actions have. We can use the Innovation/Impact Model to get an idea of where we fall in this context, and we can use it to gain a view of how the organization relates to the variables. By analyzing the relationships between the two variables, we can group typical actions into the four broad categories shown in the chart.

Lost Opportunities

An individual or organization whose actions tend to lie in the *low/low* quadrant rates low in innovation and also low in impact. Organizations

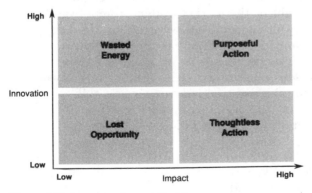

Figure 1-7. Innovation/Impact Model.

and individuals that stay in this quadrant will not be the innovators. They may not even be the survivors. This quadrant might be a useful haven between forays into the "Purposeful Action" quadrant. But in today's environment, we must not remain here for long. For example, we may decide that innovative initiatives constitute such a risk right now that we dare not attempt them. We might categorize those that remain in this quadrant for extended periods of time as *imitators*. An imitator does not play the role of an innovator and does not have a great impact on the organization or the industry.

Wasted Energy

In the *high/low* quadrant are those individuals or organizations that rate high in innovation but low in impact. If we find ourselves here, it had better be only for a short time in response to some clear market need. For example: "Everyone else is doing it." Change and innovation is costly, and we want to avoid being forced to enter this quadrant in re-action to some external pressure. We might categorize those that re-main in this quadrant as *problem solvers* who are constantly reacting to external forces rather than creating real change. They may have inno-vative ideas, but they do not have enough impact to drive the new ideas into the market. These individuals or organizations may not be in a po-sition to take the required risks to exploit their ideas.

Thoughtless Action

Those whose actions are in the *low/high* quadrant rate low in innovation but high in impact. An organization in this category might be one that continues to run current operations with higher and higher efficiency, even though the lifetime of the product or service it offers may be com-ing to an end. These might be the market leaders from a bygone time who will soon have difficulty keeping up with the new leaders. Many companies were innovators in the past but have been unable to produce new innovations to continue their growth. We might call those that re-main in this quadrant *problem creators*. Organizations in this category are usually unwilling to take required risks or are not able to take an innovative role in planning the organization's future. Individuals com-fortable in this quadrant of the chart include those "process caretakers" in jobs where reward and promotion are based on their ability to avoid making mistakes. Some of the comments heard from individuals in this quadrant include, "Don't make waves," or, "If it ain't broke, don't fix it." However, as Will Rogers once said:

> **Even if you're on the right track,**
> **you'll get run over if you just sit there.**

Purposeful Action

Those whose actions are largely in the *high/high* quadrant rate high in innovation and also have a high impact on the environment. Organizations that remain in this quadrant have the innovative ideas and are able to exploit them. If we can place ourselves into this category, we will be positioned to help the organization reach new levels of effectiveness in achieving strategic advantage. We might categorize organizations in this quadrant as the *innovative leaders* that use novel ideas to change the very structure of their industry and to find new ways of competing. Taking yourself and your organization into the purposeful action quadrant is what this book is all about.

Conclusion

Where are you and where is your organization with respect to the two key variables in the Innovation/Impact Model? Are you willing to step up and take the necessary risks and accept the challenges that are necessary to revitalize your organization and become an innovative leader? Has your organization begun making the necessary investments in time, capital, and technology? Does your organization have a strategic vision? Has your organization made an effort to communicate its vision throughout the organization? Is the vision understood and can it be clearly articulated by the entire management team? Strategic advantage is not achieved in one step; but by executing all the steps in the innovation arrow. It cannot be achieved in a one-time, one-step event. In order for it to be sustainable, the process must be continuous and must be used by all members of the organization. The remaining chapters of this book focus on specific methods for enhancing the effectiveness of the organization and helping to achieve strategic advantage in today's chaotic environment.

References

1. Thomas Peters. *Thriving on Chaos: Handbook for a Management Revolution.* New York: Alfred A. Knopf, 1988.

2. Al Ries and Jack Trout. *Bottom-Up Marketing.* New York: McGraw-Hill, 1988.

3. George Stalk. "Time—The Next Source of Competitive Advantage." *Harvard Business Review,* July–August, 1988.

4. James C. Abegglen and George Stalk Jr. "The Japanese Corporation as Competitor." *California Management Review,* Spring, 1986.

5. Wilton Woods. "The U.S. Must Do as GM Has Done." *Fortune,* February 13, 1989.

6. Walter Kiechel. "How Executives Think." *Fortune,* February 4, 1985.

7. Henry Mintzberg. "Planning on the Left Side and Managing on the Right." *Harvard Business Review,* July–August, 1976.

PART 1

Vision

In the chapters in Part 1, we discuss formulating a shared strategic vision—the first phase of the *innovation arrow* (Figure P1-1.). These chapters lay out steps for changing your view of the business environment and for assessing and visualizing the strategic position of the organization. An important objective of Part 1 is to provide us with a common vocabulary. This vocabulary will allow us to better describe a strategic vision and communicate it to others. There are five steps that lead toward formulating a strategic vision:

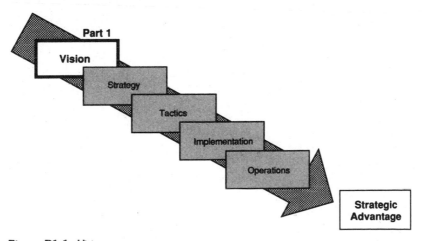

Figure P1-1. Vision.

1. Understanding the *waves of innovation* through which the enterprise is passing with respect to applications of technology. The objective of this step is to determine the organization's level of innovation compared with that of the competition. (Chapter 2)

2. Determining new ways in which the organization can exploit industry and functional *experience curves*. This involves learning new ways of thinking about experience curves and discovering how the organization's experience curves compare with those of the competition. (Chapter 3)

3. Examining the *power relationships* that exist in the industry. The objective here is to visualize the important linkages that predominate in the industry, to determine how the industry's structure is changing, and to identify how the organization can take advantage of innovation and technology in exploiting these changes in industry power relationships. (Chapter 4)

4. Expanding our view of the enterprise and visualizing it in the context of an *extended enterprise*. The extended enterprise is made up of not only the organization itself but also those organizations with which it interacts. (Chapter 5)

5. Visualizing how the organization can use technology to create *electronic channels* that tie together all the elements in the extended enterprise. Electronic channels form a major tool for restructuring the extended enterprise to achieve strategic advantage and for linking every key function in the organization, including suppliers, customers, and employees. (Chapter 6)

2

Understanding the Waves of Innovation

Introduction

An important step in developing a new vision of the organization involves examining the ways in which the technologies used to produce products and services has evolved and matured over time. The uses of technology have evolved differently in each industry and in each enterprise. It is important to understand how the technology employed by the organization compares with that of the competition. Innovation, and the technology used to create products and services, tends to evolve in *waves*, with each successive wave of innovation built on the previous ones. An analysis of these waves of innovation will provide a new lens for viewing products and services and for viewing the uses of technology as a competitive weapon. An analysis of the waves of innovation also provides the beginnings of a model or framework for visualizing and communicating the strategic vision.

Substantial and Sustainable Competitive Advantage

Brandt Allen, in the December 1982 issue of the *Harvard Business Review*, showed that many enterprises are outperforming their competitors by a wide margin mainly owing to their ability to use technology to create new products and new services that are of strategic importance to the enterprise. These products and services often use innovative forms of technology, such as advanced information systems, that are qualitatively different than the technology that has been used in the past. Allen stated:

> Senior executives must become closely involved with their information systems to reassess and perhaps reorganize their computer resources...Matters are at the crisis point in computing for many corporations. Technology, by itself, is not enough...Key to these solutions is the formulation of a comprehensive strategy for the deployment of information resources within the company...An unmanaged computer system can stop you dead.[1]

Michael Porter and Victor E. Millar in a later *Harvard Business Review* article stated:

> Every company must understand the broad effects and implications of the new technology and how it can create *substantial* and *sustainable* competitive advantages. [Emphasis ours.][2]

Porter and Millar then went on to identify three specific ways that technology affects competition:

- It alters industry structures.
- It supports cost and differentiation strategies.
- It spawns entirely new businesses.

These three results of using innovation and technology to create substantial and sustainable advantage are key themes that we continually emphasize. At all stages of business planning, managers must ask themselves whether a new product, a new service, or a new application of technology meets the above tests in creating competitive advantage:

Is the advantage both *substantial* and *sustainable*?

The techniques for strategic thinking that we present in this book will provide the tools needed for identifying and exploiting such strategic opportunities.

The Porter Competitive Forces Model

Michael Porter developed a model, shown in Figure 2-1, that is useful in beginning to identify and analyze the competitive forces that exist in an industry.[3] According to Porter, the five competitive forces shown in the model determine the long-term profitability of an enterprise. One of the first steps in strategic thinking is to develop a Porter-type competitive forces chart for the industry. Such a chart can be a powerful tool to use as a starting point in identifying threats to the organization's position in the industry and in pointing out potential opportunities.

Interorganizational Systems

In a *Harvard Business Review* article entitled "IS Redraws Competitive Boundaries," the authors stated:

> Today the most dramatic and potentially powerful uses of information systems technology involve networks that transcend company boundaries. Some of these interorganizational systems (referred to hereafter as IOSs) also have important social and public policy implications. These systems, defined as automated information systems shared by two or more companies, will significantly contribute to enhanced productivity, flexibility, and competitiveness of many companies.[4]

Interorganizational systems create *electronic channels* that can be used to cross traditional company boundaries in order to enhance productivity, increase flexibility, and create competitive advantage. We discuss electronic channels further in Chapter 6, and then in Chapter 9 we

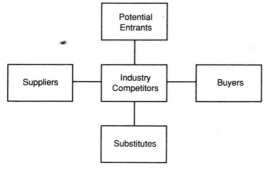

Figure 2-1. Michael Porter's competitive forces model.

show how they can be used to create substantial and sustainable competitive advantage. We introduce them briefly here because they play a major role in shaping the competitive forces that operate in an industry and are important parts of the advanced technology that organizations are using.

Identifying Waves of Innovation

In most applications of technology, the focus of the uses of technology in solving business problems has shifted as time goes on and will continue to shift in the future. As we mentioned in the introduction to this chapter, innovation and technology tend to evolve in the form of waves. Figure 2-2 shows the first two major waves of innovation that are associated with most uses of technology.

Wave 1: Reducing Costs

The initial focus of management in using technology was on the automation of routine functions. For example, most of the early use of computers in the 1960s were applied to applications that were highly controllable and that had limited interfaces—they automated the basic accounting and clerical systems of the organization, such as order entry, accounts receivable, accounts payable, payroll, and general ledger. First-wave information systems concentrate on enhancing the productivity of individual business areas and are generally associated with clerical and administrative savings. Early efforts at streamlining manufacturing operations in many industries can also be classified as first-wave applications of technology. For example, early efforts aimed at the use of assembly lines in manufacturing were focused on the cost reductions that are associated with mass production.

Wave 2: Leveraging Investments

In the 1970s, technology was applied in more sophisticated ways. For example, computer systems were created that used online terminals to

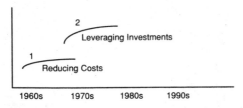

Figure 2-2. The two lowest waves of innovation.

perform asset turnover management, cash management, sales analysis, and resource scheduling. Second-wave information systems concentrate on the effective use of corporate assets and with leveraging expenditures in order to enhance profitability. Second-wave applications of technology in manufacturing were also associated with leveraging of investments and concentrated on streamlining manufacturing operations and enhancing control over inventory. The justification of these systems was based on financial considerations, such as measuring return on investment and performing cash flow analyses.

The first two innovation waves share a single characteristic. They were designed to reduce the costs that were associated with performing earlier manual functions. The focus was on *productivity* of people and resources. Although such applications of technology are valuable and are vital to the running of today's enterprises, they do nothing to increase the revenue flowing into the organization. The business justification of these systems was to *save* money, not to *make* money.

Wave 3: Enhancing Products and Services

Our attention turned next toward using technology to solve more complex problems. This was concurrent with significant reductions in the cost of many forms of technology, including computers, communications technology, and robotics. Advanced technology, especially in computers and communications, tends to be less expensive than earlier forms of technology and is also generally much more capable. Beginning in the 1980s we started to see enterprises install new types of information system that, instead of simply saving money, opened up new avenues for producing revenue. (See Figure 2-3.) Third-wave systems use technology to gain strategic advantage and often create entirely new businesses. These systems employ comprehensive communication net-

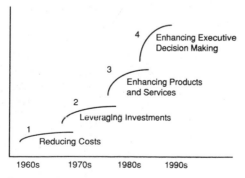

Figure 2-3. The next two waves of innovation.

works and information storage and retrieval techniques to perform such functions as consolidation of financial functions, expansion of credit card services, hotel, travel, and theater ticketing, elimination of the intermediary functions in many enterprises, and online catalog shopping.

Third-wave systems concentrate on using technology to increase both market share and profitability. For example, third-wave applications of technology in manufacturing concentrated on such techniques as just-in-time inventory management and the creation of flexible manufacturing systems. Using advanced technology to restructure manufacturing operations allows plants to create entirely new types of product and to rapidly shift from one product to another to better respond to changes in customer requirements.

Wave 4: Enhancing Executive Decision Making

Even later in the 1980s, some forward-looking enterprises began to use technology to create systems for improving the way in which top-level decisions are made concerning such things as acquisitions, strategic planning, and corporate transformation. Fourth-wave systems typically use advanced computer and communication technology to create systems that help top management improve the decision-making process. The installation of fourth-wave systems was accelerated because of the proliferation of the use of personal computers in industry during this period. In manufacturing, fourth-wave applications applied technology to all the organizations involved in the creation of a product or service and extended the reach of management control to beyond the traditional boundaries of the organization. Simulation and modeling of the product flow and resource requirements in the manufacturing process became prominent for industry leaders. The business justification for these types of system was to improve the organization's effectiveness by enhancing the management process.

An organization generally had the luxury of choosing the time frames for installing first-wave and second-wave forms of technology. These forms of technology tended to be negotiable with respect to time because of their inward focus. Unlike first- and second-wave technology, third-wave and fourth-wave technology is not optional, and time frames for implementation are often set by the leaders in the industry. As soon as the industry direction is set, competitive advantage and survival becomes the issue with these new applications of technology. *Once the leader in a given industry has established a new innovation wave, it is then no longer optional for the other players in that industry to also enter that wave.*

Wave 5: Reaching the Consumer

We are now beginning to see examples of a fifth innovation wave, in which computers, communications, and other new forms of advanced technology are converging and are being used jointly to directly reach the end consumer of products and services. (See Figure 2-4.) These systems use highly advanced technology such as home computers, full motion video, touch screens, and consumer databases.

In an era when strategic advantage is focused on reaching the consumer, it is important to make a clear distinction between the term *customer* and the term *consumer*. A customer is any person or organization that buys a product or service. A consumer is the person or organization that is the *ultimate* consumer of a product or service. An organization's customer may or may not be the ultimate consumer. Until recently, the customer was not the consumer in the most organizations. However, in many industries, strategies for reaching the consumer directly have the biggest potential for growth.

It is clear that fifth-wave applications of technology will ultimately be the most important innovation wave for successful enterprises. The use of such technology will have far-reaching effects on the organization. These changes will significantly alter the way in which people are managed and trained. New marketing, distribution, and service strategies will change the rules of competition. It is possible that the first organizations in an industry to apply highly advanced technology to directly reach the ultimate consumer will set new standards and establish new rules for survival in that industry.

It is interesting to note that in the area of computer and communications technology, the focus of fourth- and fifth-wave information systems has changed dramatically, and the focus is now outside of the in-

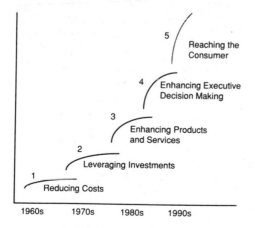

Figure 2-4. The fifth wave of innovation.

formation systems department; these information systems operate where the business is actually transacted. Leaders have been able to expand their businesses by substantially increasing market share in order to create sustainable new revenue streams. Two examples of companies that are doing this today are Federal Express, discussed in Chapter 3, and American Airlines, discussed in Chapter 9. The reader can probably think of many more. Today, the business justification for advanced forms of technology is to *make money*.

In the future, the business justification of the fifth, reach-the-consumer, wave will be to *remain in business*.

It is important to realize in assessing the organization's position with respect to the waves of innovation that it can be very difficult, risky, and expensive to jump over or bypass a wave in an attempt to catch up with the competition. It may not even be feasible to do so in some instances. This is true not only for the waves of innovation in the information systems realm, but in any high-technology area.

Achieving an Above-the-Line Orientation

Figure 2-5 shows how we can classify the waves of innovation as being either *above the line* or *below the line*. Those that are below the line concentrate on *saving money*; those that are above the line concentrate on *making money* and *remaining in business*. In the 1990s it will be of critical importance that top management change its focus from below-the-line applications of technology—those that focus on administrative savings, financial, manufacturing, and services functions—to an above-the-line orientation—the waves of innovation that focus on marketing, distribution, customer service, megadecisions, and people systems that are designed to reach the ultimate consumer. Throughout the remainder of this book, we will constantly emphasize:

An above-the-line orientation must become a *fundamental management belief*.

It is essential that this fundamental management belief become an integral part of the underlying management culture of the organization.

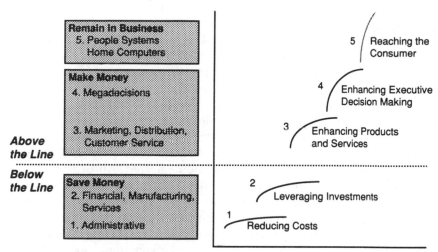

Figure 2-5. Classifying the waves of innovation.

Whenever we use the term *above-the-line* in the remaining chapters in this book, we refer to strategic thrusts that are oriented to achieving substantial and sustainable competitive advantage in the way that Porter and Millar have defined it.

We can construct a set of wave charts that will help us to analyze how the organization stacks up against the competition. It is important to ask how much time and capital is being invested in new applications of technology that fall in the two lowest waves of innovation and how much is being spent in the far more important upper waves. As we have seen, it is in the upper waves where innovation offers opportunities for generating new revenue sources and for significantly increasing profitability.

- Above-the-line innovation involves the building of organizational and technology capabilities.
- Above-the-line innovation represents the long-term view.
- Above-the-line innovation represents continual strategic planning and industry reassessment.
- Above-the-line innovation affects top management style and skills.
- Above-the-line innovation shifts the management focus from an internal organizational focus to an external strategic forces focus.

In analyzing innovation in an organization, it is interesting to examine the information systems function to see how the budget for computers and communications is allocated in most organizations. We have found that 60 percent to 70 percent of the information systems development budget is spent today in maintaining and enhancing first and second wave systems for which the enterprise is no longer getting a big payback. It is necessary for forward-looking organizations to re-evaluate how the information systems budget is being spent. In today's environment, it is essential that the focus of the information systems department change to the upper-innovation waves.

However, it is important to note that before above-the-line systems can be developed, effective below-the-line operational systems must already exist and must continue to evolve for an organization to sustain an advantage over competition. Below-the-line uses of technology will continually be important and must not be neglected. An organization's information systems can be viewed in the form of a pyramid, with the great bulk of the systems dedicated to mundane, below-the-line functions. Although these systems are important, they must not be the primary focus of top management. Responsibility for below-the-line systems should be delegated to middle management so that top management can focus on those few strategic applications of technology that will make the real difference. New applications of technology are best managed in the context of above-the-line strategic thrusts that are based on a solid below-the-line foundation. In many cases, even below-the-line investments are being justified by their above-the-line impact. Once effective below-the-line systems are in place, the management focus should shift to above the line and to the exploitation of the below-the-line investments. It is critical that the organization adopt this attitude as a key part of its culture:

The appropriate focus of *top management* is on above-the-line issues that have the greatest impact on the future success of the organization.

Analyzing Return on Investment

Notice that the slopes of the curves toward the bottom of the chart in Figure 2-5 are flatter than those at the top. This is because there is a declining marginal return on the investments at the lower waves. The curves are steepest at the top because advanced technology generally has the biggest impact on profitability. The biggest return on investment with first- and second-wave information systems comes as soon as the system is fully productive and functional, and cost savings diminish after the first day of full productivity. This is because the major enhancements or benefits have then been achieved. The management focus, and the focus of the information resources in many organizations, has remained on these types of systems, which are already productive and have achieved their major benefits. For example, how many organizations are now in the process of redoing their payroll system? Changes are being made to existing systems, such as changing screen layouts and report formats, and no significant return on investment is being derived by the organization from these activities. These changes may be nice things to have, but from the viewpoint of top management, who probably never see these screens or reports, these changes are not bringing any significant payback to the organization. Extremely valuable resources and significant time are being devoted to efforts that do not create strategic advantage.

We must begin to ask: "Why is this happening?" The problem is that many organizations do not realize that they are in a transition period between the "save money" waves and the "make money" waves. They do not yet fully understand this distinction, so they often continue to work on what they have always worked on in the past. In many cases, no vision or direction is being sent to the information systems department. More important, top management has not recognized its change in responsibility. If top management begins to fully understand the implications of going above the line to making money, then they will get directly involved in these systems, rather than taking a hands-off approach. The information systems department does not fully appreciate the value of these new types of system, because they do not fully understand the business; and top management has not determined that they must get involved in establishing a strategic vision for innovation in the organization. Another way of saying this is that technical managers often understand the technology but lack the vision; top management may have the vision, but too often fails to understand the technology that is necessary to achieve it. When an organization shifts to the "make money" innovation waves, the level of top management involvement in decision making must be changed. Direct joint top management and information systems management planning must take place. Information technology must be part of the organizational plan. It cannot be reactive, it must be proactive. Information systems management must be able to explain to top management how technology can be used for business gain, and together they must develop the strategies that are required for exploiting the technology.

It is our experience that most organizations do not involve the information systems department in the business planning process. Information systems normally gets involved after the fact. When the organization begins to go above the line, this approach will no longer work. For these reasons, we say again that it is essential for top management to devote most of its resources to above-the-line issues and should have minimal involvement with below-the-line concerns. An above-the-line orientation is required for success in the 1990s.

Evolving the Management Culture

The management implications inherent in the waves of technology growth leads to an analysis of how the management culture and philosophy of the organization must change as it begins to innovate and use highly advanced technology. Figure 2-6 shows how the functional uses of technology (on the left) can be compared with the management focus that characterizes each wave (on the right).

The two "save money" waves have a management focus that is oriented to process management or asset management. Organizations that have their primary focus on below-the-line applications of technology tend to have a restrictive management culture that perpetuates a status quo, cost-saving orientation. As we move up in the waves, the waves associated with marketing, distribution, and customer service have a more sophisticated management focus that is oriented to growth and increasing market share. The wave associated with megadecisions requires an even more sophisticated and complex management mentality that focuses on changing the fundamental structure of the organization and on creating realtime executive business management systems. The fifth wave of people systems that reach the ultimate consumer of products and services has the most complex management focus and is concerned not only with the restructuring of the organization but with changing the structure of the industry of which the organization is a part. It is at this level that management focuses on creating entire new businesses that have order-of-magnitude greater potential for growth.

In those innovative organizations that have been able to achieve an above-the-line orientation, the management culture and philosophy tends to be focused on providing individuals with degrees of freedom that allow them to freely innovate, but within the context of centralized

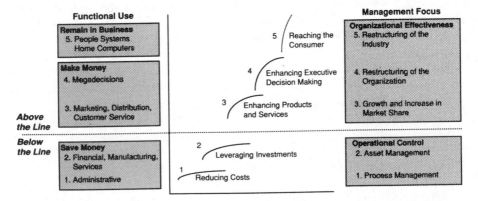

Figure 2-6. Comparing functional uses with management focus.

control. The management culture should combine top-down vision with bottom-up implementation. Such a management culture is the basis for achieving buy-in and ownership of strategic plans and for empowering individuals in the organization to think and act strategically. It provides for a degree of centralized control while allowing for innovation in the implementation phases.

It is extremely important that the management culture of the organization evolves appropriately as the organization moves upward through the waves toward above-the-line innovation. There are many examples of organizations trying to use outdated and restrictive management methods while attempting to evolve toward advanced applications of technology. This can be a recipe for disaster. An older, restrictive, inflexible management culture does not provide managers with the degree of autonomy that is required to encourage innovation. It is interesting to note that Roger Smith, chairman of General Motors, recognized this fact when discussing the new factory then being built to produce the Saturn car:

> I've never set foot in the place, by the way, because I want them to have the maximum degree of independence. It's difficult, but I'm not going to go until I'm able to drive out in their first car.[5]

With the management culture that is most appropriate for managing advanced technology, the focus is often external to the enterprise itself. Organizations that have a flexible management culture are best able to focus on above-the-line applications of technology that create strategic alliances with other organizations. The focus then becomes a redesign of processes and relationships that culminate in competitive advantage for all the organizations concerned. Such win/win forms of relationship will be increasingly important, and we will discuss them more thoroughly in Chapter 4.

Assessing the compatibility of an organization's management culture with the forms of technology it employs is as important as assessing where the organization stands with respect to the waves of innovation that characterize the industry. We must determine not only where the organization as a whole is with respect to the waves, but also where the management culture is. It is important that the functional uses of technology and the appropriate changes in management focus should come together at the same time. If we have all of the technology in place, but top management has not yet determined how to exploit it or, worse yet, is afraid of it, then it will not be effective. If management thinks that the organization is moving up to the top waves, but the implementation of the technology is lagging behind and has not yet taken place, then the organization cannot get there either. The important topic of management culture is discussed further in Chapter 11.

Implications of the Waves

The top management must assess where the enterprise is in relation to the waves of innovation in those aspects of technology with which it is involved and must understand the tradeoffs in investing above and below the line. Top management must also clearly understand the position of the industry as a whole and the position of the competition. Top management must determine when it will be necessary for the enterprise to cross from one wave to another to either stay a leader in the industry or to at least remain competitive. To fall too far behind on a new wave is betting that the organization can catch up.

> In some cases, "catch up" is no longer an issue,
> the real issue can quickly become "locked out."

Examples of this are American Airlines in the airline reservations industry, the Japanese and Koreans in the television/VCR industry, and Budweiser in the beer industry. Who can knock out "the King of Beers"? When we consider global competition, as in the television/VCR market, the issue can be more serious because management does not see the shift to the new wave quickly enough. As world demographics change and distance becomes less and less of a factor, many organizations will not survive if they attempt to play the "catch-up" game.

With respect to information systems, most companies today are at the top of the second wave. Most have not yet crossed the line from information systems that save money to systems that make money. Top management must realize that the leaders in some industries crossed the line some time ago. In order to cross the line to revenue-producing information systems, top management must get involved in managing the new business environment that exists when strategic information systems are employed in running the business.

Analyzing Risk

In analyzing case studies that relate to the ways in which innovative companies have employed advanced technology to achieve competitive advantage, one point stands out very clearly. It is quite possible to implement above-the-line information systems or above-the-line factory automation techniques that are extremely expensive, yet fail to deliver the promised results. It is important in analyzing investments to assess both business risks and technical risks. The technical risk/business risk

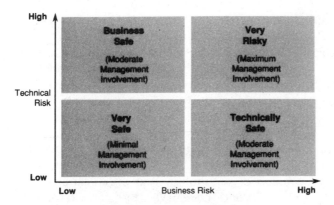

Figure 2-7. Technical risk/business risk model.

model, shown in Figure 2-7 is useful in contrasting the two types of risk. Top management is familiar with analyzing business risks in making investments. However, when we begin to use advanced technology in attempting to achieve competitive advantage, we introduce technical risk as well.

The application of advanced technology in the business context can combine business risk with technical risk, thus making certain applications of advanced technology extremely risky. However, the leaders will often be those that are best able to manage these risks. It is important to analyze both types of risk in attempting to identify those uses of advanced technology that will pay the highest dividends. As both business risk and technical risk increases, then top management must devote more attention to those issues in order to manage and control them. It is important to realize that risk, in itself, is not necessarily bad. In many cases, some element of risk cannot be avoided when making a business decision. The important point is that both business risk and technical risk must be appropriately *managed* and *understood*.

Conclusion

An understanding of the waves of innovation provides us with one of the new lenses that are required for viewing the changes that are occurring in the organization, in the industry, and in technology. This is the first step in strategic thinking. Where the industry is and where we are with respect to the waves of innovation are questions that we must answer. We must ask ourselves whether the organization's competitiveness is substantial and sustainable. As we begin to analyze the waves of innovation, we should begin to position the organization with respect to both uses of technology and the management culture that predominates. Below-the-line issues that concern mainly budgetary decisions often do not require the involvement of top management. As we go above the line, new management thought processes become important and top management needs to be involved in new issues, such as changing markets, restructuring the organization, and ensuring that the below-the-line systems remain competitive and capable of supporting above-the-line strategic thrusts.

Analyzing the waves of innovation allows us to determine how the organization and the competition are positioned. In Chapter 3, we take a closer look at the specific forms of technology that organizations use and learn new ways for viewing experience curve strategies. Chapter 3 discusses new approaches for clearly seeing the individual steps that are available for exploiting the waves of innovation that we have just described.

References

1. Brandt Allen. "An Unmanaged Computer System Can Stop You Dead." *Harvard Business Review.* November–December, 1982.

2. Michael Porter. "How Information Gives You Competitive Advantage." *Harvard Business Review,* July–August, 1985.

3. ——— *Competitive Advantage.* Free Press, 1985.

4. James I. Cash and Benn R. Konsynski. "IS Redraws Competitive Boundaries." *Harvard Business Review.* March–April, 1985.

5. Wilton Woods. "The U.S. Must Do as GM Has Done." *Fortune,* February 13, 1989.

3
Exploiting Experience Curves

Introduction

Once we have determined where the organization stands with respect to the waves of innovation, the next step in strategic thinking is to assess where the organization stands with respect to the *experience curve strategies* that predominate in the industry. An analysis of the waves of innovation provides a general view of the way in which technology is evolving and serves as a statement of direction. An analysis of experience curves provides a new lens that can help in determining how to exploit the trends that are the basis for the waves.

Traditional View of Experience Curves

Experience curve strategies have traditionally been viewed from a cost or efficiency viewpoint. Experience curve strategies suggest that with any given level of technology, because of economies of scale, learning experiences, and production efficiencies, the cost of providing goods and services should decrease as volume increases. This will generally be true as long as the cost of capital and labor has not substantially increased and good management judgment is applied to the process. The logic of experience curves is heavily used in manufacturing and reflects organizational learning as well as economies of scale and scope. Experience curves are traditionally based on accumulated output, not on time. This suggests that higher volumes are associated with lower costs. Before the advent of flexible manufacturing, market share was the key determinant in the decision process to be the low-cost provider. With this cost reduction in mind, we can examine a typical experience curve example.

Suppose Traditions, Ltd., invests $100 million in new equipment for producing magic markers aiming at a 90 percent experience curve. Traditions, Ltd., then produces markers that cost $1 to manufacture on the first day. A 90 percent experience curve means that after the first million has been produced the cost is 90 cents, after the second million, the cost is 81 cents, and so on. Tradition's major competitor, Futures, Unlimited, at the same time invests $120 million in a new high-technology plant that uses robotics and flexible manufacturing that aims at a 70 percent experience curve in magic marker manufacturing. (See Figure 3-1.) With a 70 percent experience curve, the product that initially costs $1 to make costs 70 cents after the first million, and 49 cents after the second million. Traditions, Ltd., whose magic markers cost 81 cents will find it difficult to compete with Futures, Unlimited, whose magic markers cost 49 cents.

Does this actually happen in real life? Do such experience curve gaps really occur, even with this traditional view of experience curves? We think they do. We have identified many companies who have found that the experience curve gap has become so great that they could not afford the shift to a new curve. Many of these companies have decided, since they were unable to compete in their original businesses, to change the company name and enter new fields: U.S. Steel finds it is no longer the leader in the steel business and becomes USX; International Harvester withdraws from the farm equipment business and becomes Navistar; Firestone decides it can no longer profitably make tires and enters the

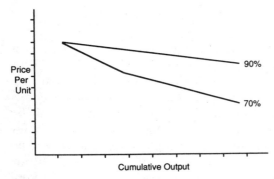

Figure 3-1. Experience curves.

automobile repair business; RCA and General Electric no longer manufacture the television sets they sell; American Can leaves the can business and becomes Primerica, on and on and on. The question is, did the experience curve gap simply get too wide to bridge and did this happen in the last 2 or 3 years, or has this been happening over the last 10 or 15 years? Even on a 90 percent experience curve, revenues can be going up and costs can be coming down. But if the rest of the industry happens to be on an entirely different experience curve, the revenue and cost figures can be misleading. The real message of the experience curve game is that if we start falling behind and do not make the required investments in capital and plant at the right time, it can become too late to catch up. Most enterprises are on experience curves in the 70 percent to 90 percent range. Companies that are working with experience curves in the 90 percent range tend not to measure their experience curve results, and most service-oriented companies do not analyze experience curve strategies.

New View of Experience Curves

With the traditional view of experience curves discussed above, costs go down because we learn to manufacture a product or provide a service more efficiently over time. We believe that in the 1990s it will no longer be useful to view experience curves as continuous curves. Instead, we must view them as sets of connected curves, as shown in Figure 3-2. With this view of experience curves, each new curve represents fundamentally different technologies—often both the technology used to create the product or service and the technologies embodied in the product or service itself. It generally requires substantial investments and

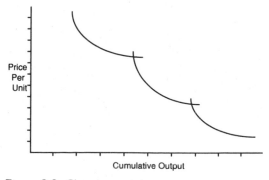

Figure 3-2. Changing experience curves.

substantial risk in choosing the technology required to switch from one experience curve to another. Instances of such new views of experience curves can already be found in many industries. For example, the microprocessor vendors, such as Intel, jump from one curve to another with each new chip generation: 8086, 80286, 80386, i486; some automobile manufacturers, such as Honda, do much the same with each new model generation: Civic, Accord 1, Accord 2, Acura, and so on.

An important part of strategic thinking involves determining where the enterprise stands with respect to the experience curves that predominate in the industry, including where the competitors are and what are the evolving technologies. The enterprise must then determine when it must switch from one experience curve to the next. This can be extremely difficult to do. In some cases, logic alone does not lead us to the correct conclusions, and a highly developed sense of intuition is required. For example, remember when audio tape technology began to capture a significant percentage of the audio recording market? At that time there were two competing tape technologies—8-track cartridges and cassettes—that together were attempting to capture market share from the LP record segment of the industry. In an attempt to apply logic to aid in making a purchasing decision, many analyzed the benefits of the two competing technologies and confidently installed 8-track players. It seemed logical to one of the authors at the time that the medium that required no rewinding, no flipping over of the cassette, and would play endlessly, was the clearly superior choice. As the reader is no doubt familiar, this logic proved faulty, and the marketplace chose the cassette as the winner. As shown in Figure 3-3, the cassette tape is now beginning to be overtaken by the compact disc. However, the digital audio tape (DAT) medium seems to offer better technology due to its ability to record. And the medium of video tape offers the ability to record full motion video as well as high-quality sound. It is difficult at this time

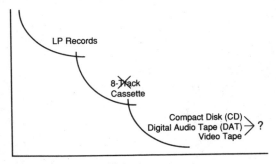

Figure 3-3. Recording industry experience curves.

to predict the winner in this shift to a new experience curve. The players in the audio recording industry have much at stake in choosing the correct new experience curve. The consumer also has a stake in trying to pick the winner. It would be nice to know which one to buy.

Decision-Making Criteria

Why have we presented this example? It is important to realize that there is a difference between decisions made at home and decisions made at work. At home the decision to invest in new audio playback technology is not of critical importance to most of us, and we may feel that we can wait until the technology has proven itself. The danger in this kind of thinking is that we tend to carry this attitude over to decisions we make at work. But in today's business environment, the decisions we are making today at work are very different from the decisions we are making at home. At work, it may be critical to make a decision today to shift to a new experience curve, probably before the technology has had a chance to prove itself. If we wait until the technology has been proven, it may be too late to switch and it may be impossible to catch up to those who have done the pioneering. If *we* wait, who will prove the new technology? It is often the runaway winner. How long do we wait to see if the new technology has been proven? Until we lose 10 percent, 20 percent, or 50 percent of the market?

Here is the important question: "When do we begin investing in a new experience curve?" Figure 3-4 shows that the point at which we must recognize the need for a new experience curve occurs far ahead of the time that we actually switch from the old curve to the new one. Notice that investments must generally be made long before we can switch over to the new curve. The cost of converting to a new experience curve has many components, including capital cost of production, management time, personal emotions, and the cost of overcoming inertia.

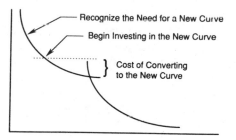

Figure 3-4. Recognizing and changing to a new experience curve.

False Assumptions

As with the waves of innovation, we must *make no assumptions* concerning experience curve strategies. In fact there are *many* false assumptions that executives tend to make with respect to the experience curves that predominate in an industry. Here are a few:

- Competitors are on the same experience curve as we are. (*False. In many cases they are not; the industry leader may be on an entirely different experience curve.*)
- Competitors have the same profit motive for the short run. (*False. Industry leaders may take a longer view and may be willing to sacrifice short-term profits in order to shift to a new experience curve to increase the likelihood for long-range survivability.*)
- Outside forces will not affect the cost curve, such as currency devaluation, consumer trends and style changes, and so on. (*False. Dangerously so in many environments.*)
- Technology does not change. (*False. New production and information systems technologies appear with increasing frequency.*)

Time and again it has happened that an innovative leader has paved the way in shifting from one experience curve to another, has been outstandingly successful, and has then ultimately lost market share and industry leadership when it is unable to identify the next experience curve shift. In some cases, the entrepreneur has such an emotional stake in the existing curve that the personal cost of change is too great when measured in human terms, such as emotion or personal energy. A classic example of this is Henry Ford and his Model T. The experience curves predominating in the early automobile industry are shown in Figure 3-5. Henry Ford's strategic vision allowed him to pioneer the use of manufacturing technology to produce a reliable car that a large segment of the American population could afford to buy. This represented a major experience curve shift from the methods used at the time to manufacture the then typical hand-built automobile. Ford's Model T is one of the most spectacular success stories in American industry. The Model T is widely acknowledged to have changed the very fabric of life in the United States.

As the United States entered the relatively affluent 1920s, Ford was unable to make modifications to his vision and did not recognize the need to shift to a new experience curve. General Motors, however, at that time began to introduce technical innovations such as completely enclosing the car, painting the car in colors other than black, and offer-

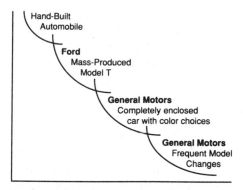

Figure 3-5. Automobile industry experience curves.

ing a choice of four or five pieces of optional equipment. These innovations gave the customer the feeling of having something unique and different from everyone else, and customers were willing to pay more for these innovations. The new experience curve emphasized *style*. By the time that Ford responded to the strategic thrusts that General Motors was making concerning style, General Motors began introducing frequent model changes, an experience curve the industry is still on today.

Peter Collier and David Horowitz describe an attempt that Ford employees made at trying to improve on Henry Ford's Model T:

> Harold Wills and others decided to welcome Henry home with a present—a new and streamlined version of the Model T which one employee felt was "so much over the original it was like night and day." When Ford returned to Dearborn, he went immediately to Highland Park, saw the car and asked what it was.
>
> Well, Mr. Ford," said an employee, "that's the new car."
>
> "Ford car?"
>
> "Yes, sir."
>
> "How long has it been standing there?" Ford asked.
>
> "Well, about two weeks. They just finished it. It's just going into production."
>
> "It's going into production?"
>
> "Yes, sir." The employee didn't catch the signs of Ford's rising anger in the flattened irony of his responses. "It's all tooled up and the orders are placed for the new car."
>
> Ford circled the car a couple of times with his hands in his pockets, then suddenly released them and sprang on it with a fury, opening the driver's door and ripping it off its hinges. He did the same for the passenger side. Then he jumped up on the hood to kick in the

windshield, and, yelling all the time, climbed up onto the top of the car and began to stomp down the roof.

As observer said later on, "We got the message. As far as he was concerned, the Model T was God and we were to put away false images."[1]

Not soon afterward, General Motors was able to capture from Ford the role of industry leader—this in an industry that Ford practically invented. Ford was so obsessed with the success of his vision of providing low-cost, basic transportation for the common person, that he was unable to make modifications to that vision, even in the face of evidence in the market place that the consumer no longer wanted the Model T. The style that General Motors offered became more important to the consumer than cost. Ford finally caught up with GM again in the 1986–1987 time frame on a profitability basis—more than 60 years later. How did Ford do it? The answer turned out to be the same: *style* again. Now the question can be asked: How long will it take GM to recover from *its* mistakes, especially in view of the foreign competition that has increased? According to Roger Smith: "As for the market for cars and

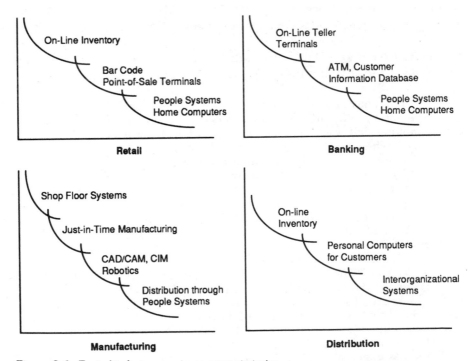

Figure 3-6. Typical industry experience curve strategies.

trucks, I just don't know whether we'll ever recapture the near 50 percent domestic share we had ten years ago."[2]

It can be extremely expensive to fail to recognize the need for making a shift from one experience curve to another. If the vision of top management does not encompass new technologies, it will not be possible for them to exploit them, and the enterprise will be left behind when its competitors begin to innovate. It is one thing to make technology decisions that are consistent with an already stated corporate strategy; but it is quite another to integrate technology issues into the strategic planning process itself. This is where the real payoff lies. In many cases, outside forces and technology can be more important than cost considerations. An example of such an outside force can be found in the sound recording industry in the controversy surrounding the digital audio tape (DAT) recorder. Record publishers in the United States fought the introduction of the DAT recorder because of its ability to make duplicate tapes with no generation loss. They fear that the perfect reproduction capabilities of DAT recorders and players may cause counterfeiting operations to spring up that would have a detrimental effect to their revenue streams.

Figure 3-6 on page 48 shows typical experience curve charts for a few major industries.

New Experience Curve Strategies

What is needed today are fresh strategies that are based on the new view of experience curves that we have been discussing. Instead of looking at experience curves from a purely cost-savings viewpoint, we need to look at them from the viewpoint of new technology that allows us to change the rules of competition, to significantly alter a process, to eliminate expensive functions, or to radically alter the structure of the industry when we shift from one experience curve to another. This may take some adjustment in the management mindset. With the advent of the new technologies of the 1990s we need to acquire these new mindsets quickly.

In the 1970s and 1980s experience curve strategies were used mainly to reduce costs and save money. For example, almost all enhancements in information systems have been aimed at lowering cost and maintaining quality. In today's environment, however, the emphasis has shifted. Corporations are now beginning to change to entirely new experience curves to enter new markets, to change the rules of competition in the industry, and to gain strategic advantage.

Analyzing Information Systems
Industry Experience

Analyzing the experience curves that exist in the information systems industry is a useful exercise in seeing how quantum jumps can occur in switching from one experience curve to another. The experience curve chart in Figure 3-7 shows that we began using computers to store *data*. Database techniques then allowed us to store data more efficiently and to begin retrieving *information*. An indication of the significance of this particular experience curve change is that we no longer use the term *data processing department*; instead we now refer to the *information systems department*.

Many people have not yet realized that another very significant experience curve change is just beginning to take place. The experience curve change through which we are passing with respect to information systems will prove to be much more significant than the change from a data to an information orientation. The changes that are occurring today represent the first really significant change in the storing of data in the 40-year history of the computer. For the first time, we are beginning to store something different from words or numbers. With advanced technologies like relational databases, personal computers, expert systems, CD-ROM, video disc, and touch screens, we are beginning to use computers to store charts, graphs, images, audio, full motion video, and complex financial models. These represent concepts in people's minds. We are storing *knowledge*. This change will have a profound effect on how we use computers and on the amount of computing power that will be required in the future. The management of some organizations have

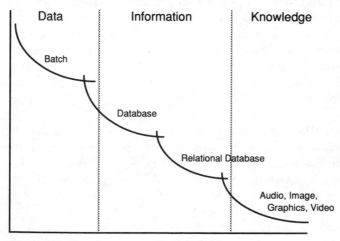

Figure 3-7. Experience curves for the use of computers.

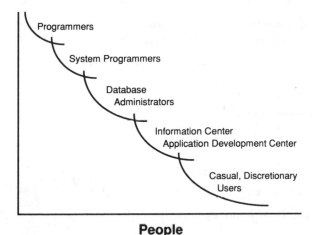

People

Figure 3-8. People-oriented information systems experience curves.

not yet acknowledged the importance of the traditional data processing uses of computers. What will happen to those organizations now that we are entering the knowledge-distribution age?

Figure 3-8 shows the experience curves for information systems that are related to people. Cost curves have dropped for employing the power of computers. The level of special education required to use computers has also dropped. Artificial intelligence and the personal computer have been significant forces driving this trend. Because of these changes, we have seen the programming of computers go from computer programmers doing everything in the early days, to specialization of functions in today's information systems departments, and finally to everyone being a programmer. To use a microwave oven or a refrigerator, the consumer now has to know how to program the device!

Anticipating New Experience Curve Strategies

One of the questions that always comes up in discussing this new view of experience curve strategies is "How do I find the next curve?" There is no simple answer to this question because management will always be working with limited information. A quote from the book *How Children Fail* provides an insight into how difficult it is to apply insight and intelligence to choosing when to shift from one experience curve to another:

> **Intelligence is not a measure of how much you know,**
> **rather it's how well you do when you don't know.**[3]

Choosing a new experience curve strategy is one of those areas where intuition often plays a greater role than logic. Having said that, we *can* identify some methods that often bear fruit in identifying changing experience curve strategies:

- Investigating parallel or similar industries
- Studying classical business linkages
- Analyzing industry and functional experience curves, often across dissimilar industries

Parallel or Similar Industries

It is often possible to identify parallel industries or related functions that suggest the way in which technology is beginning to evolve. For example, today's advanced personal computers had their beginnings in the once expensive technology of engineering workstations used for computer-aided design (CAD). Early developers of desktop publishing technology, such as Apple Computer, were able to identify the experience curve strategies that applied to the expensive workstations and were able to determine when this technology would be cost-effective on less expensive desktop machines. Many companies are now playing catch-up with the early developers of desktop publishing technology. Some are targeting the existing graphics curve, while some of the leaders are going after multimedia, image, voice annotation, and motion video.

In your own environment it is possible that the future technology is already being used, and you can see it; but perhaps it is being used in a different industry. A great many technologies that had their birth in the aerospace industry eventually came into common use competitively in other industries. We need to identify those ways in which we are like and those ways in which we are different from other industries. Analyzing what is going on in other industries that might be employing similar technology represents one way that we can anticipate the need to change to a new experience curve.

Classical Business Linkages

An analysis of the classical business linkages that exist in an industry can also often help to anticipate experience curve trends. Such a chart is

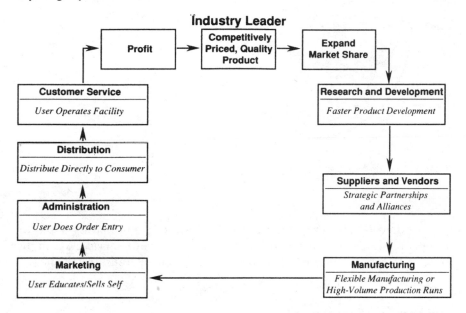

Figure 3-9. Classical business linkages.

shown in Figure 3-9. In today's business environment, many of the traditional intermediaries are being eliminated. Notice that the functions listed on the left in the classical business linkage chart shows functions (and, therefore, costs) that are beyond the traditional research and development, materials, and manufacturing functions. Opportunities for the use of information systems technology to jump to a new experience curve exist because many of the communication channels that are used in industry are subject to enhancement. Many customers have applied technology to vendor, manufacturer, and administrative applications, but not to other areas. The bottom of each box in Figure 3-9 indicates possible steps that might be taken in that function for improving the product flow. It is now clear that information about experience curves must be used across all functions of the product or service flow, beginning with the initial stages of the creation of the product or service to the final stages of delivery to the ultimate consumer.

For the most part we have applied technology only to manufacturing and upstream functions, plus perhaps some to administration. We have left relatively untouched other functions, which may represent 75 percent or more of the opportunity. These functions, such as marketing, administration, distribution, and customer service involve the same types of activity that we have traditionally associated with the *service sector* of the economy. Lack of attention to improving these activities is one of the reasons for today's negative productivity growth in the service industries. The service sector of the economy is information intensive and

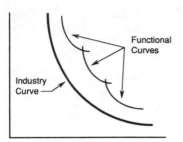

Figure 3-10. Industry and functional experience curves.

people driven. Therefore, if we can find ways of eliminating some of the people-intensive costs associated with a product or service, we might be able to significantly increase productivity and overall effectiveness.

Industry and Functional Experience Curves

Inside each of the industry curves that we have been discussing, we can usually identify a collection of *functional curves* that operate within the overall experience curve for that industry segment. (See Figure 3-10.) Changes that are occurring to the *functional* curves in our own industry can sometimes help us to determine when a new *industry* curve will be required. Often, by studying the individual, detailed functional curves that characterize the industry, we can discern an early indication of the formation of new strategic industry curves. These may someday result in the creation of new markets and in the restructuring of the industry.

Learning from the Shipping Industry

Figure 3-11 shows the industry and functional curves that characterize what happened a few years ago in the shipping industry. The first industry curve shown is for the trucking industry segment. One of the functional curves within the trucking industry curve concerns the point-to-point shipping of full truckloads of goods. In order to handle trucking to points not served by the point-to-point shipping of entire truckloads, many companies in the shipping industry established distribution centers and other techniques to handle the trucking of goods to destinations they did not then serve.

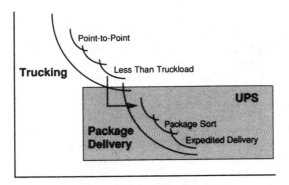

Figure 3-11. Industry and functional experience curves for the shipping industry.

Package Delivery

Another functional curve in the trucking industry concerns the shipping of quantities that are less than a truckload. Many companies gained experience with handling less-than-truckload (LTL) shipments, but United Parcel Service (UPS) was the first to create an entire business based on this type of shipping. In effect, what UPS did was to identify one of the individual functional curves in the trucking industry, which it then exploited to create an entirely new industry curve for what became the package delivery industry segment. The end result of this shift to a new experience curve was that UPS created new markets. It eventually changed the structure of the shipping industry and became much larger than any of the trucking companies associated with the industry curve discussed earlier. It was able to do this because UPS recognized a strategic business opportunity to fill a need that none of the trucking companies were willing to take the risk to fill.

There are a number of functional curves that can be identified in the package delivery industry segment created by UPS. One of the functional curves concerns the sorting of packages at distribution centers in routing a package to its destination. Efficient sorting of packages was one of the keys to the success of UPS. Although the sorting process worked efficiently, it was oriented toward maximizing the utilization of UPS trucks, and there was no way to guarantee a particular delivery time. In addition, it was not possible to track a package through the UPS system. Once a package entered the system, there was no way to tell where it was until it arrived at its destination. Two functional curves within the package delivery industry segment, then, concern delivery time and shipment tracking.

Overnight Delivery

Federal Express was the first company to capitalize on these two functional curves (first 24-hour delivery and later shipment tracking). (See Figure 3-12.) By initially limiting itself to 24-hour shipping, Federal Express was able to create an entire new industry curve from one of the functional curves in the package delivery industry segment. This segment of the shipping industry is now known as the overnight delivery industry. Federal Express and UPS are now the two biggest players in the overall shipping industry.

Inventory and Distribution Management

Another functional curve within the overnight shipping industry that was important to Federal Express was shipment tracking. Federal Express has invested heavily in information technology to be able to track each shipment. They can now tell at any time where any package is within the system. An outgrowth of the information systems that Federal Express built to handle the tracking of packages was an attempt at creating a new functional curve to handle the facsimile transmission of documents. Because of a number of factors, including missing the emergence of inexpensive fax machines, its initial attempt to create a new industry curve from this functional curve was not successful. However, much of the networking capability that Federal Express installed

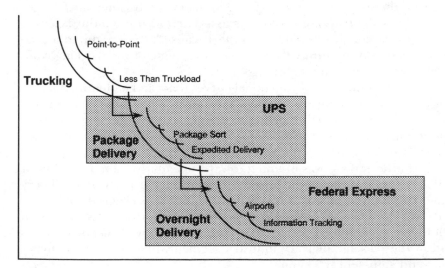

Figure 3-12. Federal Express and the overnight delivery industry.

to handle electronic mail was used in creating the inventory/distribution management system that Federal Express is now offering to large corporate clients. In this service, Federal Express handles a portion of the inventory function for a company and agrees to deliver any inventory item to its destination within a 24-hour period.

It is relatively easy for companies to drop down from the package delivery industry segment to the overnight delivery industry segment. UPS did that as soon as Federal Express demonstrated how lucrative this industry segment could be. But with the more advanced industry curves, which require the creation of a complex and expensive information infrastructure, it has become much more difficult to compete with Federal Express.

The Future of the Shipping Industry

To extrapolate into the future, we can make some guesses as to what the next industry curve might be in the shipping industry. An obvious one is to increase the penetration into international markets, and this is being done by many of the major players in the shipping industry, including Federal Express. Another potentially lucrative functional curve for Federal Express may involve capitalizing on the information infrastructure that it has built to handle the inventory and distribution functions for its corporate customers and expand this to reach individual consumers.

Federal Express would seem to be ideally positioned to reach the consumer directly because of the access it has to both corporate clients and individual homes across the country. Federal Express has already established access to inventory and distribution information for many of the companies with which it does business. And, their network of airports, distribution centers, and delivery trucks provide them with direct access to consumers in the home. It would seem to be a logical step to tie these together to perform inventory and distribution functions for companies such as large retail companies, who distribute goods directly to consumers. This is likely to be an even bigger market than any of the others as electronic marketing to the home significantly increases.

Changing Industry Structures

If we look at the entire set of industry and functional curves for the shipping industry, a key question becomes: "What is the shipping industry?" The functions that are being performed at the bottom of the chart are fundamentally different from those being performed at the top. An example here from another industry sheds additional light on this point. The *information* that American Airlines generates (airline reservations data) has generated higher profit margins in recent years than did its physical resources (terminal buildings and aircraft). If this is the case, what is the airline industry?

The same may be beginning to be true for the shipping industry. The information infrastructure that Federal Express is creating is fast becoming more valuable than the airports, planes, and trucks it has acquired. Federal Express has been enormously successful because it has been able to exploit experience curves in its industry, to take necessary risks, and to very quickly make the right things happen. It is very possible that Federal Express was not the first to think of any of the innovations that it capitalized on, but it is the company that was willing to take the risks and exploit new ideas to achieve competitive advantage. American Airlines and Federal Express each demonstrate many of the qualities of an "innovative leader." American Airlines is discussed further in Chapter 9.

Investing in Technology

It has been traditional in American business to view organizations from the perspective of the traditional management triangle, first described by Robert Anthony in 1965.[4] What has now happened in many industries is that the blue-color work force has been steadily shrinking because of the management focus on cutting costs and because of the successes of early applications of technology in the lower waves of innovation discussed in Chapter 2. This has often resulted in the "Christmas-tree" form of organizational structure shown in Figure 3-13. Many organizations are finding it to be a requirement, because of intense competitive pressures, to trim out some of the layers of middle

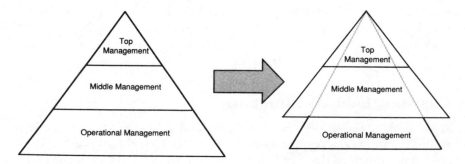

Figure 3-13. Changing management pyramid.

management. This is represented in the diagram by those areas of the pyramid outside of the shaded lines.

Many times this is referred to as decentralization of the organization, streamlining the decision-making process, or enabling the organization to become more dynamic and flexible. No matter what it is called, however, it is still *downsizing the organization*. This downsizing is not necessarily wrong. In fact, downsizing can result in significant cost savings that can generate additional funds for the organization. The question becomes, what will the new funds be used for? Will the new funds be invested back into the organization for research, development, innovation, implementation of new technologies, increasing market share, or restructuring and repositioning the organization? In other words, will the funds be used to create new levels of organizational effectiveness? What has been happening in many organizations is that the funds that result from downsizing have often been carried down to the bottom line and paid out to stockholders in the form of increased dividends or sometimes to repurchase the company's stock. Innovative organizations are instead using these cost savings to fund a switch to new experience curves in order to create competitive advantage for the future.

Experience Curve Strategies

Pankaj Ghemawat said the following in "Building Strategy on the Experience Curve":

> What distinguishes the winners from the losers in the experience curve game is their grasp of both the logic of the experience curve and the characteristics of the competitive arena that determines its suitability as a strategic weapon.[5]

The challenges are to determine the suitability of applying technology and to learn how to use it as a strategic weapon. In order to do this, we must ask ourselves whether the organization has the proper controls and structures that are required to assimilate, learn, and change. Just as in Chapter 2 we were able to plot the waves of innovation against the management culture of the organization, we can also assess whether the management philosophies of the organization enable or inhibit our ability to identify requirements for shifting to new experience curves. We must ask questions like:

- What industry and functional curves are we currently on?
- What industry and functional curves are our competitors on?
- Who is likely to be the key player in the future? Us, a competitor, or a new player?

- What will it take to effectively compete in the future?
- Does the organization have the ability to create or move to the new curves?

Conclusion

The industry leaders are implementing new industry and functional experience curves to exploit the chaotic forces at play in the environment. These new curves go far beyond the traditional cost-savings orientation and are frequently used as weapons to achieve competitive advantage. Managers must assess the organization's ability to exploit experience curve strategies in the areas of technology and competitiveness. To a major extent, it is the uses of experience curve strategies as strategic weapons that are changing classical industry relationships. We must make no assumptions concerning experience curve strategies. In many cases, leaders are both decentralizing and centralizing. In attempting to identify the need to shift to a new experience curve it is important to ask ourselves, Are managing by "The Paul Masson School of Technology"?

We will use no system before its time.

Chapter 4 provides insight into methods for understanding how power structures are changing in the industry and to properly position the organization to take advantage of strategic opportunities. Chapter 4 builds on the understanding provided by studying the waves of innovation and experience curves.

References

1. Peter Collier and David Horowitz. *The Fords: An American Epic*. New York: Summit Books, 1987.
2. Wilton Woods. "The U.S. Must Do as GM Has Done." *Fortune*, February 13, 1989.
3. John Holt. *How Children Fail*. New York: Dell, 1988.
4. R. N. Anthony. *Planning and Control Systems: A Framework for Analysis*. Boston: Harvard Business School Division of Research Press, 1965.
5. Pankaj Ghemawat. "Building Strategy on the Experience Curve." *Harvard Business Review*. March–April, 1985.

4
Redefining Industry Power Relationships

Introduction

As we pointed out in Chapter 1, the road maps are now gone and management needs a new set of lenses to view the business environment. Examining how industry power relationships are being redefined provides a lens for viewing the organization's competitive environment. An analysis of changing industry power relationships represents the third step in the strategic thinking process. We began, in Chapter 2, by looking at the broad technology waves that characterize the industry. In Chapter 3 we examined technology more closely by analyzing experience curve strategies. In this chapter, we create charts of the power relationships that exist today in the industry and then describe techniques for predicting how these power relationships can be redefined through appropriate applications of technology. We will see that an analysis of changing industry power relationships is an excellent tool for assessing an organization's competitiveness, both now and in the future.

Expanding the Competitive Forces Model

In Chapter 2, we introduced three characteristics of the use of technology that Porter and Millar have found produce substantial and sustainable competitive advantage:

- It alters industry structures.
- It supports cost and differentiation strategies.
- It spawns entirely new industries.

We also introduced Michael Porter's chart of competitive forces. We can use such a chart to begin understanding the competitive environment and to identify those uses of technology that are likely to generate substantial and sustainable competitive advantage. In this chapter, we will expand the competitive forces model of Michael Porter to create a *strategic forces model* that includes technology, demographics, converging industries, government awareness of impacts to health and the environment, global competition, the waves of innovation, and whatever else is important in our particular environment. We can use the strategic forces model, shown in Figure 4-1, to help define and assess changes within the organization's internal and external relationships. We must analyze each of the forces shown in Figure 4-1 and alert the organization to threats and potential opportunities. The challenge in the future will be to manage within a world of accelerating change.

The strategic forces model can be used as a framework to generate a number of thought provoking ideas, such as:

- What is the impact of technology on the enterprise and on the industry as a whole?
- What is the impact of current and future government regulation or deregulation?
- What important changes are occurring in the industry and what changes could occur in the future?
- What waves of innovation are emerging (see Chapter 2)?
- What new experience curves can be exploited (see Chapter 3)?

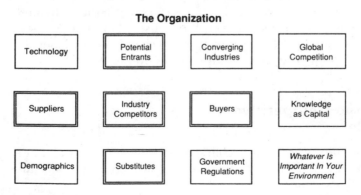

Figure 4-1. Strategic forces model.

- How can we raise entry costs to new entrants into the industry?
- Can sophisticated information systems help?
- Are customers demanding value-added information systems services?
- Are functional relationships being restructured?

Defining Industry Power Relationships

An important part of strategic thinking is to develop charts of these strategic forces to analyze the *power relationships* that exist in the industry. We can then use these charts to begin assessing how technology can be used to redefine these power relationships to shape the future for the organization's benefit. Figure 4-2 shows the traditional relationships that might exist in a typical enterprise. This chart shows a chain that runs from the supplier to the manufacturer to the wholesaler to the retailer. A chart such as this begins to point out the key *linkages* that exist within the organization and within the industry. An important part of strategic thinking is to identify these linkages, to determine which of them are most important to the enterprise, and to anticipate how they are likely to change. Management of the links and the associated relationships then becomes a critical issue that must be addressed.

Determining Who Owns the Chart

An important question to ask when analyzing any chart of industry power relationships is: "Who owns the chart?" By "owner," we mean the predominant player—the one who typically sets the rules. If the chart in Figure 4-2 represents the automobile industry and has been prepared

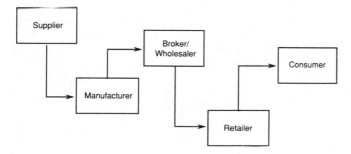

Figure 4-2. Traditional industry power relationships.

by the management of a major automobile manufacturer, we can safely surmise that *they* own the chart. But if the chart had been prepared by the management of a manufacturer of brake linings, then they do not own the chart; they are one of the *members*—a niche player. If we do not own the chart, then we must determine who the owner is, predict what the owner of the chart is going to do, and analyze the evolving rules of competition within the industry. An analysis of an industry power relationships chart can provide us with a powerful tool for visualizing where we are with respect to the competition and to other organizations with which we interact. It provides a method that we can begin to use to answer some of the questions we asked earlier.

Constructing Changing Industry Power Relationships Charts

An important step in analyzing industry power relationships is to determine how the power relationships, and, therefore, how the linkages in the chart, are likely to change in the future. As the organization begins to use advanced technology to achieve competitive advantage it is important to determine how these links must be *managed*. Figure 4-3 shows the relationships that might exist when an organization uses advanced information systems technology to establish *electronic channels* for streamlining communications between organizations. Some key questions that should be asked about this new chart of industry power relationships are:

- Who owns the new chart now? Are we a member or the owner?
- How will the linkages change in the future?

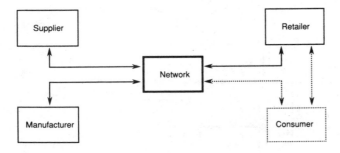

Figure 4-3. Changing industry power relationships.

- How can we more effectively exploit the organization's assets and more effectively manage the linkages shown on the chart?

- Could some parallel or complementary industry replace our products or services?

- What impact could the converging industries or strategic alliances have on the organization?

- What new innovation waves or experience curves are emerging and how might industry power relationships be affected?

In the example shown in Figure 4-3, electronic channels might permit the manufacturer to begin using "just in time manufacturing." It might also allow techniques such as "just in time distribution" to the retailer. Future technological enhancements might allow the consumer to be reached directly. The "network" box in Figure 4-3 might be today's people-driven distribution channels, it might represent a series of alliances, or it could be knowledge workers grouped together by electronic channels. Such changes in industry power relationships often have significant impacts on the players on the chart. For example, in this case the use of electronic channels facilitates a more streamlined and effective distribution system. In many cases, it is probable that some intermediary distribution functions may be eliminated, unless they can provide significant value-added services to their customers.

Part of the strategic thinking process involves drawing charts of changing industry power relationships for the organization and the industry of which it is a part. Such charts provide a powerful tool for visualizing where the organization is with respect to the environment. This phase of strategic thinking involves two important steps: *identifying* the links and then determining how to *manage* them.

Step 1: Identifying the Links

By drawing charts of changing industry power relationships, we can begin to identify the important links that exist in an industry. There are a number of questions that we can ask in attempting to understand these links:

- What are we doing, and what should we be doing, relative to gaining substantial and sustainable competitive advantage, given the existing industry power relationships?

- Are we changing the industry? Are we leaders in the industry, or simply reacting to changes caused by others? Are we using electronic channels, or are they being installed by our competitors? If our competitors are installing them, will we be able to compete in the future?

- Are we differentiating ourselves and our products from others?
- Are we entering new markets?

We must ask the question: "Who will own the chart in the future?" The answer may be:

- Those who have a vision of the future and are using technology effectively.
- Those with the ability to understand the converging and restructuring of industries.
- The organizations with the insight to form powerful alliances with important external organizations (suppliers, customers, companies having complementary products/services, and so on).
- The organizations who enter new markets to find opportunities for expanding from their mature markets.
- The organizations with a comprehensive strategy for the use of technology.

Understanding who owns or controls a chart of industry power relationships today and who is likely to own it in the future is critical to formulating strategies for cooperating with strategic partners and for dealing effectively with the competition.

Step 2: Managing the Links

It is not enough to identify and understand the linkages that exist in the organization and in the industry as a whole. Once we have identified the important external linkages, we must then develop strategic plans for actively managing these links. Managing the links is essential to achieving sustained strategic advantage. In many cases, it will happen that no one in the organization has the responsibility for managing the external linkages that we identify. When this occurs, management must ensure that strategic and tactical plans are developed for ensuring that the right individuals in the organization take responsibility for managing important linkages. The process must be formalized, and the management team must constantly assess how it is doing in managing the organization's relationships with external organizations. The failure of an organization to manage important linkages can be as much of a problem as failing to recognize a new wave of innovation or failing to implement a required new experience curve.

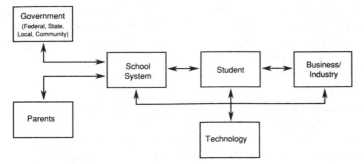

Figure 4-4. Power relationship chart for public education.

Power Relationships in Education

Charts of changing industry power relationships can be drawn up for any type of organization. For example, school systems in the United States are beginning to use the techniques we discuss here to analyze their own power relationships. (See Figure 4-4.) With respect to schools, the *supplier*—the school system—owned the chart in the past. In the future it appears that the *buyer*—business and industry—will have significantly more influence and, in a number of situations, may even own the chart in the future. For example, a state might analyze power relationships in order to use education to create the best possible workforce and thus be better able to attract new industry into the state.

Identifying Strategic Business Alliances

Another key question that we must ask in analyzing industry power relationships is this: "How might the enterprise form strategic alliances that can be advantageous?" If organizations can join forces to cause changes in industry power relationships, we must be able to anticipate these alliances. We must also anticipate strategic alliances that might be detrimental to the enterprise and weigh the tradeoffs, benefits, exposures, and investments accordingly.

The creation of strategic alliances will be an important task for many organizations in the 1990s. Strategic alliances can be a much quicker and less expensive method for achieving competitive advantage than other methods. The use of advanced technology to create electronic channels makes many new types of strategic alliance possible in which organizations are glued together electronically and not by means of bricks and mortar or through outright ownership. Such alliances enable the organization to cross traditional industry boundaries in order to compete in fundamentally different ways. Often, the way that technology will be used to enhance the development of strategic alliances will be through sharing of communication networks, consumer databases, and application functions.

This sharing of functions is taking place in two stages. First, members of alliances are beginning to share functions in development, distribution, marketing, education, and maintenance for products or services. Such sharing of functions will help to reduce development cycle times, provide economies of scale and scope, and create new opportunities not possible for any of the individual organizations working alone. Second, alliances will be formed in which organizations will work together to provide a single image to the customer organization or to the consumer. By achieving this, the members of the alliance will be able to provide a common solution. Here, we will find the members of the alliance jointly developing solutions that are designed to be tightly integrated into the customer's business operations. An example of this might be joint development of computer applications and product distribution systems that are designed to provide a single image to the customer. Today we see the beginnings of this trend with the Quik Link system, provided by the Corporate Alliance, a health care industry alliance founded by Abbott Laboratories and 3M. Quik Link provides hospitals with a wide variety of products that are required to operate a hospital. The alliance between American Airlines AAdvantage frequent flier program and other organizations, such as Citibank's credit card operation, is another example.

It is important to realize that changing industry power relationships are occurring on a broad scale in certain industries. Organizations in the *converging industries* are altering their structures and their power relationships so radically that the very nature of these industries is changing beyond recognition. In many cases, accepted industry definitions have become obsolete. Banking is a prime example of this trend.

Two Views of Changing Industry Power Relationships Charts

We can adopt two different views of the charts of changing industry power relationships when we perform this phase of strategic thinking. We can take a high-level *industry view* in which we perform a strategic assessment of the organization's position with respect to other organizations. The industry view has been the focus of this chapter thus far. Alternatively, we can take a more functional *internal view*. Here, we analyze the effectiveness of the organizational structure and see which functions are critical. Understanding this, we can then ask what enhancements can be made to these functions to provide substantial and sustainable competitive advantage. Could restructuring or enhancing these functions enhance the organization's role in the industry, or even change the industry? From a negative viewpoint, what changes in the industry would have a major impact on the key internal functions? An example of this might be the future impact of the home shopping phenomenon on the major internal distribution, warehousing, and retail store functions of large retailers such as Sears, JCPenney, and K Mart. To use the industry power relationships charts to assess internal restructuring for the future may be as critical as understanding the changes that are occurring in the industry. To be caught by significant industry shifts and not be able to respond can be a major problem. In the future, internal and external changes will no longer be separable. In many cases, in order to downsize or form alliances, we will have to off-load functions to outside the organization. We have to recognize that the traditional demarcation of functions in many cases will no longer make sense.

Conclusion

Analyzing industry power relationships can help to suggest ways that the organization can foster a feeling of innovation and entrepreneuring. We once saw the following quote of John Masters, a Texas oil executive, hanging on the wall of the Dallas/Fort Worth airport:

> You have to recognize that every out-front maneuver you make is going to be lonely, but if you feel entirely comfortable, then you're not far enough ahead to do any good. That warm sense of everything is going well is usually the body temperature at the center of the herd.

By examining and clearly understanding industry power relationships, top management can begin to have an understanding of how the enterprise must operate in the context of an *extended enterprise*. Chapter 5 introduces the extended enterprise and discusses how competitive forces are driving or enabling the restructuring of the organization.

Remember:

If you don't make dust, you eat dust.

5
Extending the Enterprise

Introduction

In the past, the relationships we have created with the organizations with which we do business have largely been arms-length relationships that operate in the context of formal rules, contracts, and procedures. There has typically been little or no interaction between companies in an individual organization's internal decision-making process. However, as organizations are beginning to integrate their operations through linkages with customers and suppliers, it has begun to happen that critical day-to-day managerial decisions within a supplier organization are now often made outside that organization in the offices of a major customer. In addition, the just-in-time environment and its requirement for quick delivery from suppliers puts customers in a delicate position if the shipments stop for some reason. We believe that in examining the realm and the extent of the organization, we must begin to look further out from the traditional legal boundaries and legal definitions as we have known them in the past.

The analysis of changing industry power relationships that we began in Chapter 4 leads directly to an understanding of how organizations operate in the context of an *extended enterprise*.

> **The concept of the extended enterprise is a key element in the formulation of a strategic business vision and is critical to the development of effective strategies.**

We cannot develop effective strategies today unless we have a clear understanding of how the enterprise interacts with external organizations. Using this lens for visualizing the organization's extended enterprise is the fourth step of the strategic thinking process we began in the previous three chapters.

Classical Management Organizational Structure

Top management has traditionally viewed the enterprise using Robert Anthony's classical management triangle, which we introduced in Chapter 3.[1] By the term *enterprise* here we are referring to the functions that are within the traditional management and legal boundaries of the organization. In the traditional organizational structure, power flows downward, from top management, through middle management, to operational managers and supervisors. At the same time, information flows upward, and day-to-day execution is at the operational levels. It is important to understand that the types of decision made at each level in the organization differ. According to Simon, the decisions made by operational management tend to be structured and repetitive. Middle management operates in an environment where decisions are semistructured and not nearly as repetitive as those of lower-level management. Top management makes decisions that are very unstructured and are rarely repetitive.[2] These distinctions can be very helpful when reflecting on the innovation arrow.

The Extended Enterprise

It is now clear that businesses no longer fit the classical model of a chief executive officer directing internal corporate operations, such as manufacturing or purchasing, without regard to customers, suppliers, competitors, and advanced technology. The new economic realities demand that we redefine the organizational structure so that it comprises not only our organization but also the organizations with which we interact—an *extended enterprise*. Figure 5-1 shows how the classical Robert Anthony view of the enterprise (the top part of the chart) is augmented by the organizations with which the enterprise does business (the bottom part of the chart). The elements of the organization's extended enterprise may include suppliers, buyers, government agencies, and all other external organizations that are important to the organization's success.

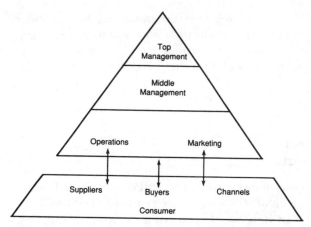

Figure 5-1. Extended enterprise.

Having reviewed the waves of innovation, experience curve strategies, and power relationship charts, we can now begin defining the structure of the organization's extended enterprise, an important part of strategic thinking. In constructing an extended enterprise chart, the three steps shown in Figure 5-2 are important. First, we must identify the key *parts* of the organization's extended enterprise. Second, we must identify the key *linkages* that exist in the external environment. Finally, we must learn how to effectively *manage* these linkages. By performing these three steps we can develop a concept of the organization's extended enterprise and begin creating the visual imagery that describes the organization of the future. The ability to visually see the structure of the extended enterprise can help us to begin communicating the vision throughout the organization.

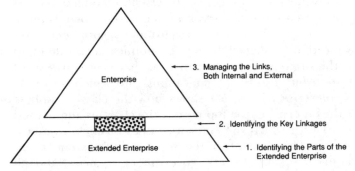

Figure 5-2. Constructing the extended enterprise.

Fundamental Insights

Perceiving the business in the context of an extended enterprise requires a clear understanding of two fundamental insights. First, the success of the enterprise depends on the existing and potential relationships that exist among all elements of the extended enterprise, including workers, managers, suppliers, competitors, and distribution channels. Second, the information content of products and services in most industries is steadily increasing. Many industries continue to price products and services and develop strategies based on the cost of raw materials, manufacturing, and transportation. This is done not realizing the following important fact of life in today's business environment:

> **Over 70 percent of the final cost of goods and services delivered to customers is dependent on information.**

Long-term success will be determined by how well the organization is able to capture, manipulate, exchange, manage and use information as a strategic tool.

New Organizational Perspective

An organization that is structured along the lines of the classical management triangle, and is managed using traditional methods, often pursues competitive advantage by focusing upward within the enterprise. This focus often results in a manufacturing and staff orientation and creates a demand-driven, transaction-oriented environment that was appropriate when stable industry structures were the norm and when there was no shortage of skilled workers. The emphasis in such an environment tends to be on developing effective management control systems. In today's environment, the ways in which leading organizations are achieving competitive advantage are changing radically. Figure 5-3 shows how strategies for achieving competitive advantage have been moving upward through the organization over time and are now moving outward into the extended enterprise. It is extremely important that these strategies move outward in order to exploit the entire extended enterprise rather than limiting the strategic view to only the internal resources that the organization controls. The extended enterprise must become the focus of new attempts at achieving *strategic* advantage.

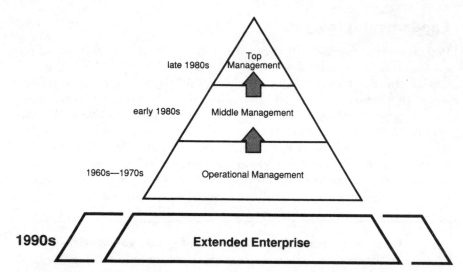

Figure 5-3. Competitive advantage is moving upward through the organization and outward into the extended enterprise.

Views of the Organization

We can view the organization using either an *internal* focus or an *external* focus. Although an internal focus is still important in many cases, adopting an external focus will allow us to identify opportunities for creating strategic advantage by looking at differentiation strategies, new markets, and changes in industry structure. As we have been stressing, success will increasingly depend on using advanced technology to create electronic channels that allow direct communication with all the key elements in the extended enterprise.

Internal View

An internal view of the organization represents the traditional view of organizational structures that we have had in the past. Strategic thinking that takes an internal focus can begin with a list of the key functions or assets that are important today for the organization. After we create such a list, we can look out 3 to 5 years and identify those functions or assets that will become important in the future. We can then place the internal functions and assets on a chart that begins to show the key linkages that exist among the important functions and assets. (See Figure 5-4.) If one or more of the functions or assets in the first list is likely to change, we can then begin to predict what will be the impact of that change on the others. It is important

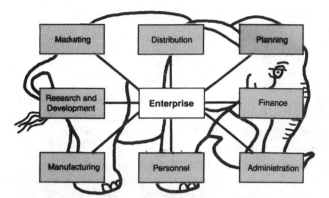

Figure 5-4. Internal analysis of the enterprise.

that the entire management team develop a single, consistent internal view of the organization. All managers and all workers must understand the key functions, important strategies, and the project priorities in order for the organization to achieve success in the environment of the 1990s. All must be looking at the same elephant. Strategic thinking techniques that focus on the internal view are still valuable, and the leaders in today's environment are those that have been able to successfully employ such techniques in mapping the way in which the organization should evolve.

An internal strategic thinking focus has allowed organizations to significantly enhance their operations in the following areas:

- Enhancing quality
- Becoming the low-cost provider
- Becoming the most effective marketer
- Increasing flexibility
- Improving service
- Enhancing innovation and creativity
- Improving profitability
- Enhancing management decisions

All of the preceding are still important. However, before analyzing the organization from an internal perspective, it is of significant value to first perform an analysis that is based on an *external* view. An analysis of external factors will allow the planning group to better understand the impact of modifications to the organization that are being demanded by the changing environment. It enables the group to better understand how to better exploit internal assets in the extended enterprise to provide strategic advantage.

External View

With an external view, the focus of strategic thinking is on a different set of factors. These are significantly different than the factors we analyze when we examine the organization with an internal focus, and these tend to be much more important as well. To analyze the external view of the organization, we draw up lists of important external functions, external assets, and stakeholders in the organization. To be most useful, we should limit such a list to the 6 or 7, no more than 10, key elements in the extended enterprise. (See Figure 5-5.)

There are two types of stakeholder in the extended enterprise that are important. One type consists of those people or organizations that are affected by decisions that your organization makes. Another type consists of those people or organizations whose decisions have an impact on your organization. It is important that in building the list that we take into considerations both types of stakeholder. We can then place the external elements that we identify in a chart that will allow us to begin characterizing the organization's extended enterprise. (See Figure 5-6.) After completing the chart, we again look out 3 to 5 years and try to identify how the stakeholders are likely to change and to find the key linkages among them. As with the charts of changing industry power relationships that we examined in Chapter 4, once we have identified the important linkages in the extended enterprise, we must then determine how these linkages must be managed. The process of identifying the important linkages in the extended enterprise and determining how these linkages must be managed are key parts of strategic

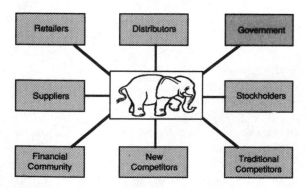

Figure 5-5. External analysis of the enterprise.

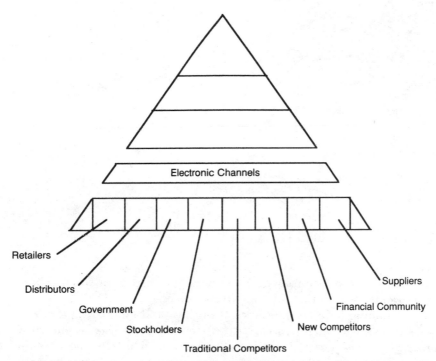

Figure 5-6. Extended enterprise view of the organization.

thinking and are important steps in beginning to formulate a strategic business vision.

When we analyze the organization from an internal perspective, the advantages we are able to achieve are focused inward on the organization itself. Although these advantages are certainly important, we have seen that they are no longer enough. When we analyze the organization from an external focus, we will find that we can achieve results that have significantly greater impact than those we can achieve with an internal focus. These results include:

- Achieving strategic advantage
- Differentiating products and services
- Creating electronic channels
- Building people systems
- Entering new markets
- Restructuring the organization
- Restructuring the industry

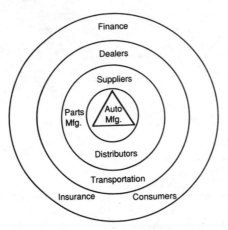

Figure 5-7. Automobile manufacturing industry.

Figure 5-7 shows examples of the elements in the extended enterprise of an organization in the automotive industry.

By examining industry power relationships and identifying the linkages that exist, we might picture the extended enterprise as shown in Figure 5-8. Such a chart allows us to begin seeing which linkages are the most important and allows us to begin asking questions about how the organization might begin to enhance market share in important supporting industries, such as auto financing and auto insurance. The

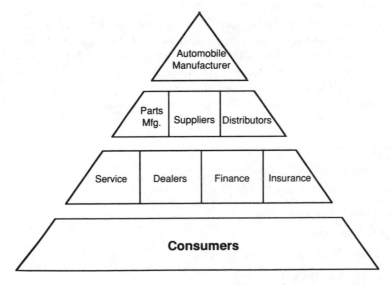

Figure 5-8. Extended enterprise for an automobile manufacturer.

chart enables us to begin identifying how the consumer can be better served in the future, for example by using such technology as home computers and touch screens to help in choosing appropriate options and to automate the ordering process. As we begin to understand these linkages, we can better see how critical internal assets and linkages need to be enhanced or offered to partners as a vehicle for improving the effectiveness of the entire extended enterprise. In fact, some of these internal assets, when shared with other organizations, increase loyalty and become barriers to switching to the competition.

Owner or Member?

Figure 5-9 shows two different ways in which we can view the extended enterprise. As we discussed in Chapter 4, we must again ask: "Who owns the chart?" The organization will have an entirely different set of objectives if we determine that the organization is the *owner* of the chart than if we decide that it is a member of some more powerful organization's extended enterprise.

Objectives of the Owner

An organization that is the owner of the extended enterprise must carefully choose members for the extended enterprise that are likely to be

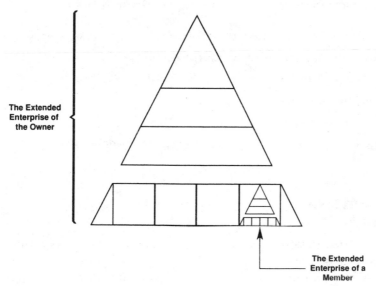

Figure 5-9. Views of the extended enterprise.

successful. The organization must then work with them to ensure your *combined* success. The success of the owner organization is tied directly to the success of the members. The following should be some key objectives for the "owner" of the chart:

- Maintain loyalty.
- Protect existing markets.
- Develop new markets.
- Cross industry boundaries.
- Reduce costs to the customer.
- Enhance service.
- Change industry structures.
- Increase the overall competitiveness of the entire extended enterprise.

Objectives of a Member

Just as it is important for the owner of the extended enterprise to ensure the success of its members, it is of paramount importance that a member choose an owner who is also likely to be successful. The organization must then work with the owner to ensure their mutual prosperity. The following are some of the objectives that are important for a "member" of some other organization's extended enterprise:

- Understand the "owner's" view of the extended enterprise.
- Understand and build your own extended enterprise.
- Take advantage of the opportunities that exist.
- Understand the exposures that exist.
- Become more efficient.
- Anticipate and respond to the owner's needs and demands.

Creating a Win-Win Environment

It is important that the linkages that exist between the members of the extended enterprise create *synergies*. The whole should become more valuable than the sum of the parts. We must optimize these synergies for the long-term survival of the entire extended enterprise. Whether the organization is the owner of the extended enterprise or a member, the following is critical:

> **All members of the extended enterprise must work together in *win-win relationships*.**

The win-win environment is key if the entire extended enterprise is to successfully compete in the changing global markets. A win-win environment means to share a common vision and to work toward common objectives. It is important to realize that win-lose partnerships inevitably become lose-lose in the long term.

Developing Management Strategies

It is important in today's environment for the entire management team to adopt a view of the organization that looks outward and recognizes the importance of the extended enterprise. This will allow the management team to begin assessing the strategic position of the organization with respect to the industry. It will also lead to identifying requirements for restructuring the organization to better use advanced technology to create the electronic channels that will be needed. In the future, the converging industries will have a greater impact on the organization and we will require a more global view of the competitive environment.

Communicating the Vision

We must ensure that the extended enterprise can successfully compete with the extended enterprises of the competition. In order to do this, the bottom line in the new environment is that we must communicate the extended enterprise vision throughout all the members in the extended enterprise, and we must also be willing to constantly reassess the vision of the extended enterprise and to make changes as they are required.

Using Electronic Channels

In order for the extended enterprise to be successful, it is important to make appropriate use of electronic channels that permit the elements of the extended enterprise to effectively communicate. The creation of strategic advantage in the extended enterprise often begins by establishing simple electronic channels that allow the members of the extended enterprise to exchange business transactions with one another. The members can then extend the reach of these electronic channels and change organizational structures to more closely integrate their business operations. The electronic channels can then be extended even further to cause a restructuring of the industry in which the extended enterprise operates. Channels that reach the ultimate consumers of products and services often create entire new industries. Examples of these types of electronic channel abound in industry. American Airlines with its pioneering work on airline reservations systems is a prime example that we examine in depth in Chapter 9. Consumers can now book airline flights, make hotel reservations, and reserve rental cars using an inexpensive home computer. The partnership of Sears and IBM in the Prodigy system that is bringing retail distribution channels directly into the consumer's home is another example. Banking has used electronic funds transfer to speed the flow of money and in some cases has brought access to banking services directly into the homes of consumers. The reader can probably think of many more examples of sophisticated electronic channels that are being used today. The way in which electronic channels must evolve is discussed in detail in Chapter 6.

Conclusion

An organization's success will increasingly depend on its ability to ensure that it is able to achieve strategic advantage by exploiting not only its own internal resources but the collective resources of the entire extended enterprise. The competitive environment today is no longer a simple one where organizations are pitted against organizations. Instead, the management team must ensure that its entire extended enterprise is positioned to compete with the extended enterprises of the competition. Those organizations that have a clear vision of their extended enterprise will have overwhelming advantages over those organizations that have not been able to articulate such a strategic view.

References

1. R. N. Anthony. *Planning and Control Systems: A Framework for Analysis.* Boston: Harvard Business School Division of Research Press, 1965.
2. H. Simon. *The New Science of Management Decision. Englewood Cliffs, NJ: Prentice Hall, 1977.*

6

Visualizing the Electronic Channels

Introduction

Having a clear view of changing industry power relationships and a chart of the extended enterprise, we can begin to develop a strategy for using electronic channels. The lens we discuss in this chapter suggests ways in which we can take action in implementing the strategies that are evolving. This discussion of electronic channels examines both the linkages that exist within the organization and the linkages that connect the organization with external members of the extended enterprise. Electronic channels constitute major tools for implementing and exploiting the extended enterprise. They are the tools we use to improve the effectiveness of the organization's external and internal links. These linkages, when they are identified and automated, will position us to achieve greater market share, provide the ability to expand into new markets, and allow us to realize marketing and cost advantages over the competition. In some cases, we may be able to use electronic channels to change the very structure of the industry. This chapter examines factors that are motivating organizations to create electronic channels. It also examines technologies for implementing electronic channels that can create significant entry barriers for the competition.

Definitions

Before we discuss how channel systems have evolved, it will be helpful to establish a common vocabulary to help guide us through this chapter.

A *channel* is a conduit or pipe that connects two or more points. A *marketing channel* or a *distribution channel* is a conduit for products, services, or information. Such a conduit can exist inside or outside of the organization; it can be either *physical* (for example, a fleet of trucks) or *electronic* (for example, a network for interconnecting computers).

Information Systems Evolution

As we have seen, information systems began as purely internal systems for supporting the enterprise and for implementing cost avoidance strategies. They are now evolving into strategic systems for producing revenue and for creating substantial and sustainable competitive advantage. It is becoming clear that those who are unable to recognize and act on the changing role of information systems will face a declining share of the market and perhaps risk being unable to survive within their industry. The information systems that leading organizations are installing today are significantly enhancing and expanding the scope of the electronic channels that early information systems implemented.

The Evolution of Channel Systems

Electronic channels have evolved in a series of stages over time from the early internal online computer systems that many organizations installed in the 1960s. The first stage in the evolution of external electronic channels occurred when internal online computer systems made the first step outward by allowing electronic communication to take place *between organizations* on a transaction-to-transaction basis. The pioneering efforts at *electronic data interchange* (EDI) are examples of this first stage.

Electronic Data Interchange

The early applications of computer-to-computer communication between organizations were called EDI. Normally, the intent of EDI systems is to eliminate time delays, save on people cost, and streamline the administrative process. The management focus on systems that use EDI is to reduce cost and save money—below-the-line functions.

The first significant industrywide system to use electronic data interchange was installed in the 1960s by the railroad industry in the United

States to implement a railroad car repair billing system. Each major type of repair to a railroad car was standardized so that any railroad could repair any car and then bill the appropriate railroad for the repair. The American Association of Railroads was instrumental in designing and implementing this system. Other examples of EDI include computer-to-computer order entry, electronic funds transfer, and exchange of shipping notifications.

Interorganizational Systems

Many organizations that developed EDI systems early have already evolved to the next step of *interorganizational systems* (IOS), first described by Cash and Kosynski. The use of interorganizational systems creates a more advanced stage of organizational interdependence. These systems go beyond a transaction-to-transaction orientation and have often caused major organizational restructuring to occur in those industries that have used them. Examples of interorganizational systems can be found in the automotive and chemical industries where organizations jointly develop just-in-time inventory, quality control, electronic billing, and engineering development systems. In the retail industry, examples can be found in quick-response, zero-balance inventory systems that interlink major retailers with their suppliers. Major opportunities for these systems exist in the more service-oriented sectors, such as insurance, banking, health, and education. The intent of IOS is to start with below-the-line EDI functions and then shift to an above-the-line, strategic orientation. The focus of IOS is toward gaining market share through creating strategic advantage. The sharing of communication networks among organizations is a major component of these systems. Interorganizational system networks provide the electronic channels that can be used to change the structure of the organizations that share them.

Electronic Channel Support Systems

Organizations that have evolved from EDI systems to IOS are now beginning to develop and use an entirely new type of channel system. As we push down into the extended enterprise, more sophisticated channel systems are required that are involved with the distribution of *knowledge* and with the support of *people-driven activities*. A key characteristics of such systems is that they are designed to leverage the shrinking knowledge worker resources that we have at our disposal. We call these advanced forms of electronic channels *electronic channel support systems* (ECSS) to distinguish them from the simpler interorganizational systems from which they are evolving. Our definition of an electronic channel support system stresses *information* and *knowledge* rather than just *data*:

> **An electronic channel support system is a system that enables an organization to electronically create, distribute, and present information or knowledge.**

The information or knowledge manipulated by an electronic channel support system can constitute a primary product or service, or it might provide an ancillary service or a complementary enhancement to a primary product or service.

Electronic channel support systems extend the function and power of electronic channels to an even greater level than IOS. Electronic channel support systems tend to focus on the information and service functions in the areas of marketing, education, and demand creation. With them the focus shifts from enhancing the common functions between organizations to exploiting changes in the very rules of competition in industries. In many cases, they are causing industries to converge, as the banking and insurance industries are doing today. Electronic channel support systems tend to shift the focus from transaction processing and the sharing of communication networks to allowing the organization to directly reach the ultimate consumer of products and services.

Figure 6-1 shows a version of the business linkages chart introduced in Chapter 3 in which we have divided the functions that are performed in producing and distributing a product or a service into two categories. Those on the right are associated with the *physical component* of the product or service; those on the left are those associated with the *information component*. Porter and Millar describe the differences between the physical component and the information component:

> Every product or service has both a *physical* component and an *information* component. The physical component includes all the physical tasks required to perform the activity as well as the product or service itself. The information component encompasses the steps required to capture, manipulate, and channel the data necessary to market the product or service.[1]

It is important to realize that there are three things associated with the channel systems that today's organizations use: the people that are associated with products and services, the physical component of prod-

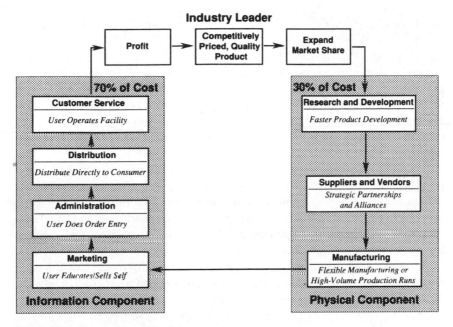

Figure 6-1. Costs associated with business functions.

ucts and services, and the information component. All three of these play a role in implementing channel systems.

Earlier forms of electronic channel focused on the linkages involving the physical component—suppliers and manufacturing. With electronic channel support systems the focus changes to the information component—marketing, administration, distribution, and customer service. The focus also changes from the use of older, more conventional technology to new forms of communications technology. In electronic channel support systems, the emergence of new technologies, such as image, fiber optics, expert systems, digital voice, motion video, and enhanced personal computer power will accelerate the development of these electronic channel applications. Chapter 9 provides additional insight into how electronic channel support systems can be used as strategic tools for increasing organizational effectiveness.

Industry View of Electronic Channels

As discussed in Chapter 3, each function in the chart of business linkages represents a contribution toward the ultimate cost of a product or service. The research and development costs, supplier costs, and manufacturing costs, which are those associated with the physical component, generally represent only 30 percent or less of the total cost of a typical product or service. The costs associated with marketing, administration, distribution, and customer service generally make up the remaining 70 percent of the cost. With some types of product and service offerings, marketing and distribution make up an even higher percentage of the total cost. For example, the cost of the product itself in the cosmetics industry typically represents a very small percentage of the total cost.

In the past, technology has been used primarily in the design of the product, in reducing supplier costs, in enhancing the manufacturing function, and on streamlining administrative functions. Those functions that represent 70 percent or more of the product cost have been relatively untouched by technology. This represents enormous opportunity for some organizations and tremendous exposures for others. Many new, dynamic organizations have found this to be true already and are growing by eliminating information component inefficiencies. A significant number of large, conservative organizations are discovering these realities at the expense of lost market share. From a global viewpoint, the realities are even more far reaching, with important implications for the entire manufacturing and service sector.

Organizational View of Electronic Channels

Examining the chart of business linkages can also help to analyze the impact on the organization of electronic channels. We can draw a business linkages chart for the enterprise using either an external or an internal focus. Both are important, but for different reasons.

External View

It is best to begin by drawing a chart of the important *external* business linkages. Such a chart helps us to understand the major functions that the organization provides from the time the product or service is created to the point of actual consumption or purchase by the consumer. If the organization does not now deal directly with the ultimate consumer, but has as its customers other organizations, it is still important here to focus on the end consumer and not end the analysis with current customers. An analysis that focuses on the ultimate consumer will help to make it clear what role and function the organization plays in the entire process, show what can happen to business linkages in the future, and indicate what new roles the organization might play. An analysis of external business linkages should provide insight into the opportunities and exposures that are associated with electronic channels and should help to identify significant changes that will be required internally to support the industry changes that are occurring.

Internal View

After charting the external business linkages, we can then take an internal focus. In charting internal business linkages, it is important to identify all important internal functions and to define the cost and the added value that is associated with each of them. The organization can then define those areas in which electronic channels have the potential for creating substantial and sustainable competitive advantage. Such an analysis of business linkages starts to point out ways to make significant changes in the organization by using electronic channels. We can then begin to determine ways in which to reposition the role of the organization in the industry as a whole. A study of the external and internal business linkages that are important to the organization should be complementary and should be part of an ongoing business planning process.

Analyzing People Costs

If we examine more closely the costs that are associated with marketing, customer service, administration, and distribution, we find that not only are these functions information-intensive, they are people-intensive as well. The growing skills shortage that American business is experiencing is making it increasingly difficult for organizations to effectively differentiate their products and services from the competition through the use of people-intensive channels. In this people-intensive environment, an observation that Marshall Field once made is appropriate:

> **It doesn't matter how long the distribution channel is.**
> **It's only the last 5 feet that count.**

It is important to always keep in mind that layers of people-intensive functions are not seen by the customer. The customer perceives only quality products and quality services that are provided in a timely manner at the right price.

As we stated earlier, the marketing, customer service, administration, and distribution functions of business are directly related to the functions that are generally associated with organizations in the service sector of our economy. It is interesting to note that the service sector, over the last 20 years or so, has been going through a period of decreasing productivity. It has been the manufacturing and agricultural sectors of the economy that have been aggressively applying technology and have seen the largest productivity gains. We have not been applying technology to the service sector, nor have we been applying it to the marketing, customer service, administration, and distribution functions in organizations outside of the service sector. The correlation between the two is striking:

Low-tech seems to equate directly to low productivity.

There are many important implications of the low productivity gains that are often associated with the service sector and the low productivity gains of the functions associated with the information component of products and services. Many of these implications become clear if we view organizational effectiveness using the lenses that the previous four chapters provide. The implications for the future of American business are severe. The demographics associated with the aging of the population, the reduction of new entrants into the professional work force, the high percentage of school dropouts, and the emergence of technology leadership of Japan and the countries of Europe all portray a different workforce and a different business environment for America. If we do not understand the changing nature of the environment, any thoughts we may have of increased organizational effectiveness will be mere dreams.

Using the Lenses

We can now begin using the lenses that we have provided in Chapters 2 through 5 to begin examining the impact on the organization of the changing environment.

Strategic Market Forces

The following are a few questions that we can ask to determine the effect of the strategic market forces that considered in Chapter 2:

- Where will the skills and people come from considering the changing demographics?

- What effect will skills shortages have on the organization and what new salary structures will be required?

- How can we leverage the organization's assets and achieve greater market share without adding armies of people?

- How can we continue to provide a competitive product or service?

- What is the impact of global competition, even in domestic niche markets?

- How can we differentiate our products, our services, and our organization?

Waves of Innovation

An analysis of the waves of innovation from Chapter 2 provides another lens for viewing the business environment that generates additional questions:

- Where is my organization, and maybe the industry as a whole, on the chart showing the waves of innovation?

- What waves will the competition be on?

- What do the answers to the first two questions mean with respect to changing the external or internal business linkages for the organization?

- What is the implication for the people and the structure of the organization?

Experience Curves

The experience curve strategies examined in Chapter 3 provide another lens and another set of questions:

- What are the new experience curves in which we should be investing in order to prepare for the future?

- What issues arise because of shortages, skills, and the training of people?

- What experience curves are the competitors on?

- How much time do we have left?

Industry Power Relationships

The analysis of industry power relationships discussed in Chapter 4 suggests questions that point the way to an understanding of the extended enterprise:

- How are industry relationships changing or converging?
- What impacts or requirements will this place on the organization?
- Will the development of electronic channels enhance or diminish the importance of the organization?
- Who are our competitors?
- What will our competitors do?
- How can we compete with them or, more important, how will they compete with us?

The Extended Enterprise

A final set of questions is suggested from the structure of the organization's extended enterprise, discussed in Chapter 5:

- What does our extended enterprise look like?
- What will it look like tomorrow?
- Is our extended enterprise a winner or a loser? (Are we the owner or a member in a losing extended enterprise?)
- What does effective use of electronic channels mean in the extended enterprise environment?
- How will our organization exploit electronic channels?
- What will this mean from a people standpoint?

This interesting set of questions is an attempt to demonstrate the impact of people-intensive channels as well as the requirements and exposures associated with a change to greater emphasis on electronic channels. The issue is no longer whether to implement these channels, but how and when?

Education and Retail Sales

The results of government studies documented in *Workforce 2000* show that retail sales and education are the two largest components of the service sector of the American economy, with education comprising

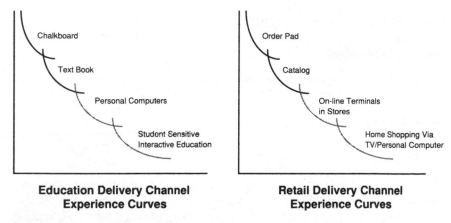

Education Delivery Channel   Retail Delivery Channel
Experience Curves   Experience Curves

Figure 6-2. Experience curves in the education and retail sectors of the economy.

9.1 million people and retail sales, 12.5 million.[2] Because of the huge numbers of people in these two sectors of our economy and the importance of them to America, it is interesting to examine the delivery channels that are most commonly used in these two segments of our economy. What major enhancements have been made over the last 50 years to the channels we use to deliver these services? It is clear that the majority of the people involved in providing these services are on the top two experience curves in the charts in Figure 6-2. For most people, no significant changes have occurred in the delivery systems in recent years. This is not to say that changes should not occur or that they will not occur shortly. It simply shows that major structural changes to the delivery channels have not yet taken place. We might ask whether this fact may not have something to do with the negative productivity gains that we have been experiencing in these areas in recent years. It is interesting to note that the experience curves shown at the bottom of the two charts in Figure 6-2 do in fact exist today. For examples in education, stop in a shop that sells software for personal computers. For examples in retail sales, stop in a Florsheim shoe store or sign up for the IBM-Sears Prodigy service.

The Home Shopping Phenomenon

An example of how industry restructuring can take place can be seen in the "Home Shopping" phenomenon familiar to cable TV viewers. This segment of the retail sales industry appeared virtually overnight and has experienced phenomenal growth, in spite of the use of unsophisticated technology and crude marketing techniques. Home shopping grew rapidly because of a simple approach to reducing the number of steps required to market and deliver an item. Traditional retail marketing works like this:

1. An organization establishes need through marketing (newspaper ads and radio and TV spots).
2. The consumer gets into a car and drives to a store that sells the product.
3. The consumer purchases the item.

Those in sales and marketing know that the shorter the time that elapses between establishing need (step 1), and the actual purchasing of the item (step 3), the higher the percentage of sales that will actually take place. Although its approach is somewhat cumbersome, home shopping has completely eliminated the second step in the process and has reduced the time interval between step 1 and step 3 to almost zero. What is really interesting in the home shopping scenario is that by focusing on the elimination of step 2, the organizations that created this industry segment were able to use technology to eliminate or significantly enhance several functions in the business linkages chart. They had the biggest impact on the marketing, administration, and distribution functions and were able to generate significant savings due to reductions in the costs associated with stores, warehouses, inventories, and administrative and marketing support people.

For the retail industry, the real question to ask is this: "What will happen to retail sales when more sophisticated electronic channels replace the telephone and the television?" For many of us not in the retail industry, the questions are:

- What will be the impact of electronic channels for our industry?
- What functions will be enhanced or eliminated?
- What does this mean to my organization and its people?

Enhancing the View of the Organization

In reflecting back on the previous sections of this chapter and on the chapter on the extended enterprise (Chapter 5), we can begin to expand our view of the organization by looking outward, beyond the classical industry and organizational functional views. We can begin visualizing the different channels that connect the organization with the various elements in the extended enterprise, including all the players who have a vested interest in the organization, such as stockholders, employees, suppliers, and customers. In focusing on the channels, we must pay attention to the magnitude of the distribution cost—the cost associated with moving products or services through the channels to the ultimate consumer. These costs can only increase in the future because of increasing people costs. The issue is not one of preventing these new requirements from occurring but one of streamlining the channel delivery systems needed to accommodate the new developments in the changing extended enterprise.

Controlling the Channels

In order to gain strategic advantage, the organization must establish and control the information channels by integrating operations throughout the extended enterprise. We must also gain control over and win the loyalty of each member of the extended enterprise by providing them with enhanced products and services. The organization must seek to share responsibilities and to also share benefits through electronic channel support systems in working toward a win-win environment.

You cannot win in the long run if the members of your extended enterprise are losing.

Learning from the Automobile Parts Industry

We can examine the extended enterprise associated with the automobile parts after market for an example of how the use of electronic channels can cause industry restructuring to occur. Figure 6-3 shows a view of the many functions that are important in the automobile parts industry. By examining the chart carefully, we can spot a number of sources of overhead, bottlenecks, vested interests, people-intensive costs, and so on. Such a chart shows that it is difficult to move products and services through the complex, people-intensive channels that exist today in the industry. In the customer's mind, the various players in the industry should exist to supply his or her needs. In reality, the consumer is frustrated because it is so difficult to work through such a complex structure. Such a complex industry structure also has an impact on the ability

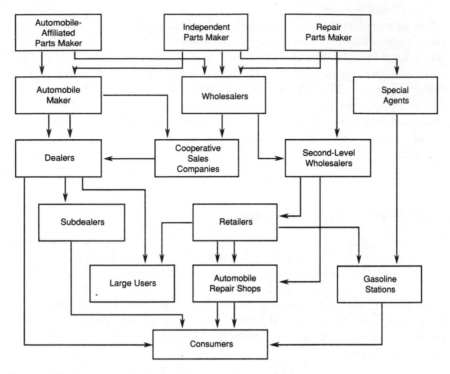

Figure 6-3. Linkages in the automobile repair parts industry.

of the parts manufacturers and the automobile manufacturers to operate efficiently. It is very difficult for a manufacturer in this industry to receive unfiltered customer feedback. An analysis of the diagram in Figure 6-3 raises a number of questions, including:

- What are the roles and objectives of intermediaries, and what value do they add and at what cost?

- How can a manufacturer get a new product or a message through these distribution channels quickly?

- What are the limiting and inhibiting factors to growth in this environment?

- How might these relationships be changed in the future?

- How can new products be introduced into these channels in order to generate the correct results at the bottom?

- How does the consumer (the owner of an automobile) resolve a problem?

If you have ever had to resolve an automobile repair problem, you should now have a better idea of why it may have been difficult. The major automobile manufacturers are striving to implement a major restructuring of their industry. One element in this restructuring involves the creation of new, sophisticated electronic channels. Here is an example of a system that automates a service channel is the General Motors Computerized Automotive Maintenance System (GM-CAMS):

> ...using a personal computer with a touch screen that is designed to quickly and accurately diagnose and isolate electronic problems in GM vehicles. When linked to GM's centralized system, the personal computer will receive current diagnostic software and repair information and provide GM with valuable feedback on repair activities.[3]

Such an electronic channel links an automobile manufacturer with those members of the extended enterprise that are responsible for servicing the automobile manufacturer's products.

Leading automobile manufacturers are trying to restructure the entire automotive industry into an extended enterprise that looks something like that shown in Figure 6-4. This view of the extended enterprise is different than the one shown in Figure 6-3 because it considers

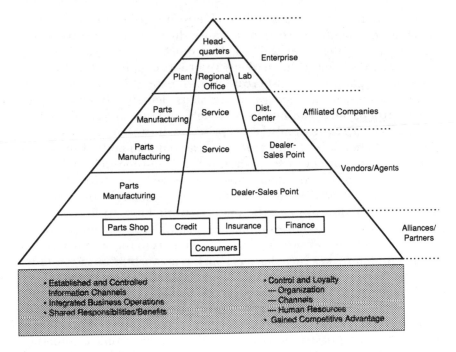

Figure 6-4. Automotive industry extended enterprise structure.

the information component along with the physical component. What is needed are electronic channel support systems that efficiently move product information and service through the existing maze of people-intensive functions. A major goal of these electronic channels is to eliminate the significant numbers of barriers that currently inhibit competitive responses to the market demands and that prevent organizations from receiving customer feedback.

It is interesting to note that organizations like General Motors, Otis Elevator, and IBM are designing new products to interface with these electronic channel support systems. These new products will provide new sources of service-oriented revenue and at the same time create an environment in which the consumer and the organizations involved in the industry can all be happy—a win-win deal. These companies will generate greater revenue from their service functions, and the customer will be willing to pay these increased costs because of the greater availability and reliability of the products.

Implementing a Win-Win Environment

The real leaders in the 1990s will be able to use control of electronic channels as a competitive weapon. Because they will have control over the electronic channels, they will be able to quickly adjust to and exploit the constantly evolving niche markets. In order to gain competitive advantage, the organization must create its own extended enterprise and implement a *win-win environment* across all its elements. In order to facilitate control of the organizations, channels, and human resources that are associated with the extended enterprise, we must share both responsibilities and benefits. The only real way to accomplish both of these objectives is to integrate business operations. Just-in-time delivery at the plant floor creates a zero-balance inventory environment for the supplier. Because this is a positive situation for the manufacturer and a negative one for the supplier, the manufacturer must try to turn this into a win-win situation. For example, the manufacturer might offer an electronic funds transfer system to make payments to the supplier at the time the supplier makes each delivery. Such relationships must continue all the way down the supplier chain. If the links to the members of the extended enterprise are not controlled and managed, chaos will prevail. Therefore, the implementation and control of the information channels is critical. As we evolve, we will see further examples of how organizational restructuring based on the increased use of electronic channels is one of the primary tools we have for improving organizational effectiveness. It is important to realize that it is not sufficient to achieve significant productivity enhancements within a given function or organizational area. We must constantly look toward improving the effectiveness of the entire organization and look for new levels of synergy with the members of the extended enterprise.

Leveraging Human Resources

The leaders are now analyzing most business functions in order to find new ways of offloading non-value-added functions from people to technology. The leaders are also constantly looking for new ways to increase the amount of time people can spend on value-added tasks. The value-added processes create new products and services and increase economic wealth. Analyzing the underlying requirements of this strategy, we can begin to see the need for extending broadband, multi-media-based electronic channel support systems further out into the extended enterprise. As we reach further out into the channels the multimedia communications become more prevalent and, therefore, more critical and valuable as tools for replacing or leveraging scarce and expensive human resources. The strategy must be to save the scarce human resources for tasks that add significant value to the product or service while using electronic channel support systems to automate tasks that once were performed by people.

Conclusion

In order to gain strategic advantage, we must establish and control the information channels. We must integrate business operations throughout the extended enterprise and gain control and loyalty of all the members in the extended enterprise by providing enhanced products and services. We must seek to share responsibilities, and also benefits, through electronic channel support systems and work toward a win-win environment. The appropriate use of an ECSS can significantly enhance the organization's productivity, flexibility, and ability to compete. In the future, companies that choose not to install these types of systems may be unable to compete with businesses that do. An important task is to identify the electronic channels that will be required for the enterprise to remain in business. This requires insights at the highest levels in the organization. Applications of advanced technology to support the extended enterprise should focus on better serving the customer. A successful electronic channel support system can make it very difficult for a competitor to attract the interest of customers because the ECSS may provide unique services not available elsewhere. In many cases, companies find it difficult to compete with the company that first installs such a system:

First in may be last in.

Leading edge organizations are building new experience curves by using electronic channels to raise their level of competitiveness. The evidence is in and the direction is clear. Electronic channel support systems, implemented using advanced computer and communications technologies, will drastically restructure an organization's channels. From a global perspective, the race is on to restructure the channels and improve the effectiveness of all sectors of the economy. It is becoming clear that *knowledge* is truly the capital of the 1990s. It is becoming critical for our economy to build an information infrastructure that includes leading-edge electronic channel support systems to provide the *knowledge* to the *knowledge workers*.

References

1. Michael Porter and Victor Millar. "How Information Gives You Competitive Advantage." *Harvard Business Review.* July–August, 1986.
2. *Workforce 2000.* Indianapolis: The Hudson Institute, June 1987.
3. IBM Corporation. *Annual Report.* 1985.

PART 2

Strategy

After we have used the techniques in Part 1 to begin formulating a strategic business vision, the next step is to carry that vision forward and develop from it a clearly defined set of *strategies*. The three chapters in this part of the book emphasize the strategy part of the innovation arrow (Figure P2-1). We must *make no assumptions* about the types of strategies that will be required for success in the business environment of tomorrow. Chapter 7 discusses the new roles of management in formulating a vision and in developing effective business strategies. Chapter 8 examines the new mindsets that we must have in today's

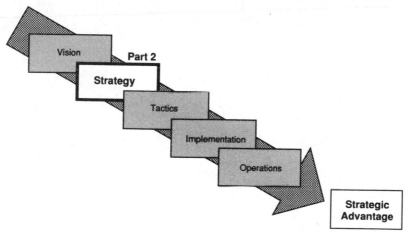

Figure P2-1. Strategy.

environment in order to identify potential threats and strategic opportunities. Chapter 9 shows ways in which we can restructure channels in order for the organization to operate effectively in the context of an extended enterprise.

7

Reassessing
the Roles
of Management

Introduction

This chapter explores the management implications associated with evolving into and exploiting the extended enterprise. Here, we analyze how the traditional roles of management must change as we become more focused outward. In formulating an effective strategy, we must analyze the information about waves of innovation, experience curves, industry power relationships, the extended enterprise, and electronic channel support systems in order to identify the strategic linkages that are important to the enterprise. We must then determine how these strategic linkages should be managed. Identifying and managing these linkages should lead to the discovery of new alliances, new partnerships, and the need for organizational restructuring. It should also lead to the identification of new product and service strategies. We must identify the implications that are associated with the waves of innovation and with the experience curves that have been identified. We must also understand the ramifications of evolving the electronic channels that permit us to distribute knowledge and allow the elements of the extended enterprise to directly communicate.

The tools and techniques for strategic thinking presented in Part 1 can be used by any manager at any level in the organization. The same can be said for Part 2; but beginning with this chapter, the real payoffs will be derived if the concepts are applied by top management in performing the strategic business planning for the organization as a whole. We begin this chapter by discussing the responsibilities of top management with respect to strategic business planning. We then make our

case for why the important job of strategic planning cannot be delegated to middle or operational management as it so often is. We then
present the steps that are involved in strategic planning and introduce
the techniques of linkage analysis planning, our approach to strategic
business planning that is discussed in detail in Part 3. We conclude this
chapter by giving our views on what the manager of the future will be.

The Responsibilities of Top Management

All too often, a "call to action" causes managers to immediately begin
focusing on tactics to solve the immediate problem. This common be-
havioral pattern is acceptable in many situations when the organization
is responding to a crisis or is playing catch-up. However, in order to
raise the level of organizational effectiveness and leap-frog the competition, top management can no longer afford simply to leap into tactical
action in response to every problem. It is the responsibility of top management to start at the top of the innovation arrow by developing a vision for the organization. Here is a challenge that we offer:

**Are you involved in activities that are designed to raise the
level of effectiveness of the organization, or are all of your
activities associated with responding to everyday problems?**

All too often, executives operate as process caretakers—managers of
form, not *substance*. As a result, many managers today have little regard
for external members of the organization's extended enterprise. They
often have little motivation to take required actions and accept the associated risks. In Chapter 1, we observed that in many of today's organizations there is too much emphasis on bottom-up business planning.
We stated there that what we need is top-down strategic *thinking* followed by strategic *action*. These strategic actions must focus on effectiveness and not just productivity. Effective strategic planning is criti-
cally important if the organization is to prosper in the business
environment of the 1990s. Ask yourself this question:

Does your organization do strategic planning?

We have found that all too often, the answer is no. If your organization is doing strategic planning, is the planning effective and is the stra-

tegic plan being used? Here are a few of the questions an effective strategic plan must address:

- How can the organization cope with the constantly changing environment that is characterized by niches that are rapidly appearing, evolving, and disappearing?
- What role does the organization play in the industry? Will it be a leader or a follower?
- What changes are occurring in advanced technology and other forces that affect the organization?
- What role will the organization play with respect to the changing industry and functional experience curves?
- Where are industries in your environment converging in the next 3 to 5 years, and how will the power relationships change?
- What role will the organization play with respect to the converging industries?
- How might the organization shift to take a new focus?
- What is the vision for the organization? How is this vision being formed and by whom?
- How can the organization encourage and enable innovation and entrepreneurship?
- How can the organization empower individuals to think and act strategically?

Because you are reading this book, you must be one of those who is thinking about the future of your organization. What do you know about the strategic planning that is taking place? If you do not know about it, there must be a problem. And the problem may be that strategic planning—real strategic planning—is simply not taking place. Some recent books have taken the view that strategic planning does not work in most organizations. For example, Ries and Trout's book *Bottom-Up Marketing* suggests that strategic planning should be done only at the bottom of the organization chart, by those in the field.[1] Peter's book *Thriving on Chaos* appears to take a similar view.[2] Although it is important to involve the frontline people in the strategic planning process, we do not agree with the view that the top-down approach is irrelevant. In today's environment, it is more important than ever that top management get thoroughly involved in the strategic planning process, while at the same time taking suggestions from managers at all levels in the organization. This chapter explains why. It is important to remember that, although strategic planning is of critical importance, what is *not* needed is an annual strategic planning event that results in a

Leather-Bound **Strategic Plan**. Remember from Chapter 1: "The thicker the planning document, the less likely it will be read." We do not need an annual strategic planning event that results in:

- A session that is long, tiring, and that no one wants to attend
- Thick, dusty planning documents that no one wants to read
- A list of action items so long that no one knows where to start
- A repeat of last year's issues and concerns
- A plan that does not consider the future
- A lack of a determination to take strategic action

What we need is a strategic planning process that works. We need a process that encourages strategic thinking at all levels of the organization.

Strategic Planning Cannot Be Delegated

In many organizations, strategic planning is delegated to middle management—to the "Long-Range Planning" or "Strategic Planning" department. These departments do not include the key decision makers in the organization. They are run by staff managers who have a limited understanding of the policies, beliefs, and values of the organization and usually have limited contact with customers and competitors. Middle management is not in a position to handle the development and implementation of strategic plans that are of real significance, nor do they have the insights that are required to identify organizational and industry changes that may be required. However, more often that not, the real source of knowledge about the operational procedures of the organization does not lie in senior management, but lies with middle and operational management. So tradeoffs are required between day-to-day operational procedures and the vision and direction that can be set only at the top.

If the focus of strategic planning remains on below-the-line issues—on a "save money orientation"—then top management involvement is often not required. As the orientation moves up and begins to focus on "make money" and "corporate survival," it becomes increasingly critical that top management be involved in the decision-making process and must help to identify strategic opportunities. During strategic planning, it is important that top management avoid concentrating on just those activities that are "below the line" in the waves of innovation. Top management must concentrate on concerns that are "above the line," as well as ensuring that the below-the-line functions remain competitive and capable of supporting above-the-line strategies and activities. These concerns *absolutely require* the involvement of top management because they tend to focus on the critical linkages that exist in the extended enterprise. Top management involvement is required for understanding the strategic forces that exist in the industry and for generating the new road maps that are required for success. Solutions that are focused above the line need a top-down view and require total integration of the organization's activities. Investments in projects that are positioned above the line tend to focus on increasing revenues, enhancing market share, and formulating alliances and partnerships. When the focus is above the line, there are no road maps. We cannot look in a book to find the answers. Each organization, and in many cases each individual, will view the environment differently as they make trade-offs in interpreting the environment, setting priorities, and formulating strategies.

> **It is on above-the-line issues where top management intuition becomes invaluable in identifying the strategic opportunities that exist in the marketplace.**

The Information Infrastructure

In the majority of cases, advanced applications of technology depend on efficient uses of computer and communications technology. It will be impossible for an organization to go forward in identifying strategic uses of technology unless the required information infrastructure, which is implemented by effective below-the-line information systems, is already in place. If the required information infrastructure does not yet exist in the organization, then top management must concentrate on putting this infrastructure into place as quickly as possible. In many organizations, since there is limited capacity for the creation of information systems, it often makes sense to fill the need for required below-the-line systems with purchased software. This allows the organization to concentrate scarce development resources on *strategic*, above-the-line systems. Since the real need is for critical strategic systems, little justification can be found today for devoting information systems resources to redoing the payroll system. The same is true for the rest of the organization's below-the-line infrastructure.

Strategic Planning Is not Financial Planning

Senior management must realize that today's "long-range planning" or "strategic planning" departments usually do not perform the type of strategic planning that is required in today's competitive environment. The typical long-range planning group has a financial focus. They perform a financial analysis, using perhaps a five-year planning horizon, by collecting financial data and forecasts on what each department thinks will be accomplished. These forecasts typically involve such things as costs, headcounts, required capital investment, and expected results. The group then consolidates the data, analyzes the economy, and makes long-range forecasts using the collected data. Based on the results of the analysis, they then make decisions on growth targets and allocation of resources within the organization in order to reach the goals that are set. The entire analysis has an internal orientation and does not take into account competitive forces and other external factors that could change the rules of competition. It is extremely rare to find organizations performing the types of analysis discussed in Part 1 of this book. The long range planning group then typically leads an annual or semi-annual "strategic planning" session, which we have already discussed. These sessions often take a week, and executives intensely dislike attending them. With some of the approaches that have been used in such meetings, the walls often become lined with to-do lists and action items. Many such sessions are heavily rule oriented. They tend to intimidate the participants rather than encourage creativity and often cause the group to focus on form and not substance. Such strategic planning is not conducive to identifying new uses of technology and to find ways for restructuring the organization to achieve competitive advantage.

The Role of the Visionary Leader

Many enterprises have achieved spectacular success, apparently without the need for performing formal strategic planning. Examples of these are Apple Computer in its formative years and many of the recent genetic engineering start-ups. In many cases, the successful organization is a new, smaller company that is lead by a visionary. In such a company, the vision is established by one powerful individual who forcefully communicates the vision and drives it through the entire enterprise. In such a case, the visionary leader is single-handedly doing strategic thinking followed by strategic action, and may not even know the process is taking place.

As often happens with a successful company that experiences a high rate of growth, the visionary leader may eventually leave. Then, as the enterprise grows, without the benefit of the strategic planning the visionary supplied, the planning process often becomes proceduralized and evolves into the annual strategic planning event mentioned earlier. The organization's strategic, entrepreneurial vision and zest for action decays with time. Because strategic planning is not often viewed as being important in such an environment, the tendency becomes "don't make waves" and get on with "more important" things. It then becomes easy to miss competitive opportunities as the process caretaker mentality takes hold. Many of today's largest organizations have been led by visionary leaders in the past but are not being led by such dynamic leaders today. You can probably generate a substantial list of these. Would you place your own organization on such a list? An important question to ask is which of these organizations will be able to make great things happen in the 1990s? Which ones will be in the Fortune 100 in the year 2000?

An important message of this book is that we must search for ways to weave into the organization's very fabric the strategic thinking process that the visionary leader automatically uses and shares. In the future, the life blood of the organization may well be a culture that fosters strategic thinking at all levels. The essence of the entrepreneur, or the entrepreneurial organization, is to do such strategic thinking and to adapt to the changing environment. This book provides methods that any organization can use to achieve the same types of results that successful organizations have achieved in the past. The process that we recommend for performing strategic planning is so simple that it can be performed by any department or division, no matter how small. Strategic planning should not be limited only to a centralized, staff strategic planning group. When strategic planning is performed properly, and the plans communicated effectively, it should be possible for the people at the very bottom of the organization chart to immediately see the vision and to visualize where they fit within the overall strategic plans of the organization. The strategic planning that is performed at all levels in the organization must interlock to form an overall vision that guides the entire organization toward meeting a common goal.

Management Thought Processes

Figure 7-1 shows how the waves of innovation can be plotted against the two forms of planning activities and thought processes introduced in Chapter 1. The planning activities and thought processes that are asso-

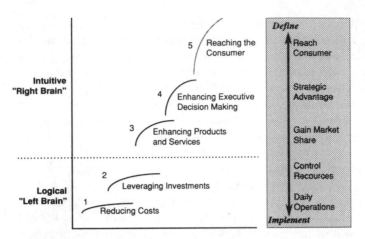

Figure 7-1. Intuitive "right-brain" activities versus logical "left-brain" activities.

ciated with the two below-the-line innovation waves are typically simple. Finding the lower-level "save money" waves tends to involve logical, "left-brain," operational thinking processes. With left-brain thinking, the approach typically involves questions like:

- How can I continue to make the company work?
- How can I reduce costs?
- How can I enhance quality?
- How can I cut development times?
- How can I do more for less?

While these operational questions are important, they should not be the sole focus of top management. If top management thinking never progresses above this level, the organization will never form a vision to guide its future direction. As we progress to above-the-line activities, it becomes more difficult to define and implement the applications of technology that are required. Finding the higher-level, strategically important waves of innovation in any environment tends to involve intuitive, creative, right-brain-oriented, *executive* thinking processes.

As we discussed in Chapter 5, top management is involved largely with decision-making processes that are highly unstructured. Higher levels of management must make these unstructured decisions using intuitive, right-brain-oriented thinking processes. Formulating broad business strategies requires the thinking of top management. Middle management works with semistructured decision-making processes and lower-level management with decision making that is quite structured.

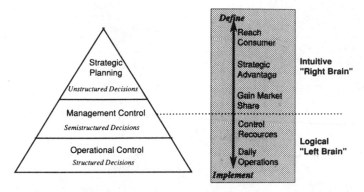

Figure 7-2. Plotting intuitive and logical thinking processes against levels of management.

Middle and lower management can use logical, left-brain-oriented thinking processes in developing the tactical plans that are necessary for implementing the strategies developed at the top. Both types of thought process are critical to the success of the organization. Figure 7-2 shows how the two types of thinking process can be plotted against the levels of management that must carry out each type of analysis.

Steps in Strategic Planning

Business planning involves a number of activities across all levels of management. The business planning that must be carried out can be described as a four-step process:

1. *Vision formulation.* Identifying and articulating a strategic business vision.
2. *Strategy development.* Developing the vision into a business strategy.
3. *Tactical planning.* Determining the best way in which to implement the vision and the strategic plan.
4. *Implementation and operations.* Implementing the strategic and tactical plans and operating on a daily basis in accordance to the plans.

The four business planning steps are summarized in Figure 7-3. What we discussed in Part 1 of this book concerns only the first step. Formulating the vision is the necessary step that must be carried out before the more traditional techniques of strategic business planning can be effectively used. It is our contention that without an effective vision,

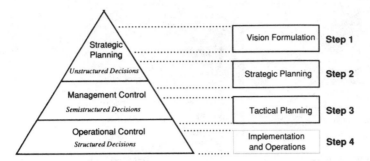

Figure 7-3. Different types of planning are appropriate for each level of management.

the remaining planning steps operate in a vacuum and do not result in the identification of strategic business opportunities.

After the *vision* has been created for the organization, top-level strategic planning becomes the next step. Strategic planning involves creating a mission statement that enables the organization to achieve the vision, articulating organizational goals to implement the vision, formulating a high-level view of the business environment, developing high-level business objectives for the extended enterprise, and identifying the information channels that are required to support the organization in the context of the extended enterprise. The two most important tasks in strategic business planning are:

- Identifying the important linkages that are important to the organization, including internal linkages and linkages to important external members of the extended enterprise.
- Developing a plan for managing these important linkages.

Identifying the Links

In formulating an effective strategy, we must first identify the strategic linkages that are important to the organization and determine how to implement them using electronic channel support systems. This phase requires the involvement and active participation of the entire top management team. In order to effectively carry out this phase of strategic planning, we must fully understand the structure and ramifications of the extended enterprise. It is critical that we understand the linkages that exist in the organization itself. However, it is even more important to identify the important linkages that exist among the external members of the extended enterprise and among the strategic forces at play in the environment.

Managing the Links

Many organizations will be able to identify the links but will fail because they are unable to effectively manage them. For example, management may make far-reaching changes to the organization but then neglect to make the necessary changes in reward systems or sales plans to reflect those changes. A formal management process must be put into place to ensure that the important strategic linkages are actively managed and that effective electronic channel support systems are put in place to implement them. This step cannot be left to informal execution or delegated to middle or operational management. In many instances, the future of the organization will rest with the execution of this step. Ensure that the organization is effectively managing the links with the external members of the extended enterprise.

A danger that can occur if we do not correctly identify the links and then manage them is graphically described by a word coined by Marina Mann's staff at the Electrical Power Research Institute (EPRI):

Infosclerosis. The condition that occurs when the information channels of an organization harden and clog, thus allowing nothing to get through.

If *infosclerosis* is allowed to take hold in an organization, the organization gradually slows down, loses its dynamism, and eventually begins to die. We can prevent this from happening by effectively managing the links and by employing appropriate electronic channel support systems to tie the organization together and to reach out into the extended enterprise.

Tactics and Implementation

Top level management must be involved in the *vision* and *strategy* steps of the business planning process, but the *tactics* and *implementation* steps can be delegated to middle and operational management. Many of the processes involved in the tactics and implementation steps can be done using methodologies that exist and are often already in place. For example, individual managers may carry out such traditional planning procedures as critical success factor analysis, goal and problem analysis, technology impact analysis, and value chain analysis. These techniques have been described elsewhere by such writers as Michael Porter[3] and James Martin.[4]

Conclusion

The manager of the future will be an active manager who performs an important role in designing the structure of the organization. It is no longer sufficient for managers to only monitor day-to-day activities and pass information about results upward. Many of these functions can today be automated and performed by executive information systems. Middle and upper management must become active decision makers, not only with respect to business policy, but to organizational structures as well. They must negotiate and establish relationships both within and outside of the organization. Their role must be to perform a continual rearchitecture of the organization. The cooperation of management is important in constructing project-oriented organizations. The manager of the future will be a team coordinator, an enabler, a facilitator. *Management must deal with the design of mechanisms for cooperative work that foster the relationships that are needed.* In Chapter 12, we see how organizations are evolving away from hierarchical structures toward more dynamic network structures that foster this type of cooperation. One of the key skills the manager of the future must have is a capability to manage cooperation across those internal and external organizations that have a significant influence on the enterprise. The acid test for the leaders of tomorrow may be the measure of how effectively everyone in the organization can form, implement, and capture a shared vision of their organization and its strategic opportunities.

References

1. Al Ries and Jack Trout. *Bottom-Up Marketing*. New York: McGraw-Hill, 1988.
2. Thomas Peters. *Thriving on Chaos*. New York: Alfred A. Knopf, 1988.
3. Michael Porter. *Competitive Advantage*. New York: Free Press, 1985.
4. James Martin and Joe Leben. *Strategic Information Planning Methodologies*. Englewood Cliffs, NJ: Prentice Hall, 1989.

8

Attaining a Mindset for the Future

Introduction

The restructuring occurring today in many industries is making it increasingly important for all managers to clearly visualize their roles. In many cases, people are moving away from headquarters, but the vision and their ability to understand the vision often does not move with them. Large organizations often see this happen as new layers of management keep pushing managers further and further away from a real understanding of the vision. Organizations in which this happens can become indecisive and ineffective. If decentralization and downsizing of the management structure is to work, the ability of leaders to communicate the vision must increase, and the ability of managers to understand and manage in the new environment must also dramatically increase. Management must understand what the focus must be. Will the focus remain on the current view of the organization and the industry, or will it shift? If it shifts, then how can the management team communicate this new vision? To do this, management will find that it is more important to instill a culture that enables the entire management team to view the future and to then focus on seeing the individual changes that will be required. It is the responsibility of top management to provide middle and operational management with the framework that is required for achieving the vision, for seeing the future, and for making the organizational changes that are essential.

> **Managers must radically change their *mindset* if the benefits of strategic thinking are to be achieved.**

If managers do not change the mindset that governs how they look at the business environment, then they will be unable to recognize the opportunities and threats that exist. As we have already stated, the techniques in Part 1 are designed to provide a new set of lenses that will help us to formulate a strategic business vision. Once the organization has formulated a strategic vision and has developed the basic strategies that will be required to achieve it, the vision must be driven throughout all levels of the organization. The first step in providing managers with the necessary mindset is to clearly articulate and communicate to them the strategic business vision and to identify the strategic opportunities that are most important. One of the biggest problems today in the United States is that we are beginning to become aware of what the problem is and what the potential solutions might be. But we often have not been able to change our organizations so that we can begin to identify strategic opportunities and take advantage of them in the global marketplace.

It is important for middle management to understand the key concepts that are communicated in the organization's vision. What is even more important is that managers use new management techniques that will allow them to take the steps that are necessary for the organization to achieve the vision. This chapter presents a set of *mindset images* that provide middle and operational managers with the tools they need to focus their efforts and allow them to help in attaining the vision that top management has formulated. It is important that these mindset images be shared with managers and workers at all levels in the organization so that everyone in the organization begins to perceive strategic opportunities at his or her own levels and begins to change his or her own parts of the operation to better fit in with the overall strategic thrust of the organization. The seven important mindset images presented in this chapter are:

- Growing the pie
- The information component
- Shelf space in the mind
- The envelope
- Happy captives

- Alliances and partnerships
- The warm frog

Growing the Pie

The mindset image of "growing the pie," illustrated in Figure 8-1, can be used to help managers at all levels gain an awareness of this fundamental truth:

> **In a shrinking or highly competitive industry,
> increasing the size of the pie is much more
> effective than protecting a slice of a shrinking pie.**

If the pie itself shrinks, your protected piece of the pie also shrinks. Although growing the pie is often easier said than done, it is important for the innovative organization to have this mindset and to continually look for ways to expand its markets. We must look for ways to change the extended enterprise in order to accomplish this. It may be possible to change the extended enterprise to such an extent that you find yourself in a position to take an entirely new view of the industry. With this new view, the industry might become much bigger than with the original restricted view. This concept also brings into question whether a defensive strategy in the long run can ever lead to competitive advantage. The authors question whether continual downsizing by itself is a viable strategy. If we agree that our world is characterized today by constant change and continually shifting niche markets, then by definition we

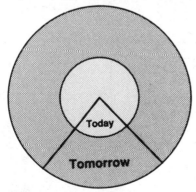

Figure 8-1. Increasing the size of the pie is more effective than protecting a slice of a shrinking pie.

will always be defending a piece of a shrinking pie. "To ensure healthy future expansion," says Drucker, "you must eliminate yesterday. If you pour money into yesterday, you prevent tomorrow."[1]

A question that immediately comes to mind is: "How do I increase the size of the pie?" Electronic channel support systems can provide an extremely effective and elastic way of growing the pie. These can provide the electronic links that are needed to reach the various members of the extended enterprise.

The following are a few additional techniques that are often useful in growing the pie:

- Redefine your view of the industry.
- Change the rules of competition in the industry to your advantage.
- Enter existing new markets.
- Develop entirely new markets by exploiting new technologies.
- Cross industry boundaries to exploit industries that are converging.
- Look for ways to exploit change.

The Information Component

The second mindset image, illustrated in Figure 8-2, concerns the information component of products and services. We are all familiar with the physical component of a product or service. We are probably less familiar with the information component. As introduced in Chapter 6, the information component is generally associated with how we market, describe, and use a product or service. Many organizations have not yet begun to contemplate the impact of the infor-

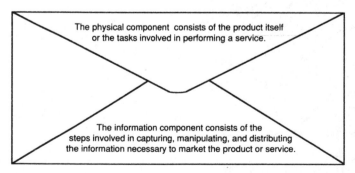

The physical component consists of the product itself or the tasks involved in performing a service.

The information component consists of the steps involved in capturing, manipulating, and distributing the information necessary to market the product or service.

Figure 8-2. Every product or service has both a physical component and an information component.

mation component when used to differentiate a product or service from the competition.

> **Focusing on the information component rather than
> the physical component can often suggest ways
> in which you might pursue strategic advantage.**

As an industry matures and products and services become commodities, then we must begin to focus on the information component in order to avoid the trap of competing on price alone. To compete only on price often leads to a no-win situation. Concentrating on the information component enables an enterprise to differentiate its products and services based on something other than price. As products or services mature and turn into commodities, the buyer tends to see no difference in your products or services and those of the competition. Focusing on the information component provides an opportunity to shift the focus away from the product or service itself to other issues, such as:

- Image or status
- Additional or complementary functions
- Explanations of how the product is used
- Saving time in acquiring the product or service
- Enhancing the customer's competitive position
- Creating user demand for the product or service
- Saving labor on the part of the user

The costs associated with the information component are dropping because of reduced technology costs. However, at the same time the number of new entrants into the skilled labor force is diminishing and thus lessening the number of people available to provide information component functions. In addition, the reach of information and communication technologies is expanding, thus creating a global marketplace for some organizations or additional competitive threats for others.

The majority of an organization's costs are associated with information-intensive and people-driven activities that lie outside the actual creation of the product or service. We have already discussed this fact in Chapter 6, but a chart that Bert Rosenblum created in his book *Marketing Channels* makes this point even more clear.[2] The "Product Flow" column in Figure 8-3 shows the flow that takes place in creating the

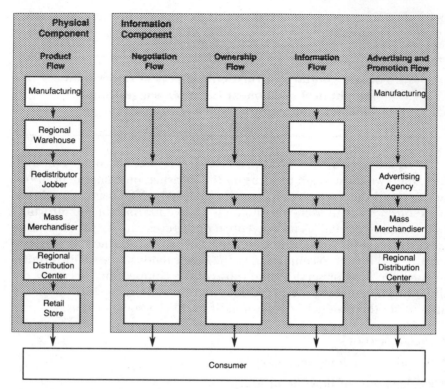

Figure 8-3. A product flow and some of its related information flows.

product and moving it through the various intermediaries in getting it to the ultimate consumer. The "Negotiation Flow" column shows the various negotiations that take place in getting the product to the market, including negotiating prices, terms, and conditions. The "Ownership Flow" column shows how the ownership of the product changes hands and how payments flow as the product moves to the consumer. The "Information Flow" column shows how the information associated with the product flows through the various steps on the way to the consumer. At the top, the information might be simple instructions for how the product is to be stored. Moving down through the flow, the information becomes more complex, such as how to best set the product up for sale, and so on. At the bottom, the information may take the form of detailed instructions on how the product is to be used. The "Advertising and Promotion" flow shows the various types of promotional materials that are required in getting the product to the market. Again, the advertising and promotional material get more complex and costly as we move down through the flow. A similar chart could be draw for a service industry. The service and production sectors of the economy now have so many similarities that it is not as useful as it has been in the past to make distinctions between them.

The chart in Figure 8-3 presents a different view of the total cost of providing a product or service to the consumer than that provided in Figure 6-1. The key message of both charts is that the actual manufacture of the product or the creation of the service actually represents as little as 10 percent to 30 percent of the total cost. This is the cost of manufacturing or creating the physical component of the product or service. The cost associated with the information component represents the remaining 70 percent to 90 percent of the total cost. However, most of today's emphasis is in improving only the Product Flow. The information component, which amounts to 70 percent to 90 percent of the cost-savings potential, has been largely left untouched. Today, then, the greatest potentials for enhancing the product lie in eliminating or reorganizing functions in the four columns associated with the information component. Information technology can provide significant enhancements to the product/information flow. The future will see the shift to increased emphasis on the functions associated with the information component.

Many European and Japanese companies have begun to focus on information and to exploit technology to enhance the information component of their products and services. Fiber optic cables are being laid under the ocean. When the appropriate information infrastructure is in place, it will be increasingly possible for distant competitors to effectively compete in what were once labor-intensive industries by focusing on the information component of their products and services. Electronic Channel Support Systems address the flows that occur in the four columns on the right in Figure 8-3. If we do not address these issues, we can be sure that our offshore competitors will.

We can expand our view of the information component of products and services if we realize that the chart in Figure 8-3 represents only one industry. If we begin to examine the charts of product flows that are associated with complementary industries, we can expand our view of our own products and services even further by enhancing the product and information flows in these industries as well. When this happens, the idea of crossing traditional industry boundaries will become a standard way of doing business.

Shelf Space in the Mind

Our third mindset image, illustrated in Figure 8-4, concerns an understanding of this fact:

Figure 8-4. Shelf space in the mind of the customer.

> **The information component of products and services constitutes "shelf space in the mind" of the customer.**

In the merchandising arena, the organization that controls the most shelf space usually wins. We can view every product or service as a commodity. If this is so, then how can we differentiate it from its competition? According to Ries and Trout, the marketing war is fought in the mind of the consumer. If we can win the consumer's mind, we win the battle. The war is not fought by knowing just what the competitors are doing but by also knowing what is taking place in the consumer's mind. If we can occupy more of the consumer's thought process and provide more of the products and services the consumer needs at the time it is needed, we win.[3] Enhancing the information component through effective use of electronic channel support systems is a way of gaining "shelf space in the mind."

The Envelope

If we do make the assumption that all products and services can be viewed as commodities, then our fourth mindset image of *the envelope* becomes important. (See Figure 8-5.)

> **One way to differentiate a product or services from the competition is to wrap it in an "envelope" of ancillary information or complementary products and services that are presented to the customer at the time of need.**

The concept of the envelope represents one-stop shopping from the viewpoint of the customer. In many cases, we can charge more for a complete envelope than we can for the individual components. In many cases, we can increase market share by using such a differentiation strategy. Value now becomes not just delivering the product or service at the time of need, but also how we deliver the complete envelope and what is its size. Most managers take the view that: "If I've delivered the product or service where and when it's needed, then I've achieved success." However, today the *size of the envelope* is becoming a deciding factor. We must ask what other kinds of information services are needed and what complementary products and services can we provide? This will start to become an important survival issue as we move into the age of sophisticated electronic channel support systems.

An example of the envelope concept can be seen in the Sears/IBM *Prodigy* system. In some areas, people who use this system can call up computer displays of all the products sold in local supermarkets. They can choose their products, and the supermarket will deliver them the next day for a small service charge. In addition to grocery shopping, the

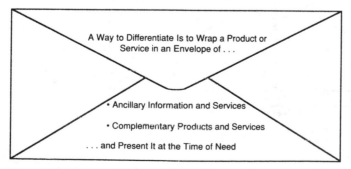

A Way to Differentiate Is to Wrap a Product or Service in an Envelope of . . .

• Ancillary Information and Services

• Complementary Products and Services

. . . and Present It at the Time of Need

Figure 8-5. Every product or service can be viewed as a commodity.

system provides banking services, airline reservations, and other information-oriented services. The Prodigy envelope is quite large.

The envelope concept can even make it possible to reduce the customer's total cost for a package of products and services. A properly constructed envelope has allowed many organizations to establish win-win relationships where the cooperating organizations all increase their margins and, at the same time, reduce the cost to the consumer. Of key importance to the customer today is the total acquisition cost of products and services. This can include a number of factors, including time, convenience, cost of carrying inventory, and purchasing costs. If we can reduce some of the customer's acquisition costs, we might be able to charge a higher price for a total package.

In developing an envelope in which to enclose our products and services, we must be concerned with timing. Figure 8-6 shows the time dimension. If I have a product or service tomorrow, it is of little use to the customer who is here today. If we had the product yesterday, again, it is of less value. But if I have the envelope exactly at the time of need, the products and services have their greatest value. We can view the envelope almost like stock on a shelf. If we put the stock on the shelf at noon, when we have the most customers, we generate the most sales. If we put the stock on the shelf at midnight, sales will be low.

In today's environment it is important for companies to make the size of the envelope part of the evaluation process for determining how they stack up against the competition. We must ask how quickly and in what manner are we delivering products and services as compared to the competition. An analysis of the converging industries becomes important when developing an envelope. For example, if you are a bank, what are the insurance companies doing with their envelopes that will begin

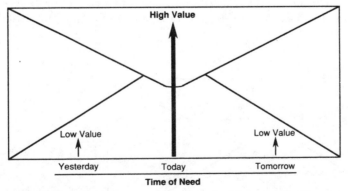

Figure 8-6. The larger the envelope at the time of need, the greater the value of the buyer.

to affect your ability to compete? How about credit card companies, such as American Express?

Service Station Example

What has been happening to gasoline service stations over the last few years provides an example of the envelope concept and the information component of products and services. Traditional service stations sell gasoline and provide repair services. Some new types of service station have eliminated the repair services and sell gasoline only on a self-service basis. Still others sell gasoline and other products, such as coffee, rolls, and a gallon of milk. All these typically accept credit cards and sell different grades of gasoline with various octane ratings. It is instructive to analyze the envelopes that service station are creating. Today, many service stations charge a higher price for gasoline purchased with a credit card than gasoline purchased for cash—they are offering the information component of credit in their envelope along with the gasoline. Service stations also sell "octane." Does higher octane really make the car run better? Perhaps. But does not "high octane" also have a "high quality" connotation—part of the information component? The service station that sells coffee and rolls is creating a larger envelope that it can offer to the consumer, and perhaps lure customers who might otherwise go elsewhere. A major oil company recently bought a chain of bakeries in order to provide fresh rolls to expand this part of the service-station business. What do you think has the higher profit margin today—gasoline or fresh rolls?

In the United Kingdom, a large number of service stations are unattended. This came about because of a below-the-line orientation that focused on saving money—reducing the people costs. Today, companies with unattended stations are finding it difficult to differentiate themselves from their competition. They must compete on price alone. The operators of the unattended service stations in the United Kingdom are finding it difficult to compete as the consumer becomes accustomed to buying more than just gasoline at the service station.

Alliances and Partnerships

As we have already discussed, an important method for growing the size of the pie is to create alliances and partnerships, our fifth mindset image, illustrated in Figure 8-7.

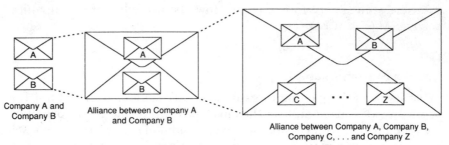

Figure 8-7. Alliances and partnerships can be used to create larger envelopes presented to the customer as one image.

> **Alliances and partnerships can be used to create a single envelope to the consumer.**

If we are going to increase the size of the envelope with the intent of going after increased market share, we might take any number of approaches. One way might be to develop a complete infrastructure, provide a complete set of products and services, and create a network for reaching out to new customers. This approach tends to be very costly, and most organizations are not big enough to do it. What we will see more of in the 1990s is an approach where organizations will form alliances and partnerships to share a single point of access to the customer. This will provide these organizations with the opportunity to provide a much larger envelope than any single organization would be able to provide. As we get into the 1990s, the challenge will be to identify opportunities for strategic alliances and partnerships and then to ensure that the links between organizations and the links out to the customer are working in the proper fashion. In other words, effective management of the links becomes the important issue. This will be a real challenge, but those who understand these concepts, and learn to create strategic alliances and properly control the links, will be the visionary leaders of tomorrow.

Two examples of strategic alliances will point out how such partnerships can change the nature of the industry and change the rules by which organizations compete.

Hospital Supply Example

In order to increase efficiency, major suppliers of medical supplies to hospitals established comprehensive electronic channel support systems to make it easy for their customers to order hospital supplies using terminals and personal computers. They were then able to use these same electronic channels to substantially increase the size of their envelopes. These organizations have formed alliances with many other suppliers so the hospital can order not only hospital supplies, but complementary medical supplies, products from office supply wholesalers, and others. All these suppliers are thus sharing a common point of access to the customer. A substantial percentage of all those products that are needed to run a hospital are now available through one easy-to-use online ordering system and are delivered with a single delivery truck. The suppliers that participate in these alliances are able to give a substantial discount for ordering in this manner. So not only is it more convenient for the customer to have a single system for ordering all types of supplies, but the cost is lower as well. This is very different from the traditional type of operation that provides only medical supplies and requires its customers to acquire other types of supplies using other means. These suppliers of hospital supplies have been able to use alliances and partnerships to create substantially bigger envelopes of ancillary products and services. Once the customer becomes accustomed to the convenience of such a system, it is almost impossible for a competitor to displace it. We can easily speculate on how such one-truck delivery systems might be expanded in the future to include the consumer.

Airline Example

Another example of a creative alliance is that between American Airlines and Citibank. When customers use certain Citibank credit cards to purchase any type of product, they receive points on the American Airlines frequent flier program. This encourages the customer to use Citibank credit cards and also enhances loyalty to American Airlines. This is a win-win situation for American Airlines, for Citibank, and for the customer as well. American Airlines is actively recruiting many types of companies to join this alliance, thereby increasing the size of the envelope each time it does so.

Happy Captives

Our sixth mindset image is happy captives:

Keep your customers happy captives.

The idea of keeping the customers that we already have is of critical importance. It must be the goal of the entire management team that every individual in the organization has this important mindset clearly in mind in every interaction with the customer. All the ideas that are generated from the highest level executive down to the lowest level manager or clerk must focus on this one important point.

While the attitudes of individuals are extremely important in achieving this goal, there are additional techniques that can be used as well to prevent customers from fleeing to the competition. In a *Fortune* magazine article by Peter Petre entitled "How to Keep Customers Happy Captives," it was pointed out that

> ...The first system to appear in a market often becomes the runaway winner. Once entrenched, it is nearly impossible to displace.[4]

Once we begin to use a particular service and are satisfied with it, we tend to remain with it. It is a fact of life that people do not tend to jump ship to a new service simply because of a reduction in cost. For example, it takes five minutes to fill out a credit card application, but how many of us have changed to a credit card that offers lower interest rates? Even if we do become sufficiently motivated to change once, it is unlikely that we will change a second time. An important method for keeping customers happy captives is to develop electronic channel support systems that destroy the customer's interest in the products or services offered by the competition. If we are able to be first in the market with such a system, the competition must generally have to shift to an entirely new experience curve in order to compete. That is not easy when an organization is already behind. We will see an example of this scenario in Chapter 9 when we see how American Airlines was able to use electronic channels to make happy captives of a significant percentage of travel agents in the United States. As organizations increase the reach of products and services into the extended enterprise by using sophisticated electronic channel support systems, these same organizations will come closer to the consumer, and the "happy captives" scenario will become even more important.

The Warm Frog

The final mindset image that we discuss concerns the "warm frog," illustrated in Figure 8-8. The warm frog concept concerns creating an environment in the organization that makes everyone aware of the fact that the business environment is passing through a period of rapidly accelerating change. The organization must be positioned so that it is able to quickly react to the changes that are occurring in the external envi-

Figure 8-8. Warm frog/cold frog.

ronment. Tichy and Ulrich made some interesting comparisons between people and frogs in the article "The Leadership Challenge—A Call for the Transformational Leader":

> This phenomenon is based on a classic experiment in biology. A frog which is placed in a pan of cold water but which still has the freedom to jump out can be boiled if the temperature change is gradual, for it is not aware of the barely detectable changing heat threshold. In contrast, a frog dropped in a pot of boiling water will immediately jump out: it has felt a need to survive. In a similar vein, many organizations that are insensitive to gradually changing organizational thresholds are likely to become "boiled frogs"; they act in ignorant bliss of environmental triggers and eventually are doomed to failure. This failure, in part, is a result of the organization having no felt need to change.[5]

Are you a cold frog, a warm frog, or a boiled frog?

We know who the boiled frogs are—they have already failed. We also know who the cold frogs are—they are the ones who have seen the changes that are occurring in the environment and have already reacted successfully to those changes: American Airlines, American Express, WalMart, Federal Express. Since you are reading this book, you are probably not yet one of the boiled frogs. But you must ask: "Am I a cold frog or a warm frog?" Do you know that the environment is changing and becoming life threatening? If you are one of the warm frogs, rest assured that you will not remain a warm frog for long. You will either take the necessary steps to become a cold frog, or the changing environment will ensure that you will be a boiled frog long before the end of the decade of the 1990s.

Conclusion

Management must ask itself if there is a mindset in the organization that goes beyond just an awareness of the vision—one that says we are going to make all levels of management start thinking differently. Are we trying to make the changes that are necessary for survival in the 1990s? If we are, this means that we must have a different view of the extended enterprise that is more than just customers and suppliers. The extended enterprise must begin to take into account strategic alliances, changing industry structures, and converging industries. We must then start to determine what the organization's role will be in the new environment.

References

1. Peter Drucker. "Peter Drucker on Management." *Management Review*. December 1974.

2. Bert Rosenblum. *Marketing Channels: A Management View*. New York: The Dryden Press, 1983.

3. Al Ries and Jack Trout. *Marketing Warfare*. New York: McGraw-Hill, 1986.

4. Peter Petre. "How to Keep Customers Happy Captives." *Fortune*. Sept. 2, 1985.

5. Noel M. Tichy and David O. Ulrich. "The Leadership Challenge—A Call for the Transformational Leader." *The Sloan Management Review*. Fall 1984.

9

Restructuring
the Channels

Introduction

The previous two chapters discussed how the roles of management must change with respect to formulating a strategic business vision, and we described a series of mindset images that can be used to drive the strategic business vision down through all levels of middle and operational management. In this chapter, we examine the primary tools that are available for differentiating the organization from the competition, changing industry structures, and possibly creating entirely new businesses. These tools consist of building electronic channels for communicating with the external elements of the extended enterprise to enhance productivity, flexibility, and competitiveness. It is these electronic channels that quickly enable the organization to restructure and, in doing so, make fundamental changes in industry power relationships. As we have been continually stressing:

> **The most important and vexing challenges executives**
> **will face in the 1990s are those associated with**
> **_continual and rapidly accelerating change._**

This change will include rapid introduction of technology in all facets of society, constant evolution of niche markets and niche competitors, and a shortfall in people and skills. Often our focus in the past has been on the nature of the products and services that we have offered to our

customers. Today the effective management of an organization's channels is of critical importance. We need to begin questioning the limited
usage that we have so far made of electronic channels. All types of organizations need to begin expanding the usage of existing channels and
to begin creating new and more powerful channels using the technology
that now exists. The evolution of global ECSSs will enable the work
force to provide new functions without having to physically cross country borders.

However, as pointed out in Chapter 2, above-the-line applications of
technology that have a strategic focus must be built on top of effective,
below-the-line systems. We cannot build electronic channel support systems that communicate with elements of the extended enterprise without having the internal infrastructure in place. Most below-the-line networks and other applications of technology have been aimed at
reporting on how well we are doing or on fulfilling orders. Above-the-
line ECSSs are often aimed at creating a need and with fulfilling the
need at the same time, in some cases directly in the home of the consumer.

Global Competition

Global competition is having increasing impact on American business.
Of great importance to the competitive environment will be the European Economic Community's dropping of their internal trade barriers
in 1992. The growing role that Japan and the Pacific Rim countries are
playing in the global marketplace is also having a significant effect in
the ability of U.S. business to effectively compete. Powerful pressures
from the rest of the world's trading countries are resulting in the constant elimination and reformation of markets, jobs, and entire organizations. These factors place intense stress on all members of the organization as we attempt to adapt to new environments. Leaders must
understand the global competitive environment and continually ener-
gize their management teams to enable the organization to make the required changes. Electronic channels will play an increasingly important
role in enhancing competitiveness in the changing environment by
allowing for the restructuring and redirection of an organization's
channels.

As the world shrinks owing to the accelerating use of communication
technologies, the further out in the extended enterprise we can reach
and the greater the need is to automate activities that do not add value
to products and services. At the same time, it becomes important to create services that *do* add significant value. Many of the leaders have already automated the activities that do not add significant value and are

beginning to create the new services that concentrate on value-add activities. They are freeing up human resources to create innovative new offerings.

Electronic Data Interchange

The development of electronic channels typically begins with efforts at installing systems that implement electronic data interchange (EDI), in which electronic transactions are shipped back and forth between organizations—one company's computers talking directly to another company's computers using communication facilities. This is often done to streamline administrative processes. From the standpoint of information systems, this is referred to as transaction-to-transaction processing. The primary focus of systems that use electronic data interchange is on manufacturing, transportation, delivery of products and services, and invoicing and collecting payments. All these can help to establish a *just-in-time* processing environment. Electronic data interchange implements the beginning of a pipeline that reaches out into the organization's extended enterprise, including customers and suppliers. (See Figure 9-1.)

Electronic data interchange can provide benefits for both customers and suppliers. Customers gain advantages from using a single integrated system to lower administrative and acquisition costs and reduce

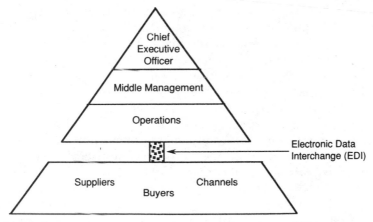

Figure 9-1. Systems that support electronic data interchange (EDI) implement the beginnings of a thin pipeline between the enterprise and the organizations with which it interacts.

inventories. Suppliers benefit from the use of a single integrated system to lower administrative and inventory costs, to enhance cash flows, and to help in differentiating products to achieve competitive advantage. As mentioned in Chapter 8, this can be done by increasing the size of the envelope through providing additional products or services. Providing the customer with the ability to order many types of products or services from one central ordering system is a way of doing this. Uses of electronic data interchange generally expand as organizations get accustomed to it. For example, a company might begin by installing a system to automate the order entry function and then move to a system that automatically handles shipment notification. A further step might be to do electronic invoicing and electronic funds transfer between organizations. As long as these types of systems remain simple systems in which there is a simple transaction-to-transaction relationship between the customer and the supplier, they do nothing to fundamentally change the way in which the organizations do business with one another, and no changes in basic structure occur.

Interorganizational Systems

As systems that use electronic data interchange expand, we begin to see basic changes occurring in business relationships. These changes in business relationships often cause major structural changes to occur. For example, suppose a group of organizations begins to use automated order entry together with shipment notification and electronic invoicing. Such a system can be the beginnings of integrated business operations. Figure 9-2 shows an example in which a manufacturer's computer sends orders to a supplier's computer. The supplier's computer then sends a shipping notification back to the manufacturer. When the material arrives at the loading dock, a worker verifies that the order agrees with the shipping notification and causes the manufacturer's computer to transfer funds directly to the supplier. Such a system causes major changes to the business operations of both the manufacturer and the supplier because such automated systems eliminate the need for many traditional business functions. The supplier no longer needs an order entry function, because the supplier's computer automatically receives orders from the manufacturer. The manufacturer has no need for an accounts payable function because it pays for orders the moment they are received. The supplier has no need of a conventional accounts receivable organization, since the funds are automatically received as soon as the order is delivered. Such systems are called *interorganizational systems* (IOS) because they change the nature of organizations throughout

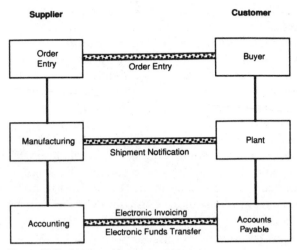

Figure 9-2. Integrated business operations.

the extended enterprise. Interorganizational systems expand the pipeline created by the first systems that began to use electronic data interchange. (See Figure 9-3.)

The primary focus of these systems remains the same as with simpler forms of EDI. However, interorganizational systems provide additional benefits to both customers and suppliers. Customers benefit from increased quality of products and services. They also gain the ability to do joint development of products and benefit from shared pricing and inventories. For example, for a manufacturer, an interorganizational system extends the manufacturer's control into the operations of its sup-

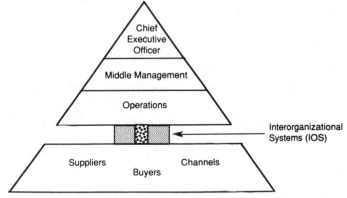

Figure 9-3. Systems that support electronic data interchange can be expanded to form interorganizational systems (IOS) that expand the pipeline.

pliers and provides the ability to cause major structural changes to occur in the manufacturer/supplier relationship.

Interorganizational systems allow a just-in-time environment to be created for both the customer and the supplier. They offer significant cost savings advantages on both sides. The extended enterprise plays a larger role when interorganizational systems are in place. Interorganizational systems make it much easier for an organization to differentiate its products and services from its competition. They also make it possible for the organization to begin changing the rules by which organizations compete in the industry. For example, when an organization that has done traditional order entry moves to just-in-time processing, it finds itself in an entirely new environment. It may find that the new zero-balance inventory techniques allow it to completely eliminate inventory control functions. The organization might ask its suppliers to supply quality control information with the goods they ship. This can eliminate the need for layers of management that were originally involved in checking quality. Many organizations also now send engineering drawings back and forth electronically to streamline the research and development function.

Instead of doing simple transaction-to-transaction processing, interorganizational systems enable the organization to concentrate its efforts on above-the-line issues and to begin focusing on creating new revenue streams rather than streamlining existing operations. When interorganizational systems begin to proliferate in the extended enterprise, the nature of the competitive environment fundamentally changes. Instead of an environment where your organization is pitted against the competition, the environment changes to one in which your entire extended enterprise is competing against your competitor's extended enterprise. Streamlining business operations throughout the entire extended enterprise can help you to achieve competitive advantage.

Electronic Channel Support Systems

Electronic channel support systems complete the expansion of the pipeline begun with EDI and IOS. (See Figure 9-4.) Electronic channel support systems concentrate on automating the non-value-added functions as well as on automating those activities that add significant value to products and services. They allow organizations to leverage their human resources and to become more innovative and creative. The primary focus of ECSS shifts to enhancing marketing and distribution functions, establishing strategic alliances and business partnerships, and understanding converging industries. Electronic channel support sys-

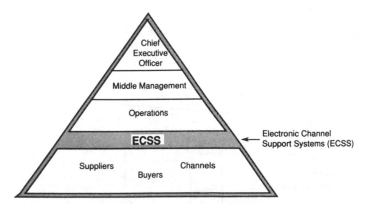

Figure 9-4. Interorganizational systems can be further expanded to form electronic channel support systems (ECSS) to complete the expansion of the pipeline.

tems allow us to exploit technology for strategic advantage in the extended enterprise environment and can cause significant management and structural changes to take place in the business environment.

Electronic data interchange and interorganizational systems typically focus on the first column of Figure 8-3, the column associated with the product flow itself—the physical component of products and services. More sophisticated electronic channel support systems begin to focus on the other four columns—those that are associated with the information component. With ECSS, we begin to ask questions like: "How do I build the envelope?" "How do I get other industries involved?" Both EDI and IOS deal with traditional business relationships, where business organizations are dealing with one another; electronic channel support systems extend the reach of channel systems. In the near future, channel systems will be primarily multimedia based and will reach directly into the home of the consumer. A major emphasis of ECSS that distinguishes it from EDI and IOS is that an ECSS enables the organization that owns a particular channel to exploit the rapidly evolving communications and information technologies for the purposes of acquiring, creating, distributing, and presenting *knowledge* rather than just data or information.

A key requirement of top management in applying strategic thinking is to understand the relationship between the waves of innovation through which we are passing and the three phases of electronic channel growth. A good understanding of these relationships, shown in Figure 9-5, can help us to exploit the technologies of people systems and develop new relationships with the consumer. In many cases we will be able to differentiate products and services from the competition and achieve substantial and sustainable competitive advantage. Before an organization begins to in-

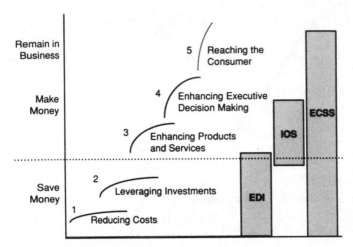

Figure 9-5. Relationships of the waves of change to EDI-IOS-ECSS progression.

stall electronic linkages to the members of its extended enterprise, it is important to understand this progression from EDI to IOS and from IOS to ECSS. This is because electronic linkages must not be employed in isolation. They must be installed with a view to the eventual installation of comprehensive electronic channel support systems. Where EDI and IOS have changed organizational structures within an organization's extended enterprise, electronic channel support systems have the potential of modifying the structures of entire industries. Electronic channel support systems begin to focus more closely on business partnerships and strategic alliances. Significant structural changes will occur first in the plant, then in the corporation, and finally in the industry as a whole.

Learning from American Airlines

The evolution of the American Airlines's *Sabre* airline reservation system provides an example of how sophisticated ECSSs have changed the structure of an entire industry. The way in which the competitive environment has evolved in the airline industry can help us to understand the value of electronic channels. The airline industry clearly shows that organizations that have the foresight to build and control electronic channels can change the structure of the industry, and in doing so, alter the rules of competition. The leading airlines have created competitive advantage by supporting cost and differentiation strategies and have created entirely new businesses. This approach is available to everyone. Anyone can do this if he or she has the vision and then develops effective strategies and tactics to implement the vision.

First and Second Waves: Online Reservations

The initial motivation for an online reservation system was to enhance the productivity of the seat reservation process. American Airlines began with first and second wave below-the-line (save money) operational systems for automating the airline reservation process. (See Figure 9-6.) The initial Sabre system went online in about 1964 and concentrated on the reduce costs and leverage assets waves of innovation. American Airlines was able to establish a competitive below-the-line information infrastructure that enabled them to switch from a manual-processing experience curve to a computer-processing experience curve. At the same time, they were able to improve service and gain economies of scale. These below-the-line systems enabled American Airlines to virtually create the lucrative airlines reservations industry. With the competitive advantage they were able to ultimately achieve, American Airlines has become a dominant player in the airlines reservation industry. It is important to realize, however, that American Airlines did not achieve a dominant position in the airline reservations industry as a result only of

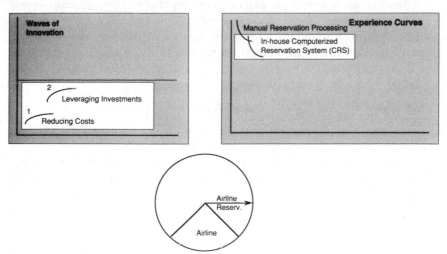

Figure 9-6. The below-the-line reservation systems that American Airlines installed in the 1960s.

its initial development of the Sabre system. In fact, in hindsight, Sabre represented relatively primitive technology that was quickly leap-frogged by other systems that were created in the early 1970s.

The initial motivation for the development of the Sabre system was to reduce the transaction costs associated with making an airline reservation. However, because the philosophy of an airline is that revenue is lost forever when a plane takes off with empty seats, it quickly became apparent that an efficient reservation system could also help to fill more seats. The Sabre system also included the function of making reservations for seats on the flights of other airlines, as did the reservation systems of the other carriers. This made it possible for each of the airlines to give the impression to the public of being a full-service provider. American Airlines may not service the final destination of the passenger, but the Sabre system allows American Airlines to provide the service of getting any passenger to any desired destination.

In 1985 American Airlines had over 40 percent of the airline reservation business and made over $100 million on its airline reservation business. Profits have dropped somewhat since then owing to the increased effectiveness of other operators of reservations systems. Regulatory intervention on the part of the Civil Aeronautics Board, which required operators of reservations system to establish nondiscriminatory pricing has also had an effect on profits. Airlines that did not have the foresight of American Airlines were charged a fee for processing each reservation transaction. Although the fee is relatively small, amounting to no more than about 1 percent of the average ticket value, a very large number of transactions are made each year. Today the airlines' reservation systems are extremely competitive. United Airlines is a leading competitor in the airlines reservation industry and now has about a third of the market. However, American Airlines has been able to maintain its over 40 percent share of the value of all tickets written.

Third Wave: Capturing the Travel Agents

Capitalizing on its experience with online airline reservations and expanding on the infrastructure it already had in place, the Sabre system moved outside, as early as 1976, to travel agencies. The services that Sabre provided to travel agencies included providing online information about schedules and fares and giving the travel agent the ability to actually make reservations using an online terminal. Toward the end of the 1970s, Sabre added new functions to provide travel agencies with useful backroom services, including itinerary preparation and basic accounting functions. American Airlines provides support for travel agents in a win-win environment that enables the agency to operate more efficiently and to attract customers away from the more poorly run agencies. Once an agency becomes used to such a service and alters its procedures to make use of it, the service tends to lock in the agency. The enhanced service becomes a "switching barrier" that prevents the agency from easily changing over to some other service. The focus here is on above-the-line systems that enhance products and services in order to generate new revenues. This focus is different from the original computer reservations systems that were designed to reduce costs and leverage investments. The new above-the-line orientation quickly leads to new experience curves for creating alliances with travel agents and other airlines, providing new forms of support for the travel agent, and developing new methods for determining optimum pricing levels for seats. (See Figure 9-7.)

By creating appropriate electronic channels, seat pricing decisions can be made on a real-time basis. The availability of information concerning every seat that American Airlines owns allows American Airlines to make instantaneous pricing decisions that permit it to maximize the revenue that is generated by each flight. It does this by dynamically varying the numbers of seats that it assigns to each pricing category based on information that it has about seat utilization and load factors on different flights. This strategic function is called *yield management.* The availability and exploitation of the yield management function is

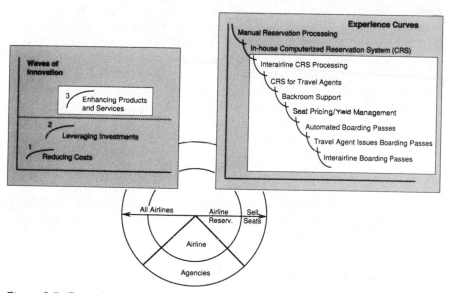

Figure 9-7. Expanding the pie with third-wave systems by moving outward to travel agents.

what makes for a pricing strategy that seems so complex to the consumer.

The new ECSSs that American Airlines has created enabled it to change industry power relationships and modify in a fundamental way the rules by which organizations compete in the airline industry. American Airlines has demonstrated the rule of "first in, last in." This rule states that the first company to enter a new industry can effectively capture and hold a significant share of the market. They effectively make it difficult for competitors to lure away American Airlines's "happy captive" travel agents. American Airlines has been able to establish an electronic extended enterprise. They have effectively created new "envelopes" to differentiate the products and services of American Airlines from the products and services offered by the competition. Their envelope allows the customer to make one call to handle ticketing to any desired destination. The envelope for the travel agent provides a single terminal that can be used for flight scheduling on all airlines and also provides support for the travel agent's business.

American Airlines has also exploited *time* to create competitive advantage, because all its new information systems made it possible for American Airlines to make solid decisions much more quickly than for the competition. Its above-the-line information systems exploit all three of Porter's and Millar's rules for creating substantial and sustainable competitive advantage that we discussed in Chapter 2: They altered industry structures and changed the rules of competition in the airline industry, they created new cost and differentiation strategies, and they created the entirely new business of online airline reservations. Not only do the new above-the-line electronic channel support systems of American Airlines create new revenue streams and substantially increase the size of American Airlines's pie, they also provide enhanced information that allows them to streamline the traditional parts of their operation and enhance their profitability. The entire American Airlines Sabre system has a win-win orientation. American Airlines wins through increased revenues and profitability, the travel agents win through the ability to better service their customers, and the consumer wins through an enhanced ability to book a seat on an airline at the lowest possible cost. It might even be said that the other airlines that use the Sabre system also win by providing them with better opportunities for filling their own seats because the reservation system is the primary marketing and distribution channel.

Fourth Wave: Megadecisions in the Travel Industry

After travel agents began installing Sabre terminals in large numbers, American Airlines further expanded the scope of the Sabre system by

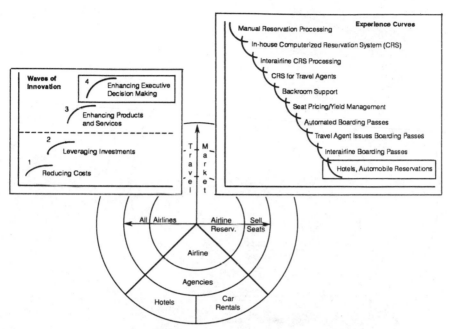

Figure 9-8. Expanding the pie with fourth-wave systems to enhance decision making and to provide complementary services.

adding complementary services. (See Figure 9-8.) By doing so, it effectively expanded the envelope with which it wraps its products and services. A traveler will often need a hotel room and a car in addition to a seat on an airplane. By the end of the 1970s, American Airlines began supplying these ancillary services through electronic channel support systems and alliances with other suppliers. The challenge of the airlines today is to redefine the industry from the "airline" industry to the "travel" industry. American Airlines is effectively using ECSSs to enhance and support its entire extended enterprise. Throughout the 1980s, the emphasis in American Airlines has been on the fourth innovation wave in which it is using technology to create new experience curves for the scheduling of ancillary services, such as hotel rooms, automobile rentals, and various types of entertainment services. American Airlines is building even larger envelopes of products and services that will allow them to provide schedules and reservations for all the travel and entertainment needs of the consumer. Figure 9-9 shows the structure of the American Airlines extended enterprise. American Airlines is continuing its efforts at expanding the size of its pie and increasing the reach and scope of its extended enterprise. New electronic channels are allowing American Airlines to increase its effectiveness, establish new win-win relationships, and add new customers who remain happy cap-

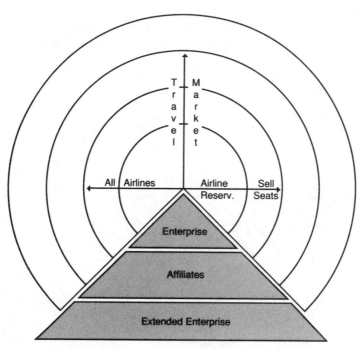

Figure 9-9. Extended enterprise view of American Airlines.

tives. It is increasing the scale and scope of its operations by constantly switching to new experience curves that generate new revenue streams.

American Airlines started with the basic sale of a service to a customer. It then made use of electronic channels to provide better service. It then differentiated its products and services by exploiting the extended enterprise, beginning with travel agents. Notice how quickly American Airlines was able to create and expand the electronic pipeline to increase the size of its pie and the size of its piece as well. American Airlines did it much more quickly than by using bricks and mortar.

Fifth Wave: Reaching the Consumer Directly

Toward the end of the 1980s, American Airlines began to provide airline reservations services directly to consumers through the EAASY Sabre system that is available to personal computer users through various information services. This will further increase the size of its pie and its own slice of it. (See Figure 9-10.) In the future American Airlines will be making it increasingly easy for the consumer to deal with American Airlines directly. The EASSY Sabre will expand as electronic linkages to

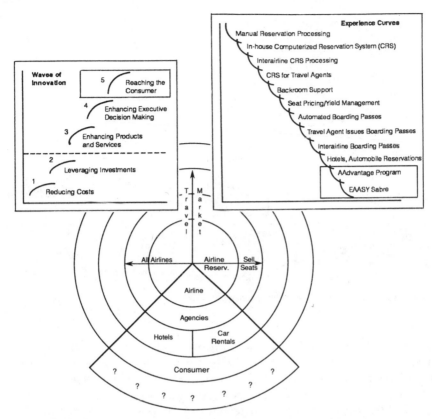

Figure 9-10. Future further expansion of the pie with fifth-wave people systems.

the end consumer proliferate. This ties back to our progression from EDI to IOS to ECSS, where the ultimate goal of ECSS is to reach the consumer and to reduce reliance on intermediaries. The new experience curves that are important here are telemarketing services, the EAASY Sabre reservations system, and the extended reach of electronic channels in providing corporate travel management services.

Outside the scope of the airlines reservation system, American Airlines is beginning to provide consumers with new envelopes by using its frequent-flier program to establish alliances with credit card companies to enhance customer loyalty. American Airlines has also established an alliance with a major provider of long-distance telephone service to provide points in the frequent-flier program each time a customer makes a long-distance telephone call. It is interesting to note that other organizations are investigating multimedia systems that will let the consumer see pictures of hotel rooms and other hotel facilities before making a reservation. American Airlines is also now providing such a service

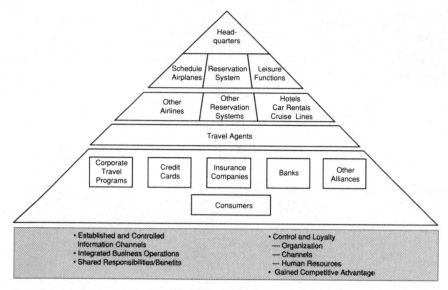

Figure 9-11. Airline industry extended enterprise model.

through a system called Sabrevision. Figure 9-11 shows a possible airline extended enterprise of the future. Notice how its scope will have expanded far beyond its initial scope of providing seats on airplanes.

What business is American Airlines in today? Transportation? Travel? The leisure industry? Information? Banking? Is American Airlines today just an airline, or is it now an information provider? What will it be tomorrow? A knowledge provider? Figure it out, and you may know where American Airlines is going in the future.

Restructuring the Channels

Competitive advantage in the future will depend on the ability of organizations to increase the effectiveness of their extended enterprises. The use of advanced electronic channel support systems that reach far out into the extended enterprise, eventually reaching the end consumer directly, will cause channels to be radically restructured. This channel restructuring will take place in four areas, but not necessarily in this sequence (see Figure 9-12):

1. *Internal department restructuring.* Restructuring of the channels will begin with an internal focus on enhancing the functions of individual departments to reduce cycle times and increase efficiency.

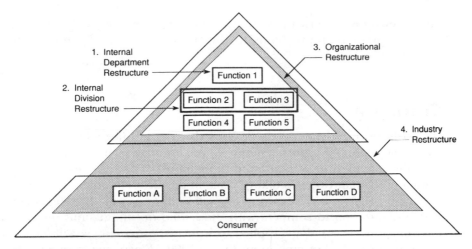

Figure 9-12. Restructuring the channels.

2. *Internal division restructuring.* Next, the restructuring will begin to affect divisions that comprise multiple departments. This will take the form of consolidation of functions and departments and may result in the elimination of some internal functions.

3. *Organizational restructuring.* In some cases, the restructuring of electronic channels will enable a third phase of restructuring to take place on an organization-wide basis. This will result in horizontal network integration, which is discussed further in Chapter 12.

4. *Industry restructuring.* The final phase of restructuring will take place throughout the entire extended enterprise and will cause entire industries to be transformed. This phase will be characterized by consolidation of functions between organizations. In some cases, electronic channels will enable cross-organizational people systems to be eliminated or consolidated. This phase will see the rapid growth of industry boundary crossing, which has already started in many environments.

There are two ownership strategies that can be applied in the context of using electronic channel support systems to support the extended enterprise. One involves the creation of strategic alliances and partnerships through the use of electronic channel support systems to implement the linkages between organizations. The other involves strategic acquisitions. Either ownership strategy involves packaging products and services in new envelopes and then presenting those envelopes to the customer for a fair price. As an example, we have seen how American Airlines, and the other airlines, are tying their frequent flier programs to the use of credit cards and other consumer services.

Conclusion

It is critical to understand the lessons that the airlines teach us about electronic channel support systems. These lessons can help you to visualize the role of your organization in its industry. If your organization cannot understand what is taking place in the airline industry, and cannot see parallels for your own organization, then it will be difficult for your organization to compete with those who do understand the new environment. Technology applied to information channels will have a major impact on all organizations in the 1990s. Electronic channels will increasingly be used to replace people channels. But those that implement these new forms of technology must have a clear understanding of the waves of technology change, experience curve strategies, and changing industry power relationships. And it is of critical importance that a coherent strategic business vision guides the application of these new forms of technology.

PART 3

Tactics and Implementation

In some organizations, strategic planners have been very successful at formulating winning strategies. In many other organizations, good ideas are conceived but do not make it all the way down the innovation arrow to implementation. Strategy requires *vision*, but implementation requires *leadership*. Strategic advantage is usually achieved at the operational level, and a strategy is only as good as its implementation. *Tactics* is the bridge between strategy and implementation. (Figure P3-1.) It is at this bridge that the two different thought and planning processes are linked together. This is where executives prove their leadership skills and earn the right to lead. On the vision and strategy side of the bridge, top management formulates a vision and develops that vision into a strategy that charts the course of the organization in achieving competitive advantage and increasing organizational effectiveness. On the tactics and implementation side of the bridge, operational management formulates tactical plans to implement the vision. It is at this bridge that effective communication plays a critical role in linking the vision and strategy team with the implementation team. What is required to achieve successful implementation is a set of management practices that help validate the strategy and develop detailed tactical plans for sharing the vision, gaining buy-in, and empowering the organization. A sense of urgency and enthusiasm is critical—in many cases, the very survival of the organization will be at stake.

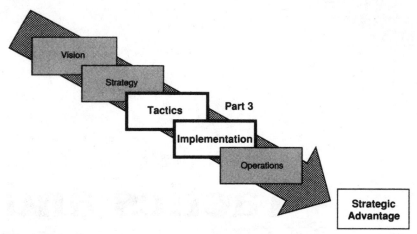

Figure P3-1

Make no assumptions about the management techniques that will be required in tomorrow's organizations. Chapter 10 introduces the mechanics of a simple planning technique, called Linkage Analysis Planning, that individuals and groups can use to formulate a vision and develop effective strategies. Chapter 11 then outlines steps for actualizing the vision, and Chapter 12 describes how to build the new organization that will be required to effectively compete in the 1990s.

10
Planning through Linkage Analysis

Introduction

In this chapter we examine techniques for conducting a linkage analysis planning session. During the planning session, the concepts presented in Parts 1 and 2 are used to formulate the strategic business vision and to develop the strategic and tactical plans that are required to implement that vision. We begin this chapter by examining the characteristics of traditional strategic planning techniques that many organizations use. We then list the characteristics of linkage analysis planning that make it a better planning tool for today's environment. We then describe the mechanics of the linkage analysis planning procedure and walk through two linkage analysis planning sessions—one with an external focus and one with an internal orientation. We then show how the results of a linkage analysis planning session are documented and list many of the benefits of this new form of strategic planning. We then conclude this chapter by asking you to work through a simple leadership exercise that shows how linkage analysis planning can be applied on an individual basis. The leadership exercise also helps to structure the information in the two concluding chapters.

Traditional Strategic Planning

Have you ever participated in a strategic planning session in which, after it was over, you felt good about it? Were the procedures easy to understand? Or did you get hung up in all the rules?

> Someone states a goal. Someone else says: "That isn't a complete sentence." So she puts a verb on it. He says: "Now it's not a goal, it's an objective." "OK," she says, "I don't care, take the verb off." "No, it's got to be a complete sentence." Someone asks: "What's our mission statement?"…"That's not a mission statement, it's a goal." "No. It's an objective."

Does any of this sound familiar? When we get finished after 2, or 3, or 5 days of this type of planning, do we feel that we have accomplished something useful, or do we feel worn down and beaten? The report that comes out of such a planning session is usually so thick that we know it will never be read.

Older planning techniques, such as critical success factor analysis, business systems planning models, data flow analysis, and the profit/impact analysis system (PIMS) usually define only a methodology; they leave it to the participants to determine how they will be able to develop plans for actually using the results of the planning session. Most approaches to strategic planning are designed to generate lists of action items. But these action items seldom lead to a strategic vision or a view of the organization's future. Existing planning techniques were developed for an era when the road maps existed and the environment by today's measures was relatively stable. In addition, they were primarily developed to enhance productivity, efficiency, quality, and financial strength and are heavily oriented toward the operational control and financial functions of the organization. They reflect an internal view of the organization and are not designed to look outward; they typically focus only on the "tactics" phase of the innovation arrow. These techniques tend to ignore vision and real strategic action. And many of these older techniques are too focused on *procedure* and do not allow the *creativity* of the group to shine through. According to George Steiner:

> Planning systems will be more flexible and less proceduralized, especially in large companies. (Planning systems today in smaller companies tend to be less formal.) Managers will become increasingly aware that too much procedure drives out the type of creativity, innovation, and imagination needed for superior strategic planning.[1]

Linkage Analysis Planning

This book is about a new kind of strategic planning that addresses the shortcomings of the old tools. What kind of capabilities do leading organizations need to win and survive in the 1990s? What are the characteristics of a good strategic planning tool? Simply stated, they should:

- Assist in raising the organization's levels of creativity, innovation, commitment, sense of shared vision, and effectiveness
- Provide new lenses for visualizing opportunities and exposures
- Be simple to use
- Provide a common language that the management team can use in communicating about strategic requirements, plans, and investments of your organization as well as others
- Foster creative participation, buy-in, and teamwork
- Leverage the creative powers of the organization's most experienced people
- Uses consistent, easy-to-understand imagery
- Be short on rules and long on creativity
- Link easily to all the organization's processes
- Help to find and develop the required new road maps that define the organization's goals in the changing environment
- Foster and encourage strategic thinking which can then lead to appropriate strategic actions
- Assess the organization's position today in the industry and on what the new role will be in the future for both the organization and the industry
- Provide new insights into strategic forces of change
- Provide the means for positioning the organization concerning applications of technology
- Succeed in developing the extended view of the organization

The key question to ask is: "Does the planning process raise the overall level of the organization's effectiveness, and does it provide the new strategic direction that is required for the 1990s?" Linkage analysis planning is a planning tool that meets these characteristics and can be used to carry us into the 1990s. Linkage analysis planning can help us to recognize the interrelationships that exist in the business environment, and takes into account the interrelationships that are involved in implementing a new organizational vision. It can assist us in forming a vision of what a strategic market thrust should look like. Linkage analysis planning is simple enough to weave into the day-to-day operational fabric of the organization. It can be used at all levels of management on a continuing basis. It is not specific to a particular industry, department, or function but is a generic tool that can enable all members of the organization to effectively participate in developing and implementing a shared vision.

Although this chapter presents the *mechanics* of using linkage analysis as a strategic planning tool, it is important to keep in mind as you read this chapter that linkage analysis planning is not *only* a methodology; it is an *ongoing process* that can help the entire organization reach new levels of effectiveness. Linkage analysis planning begins with the concepts and ideas expressed in Parts 1 and 2 of this book, and the simple methodology described in this chapter is only a part of the whole process. Linkage analysis planning is different from other planning methodologies because it is a comprehensive approach to strategic planning that takes us all the way from the first step of the innovation arrow—*vision*—to the final step—*operations*.

**The linkage analysis planning technique is
simple to understand, but is, at the same time,
deceptively powerful and complex.**

The complexity comes not from the process, but from that which we are analyzing—the organization, the extended enterprise, the industry, and the converging industries of which the organization is a part. During the linkage analysis planning process, we ask the participants to understand the organization and to determine the role the organization should play in the future. It can be used by an individual or by a group to perform strategic planning at any level in the organization. Linkage analysis planning is a generic planning technique that can be used in almost any situation. As an example, high school students are using it to identify the key linkages associated with developing into a productive adult. (See Appendix B.) The intent of linkage analysis planning is to help the planning group to:

- Identify and visualize the key forces that affect the environment
- Perform strategic thinking and creative brainstorming
- Develop and communicate a shared vision
- Identify the strategic actions that are required to implement the vision
- Leverage the team's insights, experiences, and creative skills
- Build teamwork

- Emphasize the important substance of the planning process
- De-emphasize procedure or form

Using Linkage Charts

Although we have not said so, we have already been using linkage analysis planning techniques from the very first chapter of this book to present key concepts. An important tool of linkage analysis planning consists of a set of *linkage charts* that are similar to many of the charts we have been using throughout this book. These charts help guide the strategic thinking that the group is trying to accomplish.

Drawing Linkage Charts

During a linkage analysis planning session the planning group constructs a set of linkage charts that provide important documentation of the strategic plans the group is creating. The following is a brief overview of how the process works. We describe the process in detail later in this chapter. Here is how we create a set of linkage charts during a planning session:

1. Clearly state the goal the group is trying to achieve or the question we are trying to answer and place it at the top of the chart. The goal should be one that is *strategically important* to the organization.

2. In the middle of the chart, place the organization, force, competitor, function, or whatever we are trying to analyze.

3. Put a box around whatever goes on the chart. By placing something in a box, it psychologically becomes something that we cannot ignore but must deal with. Do not use circles; circles are too comfortable.

4. Place around the center box those factors that everyone agrees are *strategically important* in reaching the goal stated at the top of the chart. Use the techniques discussed in Parts 1 and 2 to structure the group's thinking about what is strategically important.

5. Draw lines from each new box to the center box to help visualize the interrelationships and to document the important linkages.

6. Once a chart is completed, try to choose the one most important function with respect to achieving the goal stated at the top. One way to do this is to first take a vote on the top five, and then vote on the most important out of those five. If the group cannot agree on one, then choose the top two, but try never to have more than two number-one priorities. Why? Organizations can usually only swallow

a couple of hot strategic projects at a time. Having 40 number-one priorities defeats the purpose of the session; no one knows where to start.

7. The analysis can now proceed at a new level of detail using the same set of techniques. Place the most important function in the center of a new linkage chart and identify the important factors associated with this second-level function. The analysis proceeds in this manner until a level of detail is reached at which specific strategic actions can be clearly identified.

The power of linkage analysis planning lies in its ability to help the planning group to conceptualize the key issues and to allow them to focus on those factors that are critical to achieving substantial and sustainable advantage. It allows the group to discover those key issues that, after the fact, often appear obvious, but which can be so difficult to identify. A comment that is often heard in a linkage analysis planning session is: "Why didn't we think of that before?"

Linkage Chart Example

Before we describe the process in more detail, a short example will illustrate how powerful linkage charts can be in focusing the planning group on what is important. One of the authors worked with a large oil company in analyzing the company's motor oil division. The group placed the motor oil division at the center of a level 1 linkage chart. The major objective of this division was to gain market share with the automotive manufacturers—users of large quantities of motor oil. As the group added boxes to the chart, it became apparent that price, name recognition, and current technology were not going to provide increased market share. Enhanced service through conventional electronic data interchange systems for ordering were not the answer either. Image was selected as the key factor. This was placed at the center of the level 2 chart, and the group attempted to determine how enhancing the image of the motor oil division could produce the desired increased market share. After a long discussion period and after placing numerous boxes on the chart, we applied the key test. We were able to find no items that were likely to produce substantial and sustainable advantage. It soon became apparent that it was going to be extremely difficult to differentiate the oil company's motor oil product from that of the competition. We then backed up to the level 1 chart and eventually arrived at the solution of providing enhanced service to the large automotive customers by installing microprocessor sensors in the motor oil tanks of large customers. These would automatically generate an electronic order to the oil company for motor oil whenever the tanks dropped to a certain predetermined level. This eliminated the need for human intervention and reduced the work load of the automotive company's purchasing department. The end result was a number of multiyear contracts with automatic ordering. This same concept was quickly adapted to other divisions within the company.

The power of linkage charts is that they allow the planning group to zero in on the factors that have the potential for leading to substantial and sustainable advantage while also clearly identifying those issues that do not.

The Linkage Analysis Planning Procedure

We now describe the linkage analysis planning process in more detail. We begin by stating the only rule that governs the session. We then present a series of guidelines that can help focus the group and ensure success. We then describe how a linkage analysis planning session can take either an internal or an external focus; each is appropriate and has a different purpose.

The Only Rule

Linkage analysis planning has only one rule. You may already have guessed it because we have repeated this phrase many times:

Make no assumptions.

The only hard and fast rule of linkage analysis planning is that participants must bring no preconceived notions with them to the planning session regarding the organization or the environment and must focus on what is important in their own environment.

Guidelines

Although *make no assumptions* is the only rule, there are a few guidelines that, when followed, can make the session more productive. An important guideline concerns the principle of brainstorming. In constructing linkage charts during the session, whatever is important goes on the chart. All a participant needs to do is explain what he or she

means. *There are no bad ideas.* It is also important that attendees include all the key functional executives, the chief decision maker, and
other critical people. *The chief decision maker needs to be involved.* We
cannot over emphasize the importance of the chief decision maker's
role in breaking ties and ensuring that the focus stays on key priorities.
The chief decision maker has the final say on what constitutes a
number-one priority.

Asking the right questions is another key to the process. The intent of
the session is to significantly increase the value of the organization and
improve its effectiveness. The following question is one that should be
asked often:

**How will this help us to achieve
substantial and sustainable strategic advantage?**

If the group reaches a point where no one can identify anything on
the chart being discussed that can lead to substantial and sustainable advantage, the group should stop, back up, and set new priorities. This
guideline is intended to help the group zero in on those aspects of the
environment that are clearly strategic and to help avoid situations where
the group begins to focus on the wrong factors.

The session must be conducted in an environment that is conducive to
uninterrupted thought and creative, right-brain strategic thinking. The
session should be lead by a facilitator who can minimize procedure and
keep the creative juices flowing. As we have already stressed, the focus
must be on *substance*, not on *form*. The senior executives attending the session should ensure that the proper atmosphere prevails. It is hard for people to volunteer ideas and be creative in an environment that is hostile or
intimidating. During the idea generation phases, senior management
should foster an environment where rank has no privileges. Only in the
final stage of priority setting and in rare cases where the group is going off
on too many nonproductive tangents, should rank prevail.

Analyzing Waves, Curves, and Power Relationships

We will now see what is involved in an external linkage analysis planning session by walking through one in detail. The planning process
should begin with a discussion of the waves of innovation. We then try
to identify the experience curve strategies that will be important. Addi-

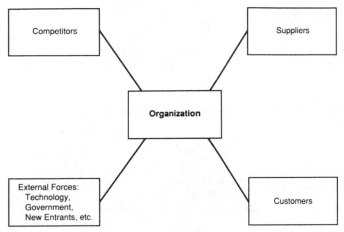

Figure 10-1. Traditional market forces.

tional experience curve strategies will become apparent as the planning process proceeds.

We then begin drawing charts that show the strategic forces that exist in the industry in an attempt to understand the present industry power relationships. A typical chart of traditional market forces is shown in Figure 10-1. We then ask questions about how the environment is likely to change in the future and draw charts that show how industry power relationships are changing. Michael Porter's competitive forces model discussed in Chapter 2 and the expanded strategic forces model introduced in Chapter 4 are useful tools in performing this analysis. (See Figure 10-2; the boxes with the double lines represent Porter's strategic forces model.) Figure 10-3 shows what a typical chart of future industry power relationships might look like.

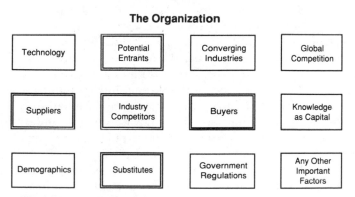

Figure 10-2. Strategic forces model.

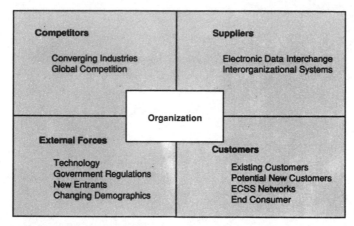

Figure 10-3. Changing industry power relationships.

Visualizing the Extended Enterprise

Our analysis of the waves of innovation, experience curves, and changing industry power relationships should begin to give us a feeling for what our external enterprise looks like. This, in turn, should begin to start us thinking about the electronic channel support systems that will be needed in the future for exploiting our extended enterprise view of the environment. Our vision for the organization should now begin to crystallize.

Conducting an External Linkage Analysis

A linkage analysis planning session can take either an internal or an external focus. Figure 10-4 shows that if we take an external focus, we look at the information component of products or services. The focus is on looking for strategic advantage and creating alliances and partnerships. In an external linkage analysis, we use the lenses and mindsets we have been discussing to begin visualizing opportunities and exposures. Notice the differences of focus between the external linkages and the internal linkages. Most existing planning processes were designed only for the internal view and do not function adequately in trying to understand the linkages in the extended enterprise, electronic channel support systems, alliances, and changing industry power relationships.

If we take an internal focus, we focus on comparative cost advantages and on the physical component of products and services. Here we focus on enhancing the processes or functions that are essential in creating or

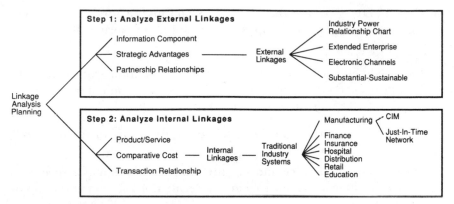

Figure 10-4. A linkage analysis planning session can take either an external or an internal focus.

providing a product or service. With an internal focus, we are trying to improve internal organizational effectiveness and position the below-the-line functions to support above-the-line investments.

It is our recommendation to begin an analysis of the organization with a session that takes an external focus. The external orientation will allow the group to identify significant modifications that need to be made to both the internal and external views of the organization. After the external analysis has been completed, an internal analysis can be conducted. Performing the analyses in this sequence can generate new insights with respect to the internal view of the organization. For example, an internal, below-the-line project may have been languishing for years in the budget authorization process. But now, when viewed through the new set of lenses that the external analysis provides, executives may ask why that was not completed years ago. The system may now be viewed as the base upon which future strategic systems will be built.

Level 1: The Organization

The next step in the linkage analysis planning process is to construct a *level 1 linkage chart* that shows those factors in the environment that are most important to the organization as a whole. The following steps are involved in creating this chart:

1. Write at the top of the chart the question that we are trying to answer.

2. Draw a box in the center of the chart that depicts the organization as a whole or whatever we are trying to analyze.

3. Place in boxes around the central box all those factors that members of the team agree are the most important in answering the question at the top.

The guidelines we discussed earlier in this chapter can be used to guide our progress in completing the chart. The two initial objectives of the level 1 analysis of the organization are to:

- Identify the major relationships related to the vision of the organization today and tomorrow.

- Understand the positive and negative impact of the major forces on the organization and their role in answering the question at the top of the chart.

We must continually ask *what is important* in choosing the boxes to place on the chart. The techniques discussed in Parts 1 and 2 of this book come into play in conducting the analysis. In preparing a level 1 linkage chart, we ask such questions as:

- What changes do we see occurring in the industry today? Tomorrow?

- What do we see as opportunities? Exposures?

- What is our view of the industry?

- Has our view of the industry changed in recent years?

- What is our view of the impact on the organization of customers? Suppliers? Partners?

- What strategic alliances might the organization form in the future?

- How might the rules of competition be changed?

- What forces may cause this to happen?

- Who might be new entrants to the market? Where will they come from?

The level 1 linkage chart that results from the analysis might look something like that in Figure 10-5.

After we achieve agreement that the chart includes all the important factors, we then focus on choosing which factor holds the *most promise* in providing a source of strategic advantage. This will be the factor that we will analyze next in detail. As we mentioned earlier, a guideline that can be used here is to try to choose the top five, and then vote for the most important from among those. In some cases, we may not be able to choose one, but might agree on two. We could then conduct separate detailed analyses on the top two. But try not to have more than two functions to analyze further. *Forcing us to choose one or two factors from*

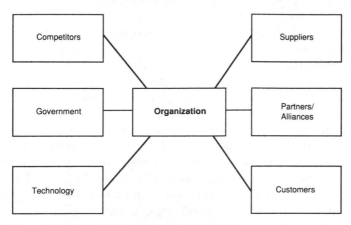

Which External Factors Are Most Important in Helping the Organization Achieve Strategic Advantage?

Figure 10-5. Level 1 linkage chart: the organization.

the chart provides insight that helps us to understand the benefits and tradeoffs involved in each decision and also helps to build teamwork.

If the group is inexperienced with the linkage analysis planning technique, it might be difficult at first to focus on what is most important. If this happens, we can simply pick one of the factors for further analysis to get experience with the technique. It will always be possible later to come back to the level 1 chart and discuss the factors further after we gain experience and confidence with the procedure.

We can now move on to the level 2 linkage analysis. For the purposes of this example, we will work through three different level 2 analyses to show the different kinds of questions that arise when different elements are analyzed. We will begin by choosing "competitors" as the factor on the chart that represents the most important factor in achieving strategic advantage.

Level 2: Competitors

In the level 2 analysis, we use the same procedure as for level 1 and focus in more detail on all the existing and potential future linkages that relate to the competition. We asked the following sorts of questions in preparing the level 2 linkage chart:

- Who are the competitors?
- What are their products and services?
- How do they differentiate themselves from us and the other competitors?

- What alliances exist or might the competition form?
- Could another industry take part of the business away?

As we begin to formulate answers to these questions, we build a level 2 chart by placing the important factors in boxes surrounding the "competitors" box, as shown in Figure 10-6. As with the level 1 chart, lines are used to link each important factor to the center box for competitors. This helps to clarify the important linkages that exist with the organization's competitors.

After agreeing that all the important issues are documented on the chart, we again try to determine which of the factors is most important. Again, hopefully one factor can be identified as most important, but no more than two number-one priorities should be identified. In this phase, we must agree on what is the most important factor to get the organization where we want it to be in the future with respect to the competition. We must achieve agreement on what is the most important linkage in accomplishing the vision. We must understand all the linkages and the important tradeoffs associated with them. At any level of the analysis, we might decide to combine two of the boxes into one for further analysis. For example, we might want to further analyze "current products and services" in conjunction with "differentiating our products and services" at the next level.

Which Factors Are Most Important from a Competitive Viewpoint?

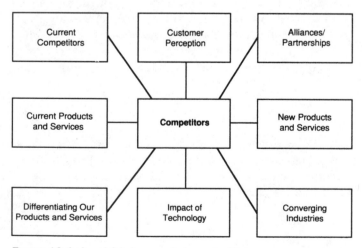

Figure 10-6. Level 2 linkage analysis: competitors.

Level 2: Suppliers

In analyzing the level 1 chart, we may have agreed that "suppliers" represented a better potential source of strategic advantage than the other factors. In constructing this level 2 chart, we might have asked a different set of questions:

- How important are our suppliers today?
- Will these same suppliers be important tomorrow?
- Could competitors form alliances with our suppliers?
- What are the alternate suppliers or alternate products?
- What are the opportunities for horizontal and vertical integration?
- How does the product flow from all of the suppliers, to us, to the customer, and then to the ultimate consumer?
- How does the revenue flow?
- What impact will technology have on these flows?
- What are the terms and conditions of contracts?
- What about title and ownership?
- What about service and maintenance throughout this chain?
- What about the information used in selling the product?
- What new experience curves are emerging? Could we use plastics rather than steel? Could we use plastics instead of gaskets?
- How can we reduce cycle time?

A possible level 2 linkage chart for "suppliers" is shown in Figure 10-7.

Level 2: Customers

We might alternatively have chosen "customers" from the level 1 chart for further analysis. In constructing the chart for "customers," we asked the following types of questions:

- Who are our customers? Who are their customers? What is important to them?
- Do the customers own the chart or do we?
- Which customer is most important today? Who is likely to be most important tomorrow?

Which Factors Are Most Important from the Viewpoint of Our Suppliers?

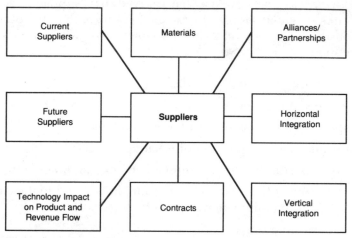

Figure 10-7. Level 2 linkage analysis: suppliers.

- Is it likely that it will be the ultimate consumer that will be important to us in the future?
- How can we grow our "shelf space" in the customer's mind?
- How can we expand the envelope of ancillary goods and services.
- Can we form alliances and partnerships that will help us reach a larger customer base?
- Can I start to cross industry boundaries?
- Can I begin to reach the ultimate consumer?

Figure 10-8 shows a level 2 linkage chart for customers.

At this point, we will choose "the end consumer" as the factor that represents the best source of strategic advantage with respect to "customers" and proceed to the level 3 linkage analysis.

Level 3: The End Consumer

To begin the level 3 analysis, we draw another chart placing "the end consumer" in the center. The level 3 analysis continues in the same manner as level 2 by identifying the key issues concerning "the end consumer" box, as shown in Figure 10-9. The linkage analysis may now be at a sufficient level of detail that we can begin identifying new business opportunities and benefits. In some cases, the function that we are analyzing in the level 3 analysis may not be at a sufficiently detailed level.

Which Factors Are Most Important from the Viewpoint of Our Customers?

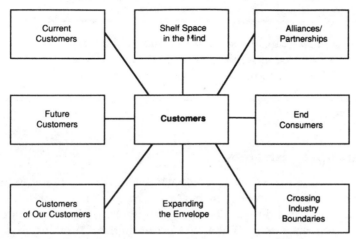

Figure 10-8. Level 2 linkage analysis: customers.

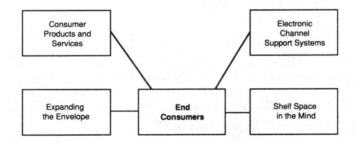

Action Plan

1. Create products and services that will appeal to the consumer and tend to lock them in.

2. Create alliances and partnerships that will allow us to offer a larger envelope of ancillary products and services.

Exposures

1. Our competitors may create products and services to reach the consumer before we do and lock us out.

2. Companies in other industries might begin to compete with us by reaching the consumer.

Future Enhancements

1. Create systems that allow the consumer to order our products and services from the home.

2. Create new alliances and partnerships that will allow the consumer to order products and services from other companies through our system.

3. Provide other types of products and services using electronic channel support systems.

Figure 10-9. Level 3 linkage chart: end consumers.

If that happens, it may be necessary to do a level 4 analysis, and in some cases a level 5 analysis to reach an appropriate stopping point.

> **At each stage the substantial and sustainable test must be applied to see whether the issues selected are strategically important.**

Documenting the Strategy

After we have reached the final level of detail, the vision for the organization should begin to become clear. As the vision materializes, it is important that we begin developing and documenting effective strategies for achieving that vision. When we decide that the function being analyzed is strategically important and that the final level of detail has been reached, we can begin to document strategic actions by adding three lists to the final linkage chart:

- Action plan
- Potential exposures
- Future enhancements

An example of a linkage chart at the final level of detail, with the three lists included, is shown in Figure 10-9.

Action Plan

The first list that is added to the linkage chart at the final level of detail is an action plan for pursuing strategic advantage in the particular area under study. The action plan must document the strategies that are required in order to achieve the organization's vision in that area. In preparing the action plan, we list benefits and opportunities. It is here that we begin making the transition from strategic *thinking* to strategic *action*. For example, on "the end consumer" linkage chart, we might try to identify information systems and new services that will allow us to reach the consumer directly. The focus here might be on providing services that tend to lock in consumers so that it will be difficult for them to switch to a competitor. We might try to define a new envelope that includes ancillary products and services that the consumer might want.

We might also try to identify functions that we might add to old services to significantly increase their perceived value to the consumer.

Potential Exposures

In addition to developing an action plan, we must also place on the lowest-level linkage chart a list of potential ways in which the organization might be threatened if it does not pursue strategic advantage in this particular area. For example, what will happen if *we* do not take steps in attempting to reach the consumer directly, but the *competition does*? What if other organizations begin to provide some of the new services that we are identifying? What will happen if players from the converging industries enter the picture with "new envelopes" and begin supplying services traditionally associated with organizations in our industry? We cannot afford to assume that the competition is not conducting planning sessions that are similar to our own.

Future Enhancements

After constructing an action plan and identifying potential exposures, we look to the future and add a third list to the linkage chart that documents additional benefits and opportunities that we might pursue later. This is where we begin to work on building *sustainable* advantage, one experience curve after another. On "the end consumer" chart, we might list completely new products and services that the consumer might want that are complementary to the products and services that we now offer. For example, we might focus on means by which the consumer might use a personal computer or terminal to order products or services from us directly. In this context, it might be important to develop a list of additional products and services that can be acquired using the same personal computer that the consumer uses to order our products or services.

Conducting an Internal Linkage Analysis

After we have completed the external linkage analysis we can then proceed to an internal analysis that focuses on the linkages that exist within the organization itself. In this analysis, we concentrate on:

- Important internal linkages
- Relationships between internal linkages and external linkages

- Economies of scale and experience
- Comparative cost
- Quality
- Effective use of resources
- Changes in organizational structure

In the level 1 internal linkage analysis, we focus on how the objectives of the organization are currently being met. We can trace the flow of products and services through the organization and ask questions about efficiency, effectiveness, quality of products and services, and the locations of bottlenecks. We should focus here on identifying the internal relationships that seem to be causing the most difficulty in meeting the organization's objectives and on ones that provide the best opportunities to meet the internal and external strategic objectives. As in the external linkage analysis, we draw a chart that shows the key internal functions for the organization that are of the most importance. Once the key functions have been identified and agreed upon, we again try to identify the most important function for further analysis with a level 2 linkage analysis. That then leads to a level 3 analysis, and so on until a sufficiently detailed level has been reached. These lower level analyses should focus on new and enhanced applications as well as functions that are critical to providing the base for meeting external and internal strategic objectives. We might conduct them using industry specialists as resources to analyze benefits, prioritize projects, and prepare action plans. These action plans might include identifying projects for performing further cost-benefit analyses, financial analyses, technical assessments, project time estimates, staffing proposals, and risk analyses. But, the analyses that are done at each level should always be guided by the same test:

**Will the function or element being analyzed lead
to substantial and sustainable strategic advantage?**

The factors analyzed in the internal linkage analysis should address such things as efficiency, effectiveness, and quality of service. Because the analysis has an internal focus does not mean that the factors being analyzed are less important. In some cases, they may be critical to achieving the strategic advantages that we have identified in the external linkage analysis.

Summarizing the Results

The output of the 2- or 3-day linkage analysis planning meeting must summarize the results of both the external and the internal analyses that we conducted. It should consist of thorough documentation of the organization's *vision* and a summary of the actual plans the organization will pursue in achieving that vision.

The Vision

As we have stated many times, a key objective of the linkage analysis planning session is to identify and articulate a *strategic business vision* for the organization that can be used to guide managers at all levels in the organization. This vision must be thoroughly documented before the planning session ends. The documentation of the vision should include charts and other documentation that show:

1. The waves of innovation in the industry that clearly positions the organization and the industry as a whole with respect to the waves

2. The experience curves that characterize the industry that shows which of those experience curves the organization must exploit

3. The organization's view of its extended enterprise that shows the organization's role (owner or member) with respect to internal and external elements

The Strategic Action Plan

We must then produce a documented *strategic action plan* that is based on plans for implementing the vision. We must also address and document the way in which business assessments of the strategic action plan will take place, including both technical and financial issues. Documentation of the strategic action plan must include the following items:

1. An overall strategy statement

2. Linkage charts for both the external and internal linkage analyses

3. Summaries of the action plans, potential exposures, and future enhancements listed on the lowest-level linkage charts

4. Documentation of the critical implementation linkages that must be managed to ensure success

5. Assignments of individual managers and/or work groups to each action item in the strategic action plan

The fifth item in the list is of critical importance. After we have formulated the vision and documented the strategic action plan that we must pursue in achieving the vision, the management team must make appropriate work assignments. Individual managers or work groups must be charged with the responsibility for studying and making detailed plans for each of the action items in the strategic action plan. Each manager or work group must be responsible for validating key business, financial, marketing, operational, and technological decisions. Risks and exposures must also be thoroughly analyzed and opportunities assessed. A well-defined strategic action plan is useful only if a specific member of the top management team accepts responsibility for each element of the strategic action plan and is held accountable for its implementation.

Follow-Up Meetings

A senior member of the management team should head each work group and be responsible for scheduling follow-up meetings. Following the initial linkage analysis planning session that all members of the top management team attend, review sessions should be scheduled by individual managers to monitor the progress of the organization toward the implementation of the strategic vision. In this key part of the process, we determine the way in which the study results of the various work groups are to be coordinated and acted upon from a corporate perspective. Management must review, prioritize, and assess the opportunities that the linkage analysis planning session identified based on an understanding of the findings of the various work groups. A business risk analysis must be done for each of these detailed plans using the results of the technical and financial analyses. The results of these detailed analyses can then be used to further enhance the strategic action plan, thus improving the likelihood of its success. The process also promotes buy-in, ownership, and understanding on the part of the entire management team of the vision and the strategic action plan.

Electronic Channel Support Systems

One of the results of a linkage analysis planning session is that we begin to have a clear understanding of what the organization's extended enterprise really looks like and how it is likely to evolve. In summarizing the results of the planning session, it is important that we take a *channel perspective*. We must document the channel flows of the organization, including electronic channel support systems and people channels. A channel perspective allows us to identify potential electronic channel support systems that will be required to achieve strategic advantage. Some of the questions that we might ask in this context are:

- Who is controlling and managing the channels?
- Who is working on the efficiencies of the channels?
- What are the significant characteristics of the channels, including revenue flow, information flow, and negotiation flow (that is, terms and conditions of payment)?
- What are additional channel services that might be important?
- How might the channels change tomorrow?

Electronic channel support systems provide the tools by which we can quickly link organizations using information instead of through significant capital investments. The overall competitiveness of the organization is a result of the efficiency and effectiveness of all the flows within the channels. These are governed to a large extent by the size of the envelope we are able to offer to our customers. The summary must include information about how channel flows can be modified to improve our products and services. Potential electronic channel support systems should also be identified. We must evaluate what parts of the channel flows are currently part of the envelope today and how we might in the future improve these channels. We must attempt to identify the constriction points in the flows where significant bottlenecks currently occur. Identifying these constrictions will often help us to identify new opportunities for achieving strategic advantage.

Benefits of Linkage Analysis Planning

An important advantage of the linkage analysis planning process is that it is highly visual, it is highly conceptual, and it can be done quickly. With a typical strategic planning session, the end result is a wall full of action items that no one can visualize or conceptualize. The key of the session is that it forces all the participants to focus on what will have a real strategic impact on the organization and on the industry as a whole instead of walls full of action items or questions to answer. Often only a few charts are needed to outline the vision or future direction of the organization.

> **The focus of linkage analysis planning is on
> issues that will help the organization achieve
> substantial and sustainable competitive advantage.**

The acid test of linkage analysis planning results is to ask the question: "Can we effectively articulate how our strategic plan will result in substantial and sustainable competitive advantage?" Forcing the management team to apply their decision-making powers to identifying the truly strategic issues is key to achieving a shared vision and generating a sense of urgency. At any point, we can decide to back up and analyze some other function in a higher level chart and perform another detailed analysis on it. The breadth of coverage can be determined by the available time, management's ability to handle multiple projects, and the available funding.

It is important to note that in order to be most effective, the linkage analysis planning process must be ongoing. Linkage analysis planning should not be viewed as a one-time event. The linkage analysis planning process should be directed at all levels of the organization, and all members of the management team should be taught to use the process. The goal should be to empower individuals at all levels in the organization with these new planning skills. This will help to create a new spirit and feeling for challenge, enthusiasm, and success. The goal must be to revitalize the spirits and energies of the entire organization. This recommitment is vital to forming the *new organization*.

Leadership Exercise

Figure 10-10 shows a linkage chart that lists many of the requirements for becoming a leader. A primary challenge for a leader is to successfully achieve results in the most efficient and effective manner. Providing a framework and a strategy for doing this is one of the objectives of linkage analysis planning.

The highlighted box at the top of Figure 10-10 summarizes the *beginning* of the linkage analysis planning process:

> **Visualize the interrelationships among the
> strategic forces that affect the organization.**

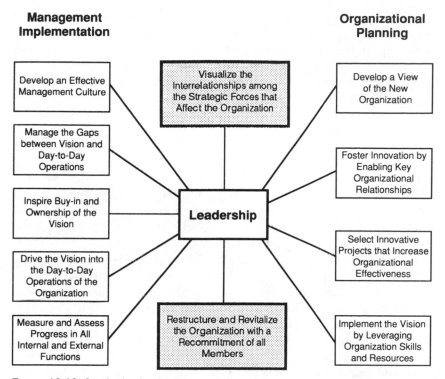

Figure 10-10. Leadership level 1 linkage analysis chart.

The boxes to the left and right in the chart are the steps that are involved in implementing the vision. The boxes on the left are related to management implementation of the vision, and the boxes on the right are related to choosing appropriate organizational structures for the 1990s.

The highlighted box at the bottom summarizes the *end result* of the linkage analysis planning process:

> **Restructure and revitalize the organization**
> **with a recommitment of all members.**

You can use the leadership chart in a personal linkage analysis planning exercise to clarify your own role as a leader. The chart shows the interrelationships between the key issues and requirements for leadership. It provides a top-down, global view of the characteristics of leadership. Any of the functions on the chart can be analyzed in more detail using the techniques of linkage analysis planning. Conducting this exercise helps to review the importance, tradeoffs, interdependencies, and relationships among the factors on the chart. In looking at a level 1 linkage chart, we sometimes find that everything initially looks important; but, as we have stated earlier, the finite amount of resources of time, people, and money that are available does not allow us to focus on all the factors. We must be able to implement a plan that addresses the critical items first, and then follow that with additional enhancements. Identifying the few critical elements is not easy, but it must be done. In analyzing the level 1 linkage chart for leadership, try to identify what are the one or two major boxes that represent the steps that you will analyze in detail. By working through this process, you will get a better understanding of the issues that are associated with choosing the most important factor on a linkage chart.

In performing a level 2 analysis for one of the factors on the level 1 chart, you will probably end up with a chart having a great many boxes. You should then attempt to determine which of *those* factors are most important to your becoming and remaining a successful leader. This then identifies the critical factors for a level 3 analysis.

At this level of detail, you will probably find that you are now in a position to identify specific tasks and develop action plans. This is where you begin to conceptualize your vision of leadership. After you have completed this step, you will be able to document your own personal vision and strategic action plan.

Conclusion

This short, simple exercise can be extremely valuable in assessing your own goals, abilities, and plans for management. It will also go a long way toward acquainting you with the power and flexibility of linkage analysis planning. Working through this exercise will help to prepare you for the next two chapters. The leadership linkage chart in Figure 10-10 is used as a tool to structure the material in Chapters 11 and 12. Chapter 11 on *actualizing the vision* concerns the management implementation steps listed in the boxes along the left side. Chapter 12 on *building the new organization* addresses the organizational planning issues on the right.

Reference

1. George Steiner. *Strategic Planning: What Every Manager Must Know.* New York: Free Press, 1979.

11

Actualizing the Vision

Introduction

The previous chapters were directed toward enabling the management team to form a strategic vision by attaining a new mindset for the future; analyzing the waves of innovation, experience curves, and industry power relationships; and creating a new view of the organization—all in the context of linkage analysis planning. In this chapter, we discuss techniques that are useful for *actualizing the vision*. As we pointed out in the introduction to Part 3, substantial and sustainable strategic advantage can be actually achieved only at the bottom of the innovation arrow, where the vision is placed into day-to-day operation and when operating results occur. Visions, strategies, and tactical plans are of little value if no results materialize. The main message of this chapter is that once you determine what it is you want to do, you must find ways of *actually doing it*.

Restructure and Revitalize the Organization with a Recommitment of All Members

The main thrust of this chapter is summarized by the box at the bottom of the leadership chart in Chapter 10 that emphasizes the end result of the linkage analysis planning process. (See Figure 10-10.) The steps in the process of achieving strategic advantage are summarized by the boxes on the lefthand side of the leadership chart in Figure 10-10.

177

Here, we look at the organization and determine the steps that are needed to build the management process for implementing the vision:

- **Develop an effective management culture.**
- **Manage the gaps between vision and day-to-day operations.**
- **Inspire buy-in and ownership of the vision.**
- **Drive the vision into the day-to-day operations of the organization.**
- **Measure and assess progress in all internal and external functions.**

Making the Vision Happen

This chapter focuses on taking the necessary steps to ensure that the vision top management has formulated makes its way all the way down the innovation arrow into the day-to-day operations of the organization. Top management can use the techniques of linkage analysis planning, described in the first 10 chapters of this book, to formulate a vision and to develop the strategies that will be required to achieve that vision. But we must then be able to communicate and share this vision throughout the organization. And, what is even more important, middle management must be empowered with the requisite skills for performing the tactical planning that is required to accomplish the implementation tasks. We must then provide operational management with the necessary skills to put into place and sustain the required changes on a day-to-day basis. Substantial and sustainable advantage can be achieved only through effective execution of *all* the steps in the innovation arrow.

Two examples will help to illustrate the difficulties that are associated with crossing over from the vision and strategy phases of the innovation arrow to the implementation and operations steps.

Large Wholesale Company

In discussing strategic planning with the president of a large wholesale company, it became clear that he knew that he had to structurally change the company to move it from a vision that was appropriate for the 1960s and 1970s to one that would be effective in the 1990s. He was going to have to make some fundamental decisions about what the company was going to be in the 1990s. Questions arose, such as: "Are we a wholesaler?" "Or are we a retailer?" His company had been primarily a wholesaler in the past, but because of the changing environment, he had recently determined that success in the future would require that it become a consumer-sensitive retailer. This meant that the organization would have to begin establishing links out to the individual stores, and to the customers of those stores, in order to understand their needs. This is not a function that is traditionally associated with a wholesaler. Major concerns for the company had always been inventory turnover, on-time delivery, lowest price, and rate of customer order fulfillment— all traditional wholesaler concerns with the retail store as the customer. To survive in the 1990s, the president realized that there would now be a critical need for a *consumer* focus directed at understanding the retail store operations and determining what services and products the *end consumer* demanded. The rules had changed, and he and his managers were having difficulty in discovering what the new rules were. The success of his operation in the future would now be tied directly to the success of his customers—the retail stores. But, his management team knew little about what would make the retail stores successful or even what products and services consumers might want in the 1990s. The president's vision had changed from that of success as a *wholesaler* to success as a *retailer*.

The president realized that he needed to communicate and share this new vision with the organization. He realized that he needed to achieve buy-in from the organization and enable them to visualize the new challenges. In the final analysis, the president realized that a complete culture change was required in order to begin doing business in a new way. The first issue that arose was how top management could communicate this new vision to people in the organization who had been thinking "wholesale" for 30 or 40 years. These people were simply not concerned with what happened *after* the product went out to the retail store.

Travel Company

The president of a large travel company had developed a vision for the use of technology within his organization. However, he was left searching for a vehicle to communicate and share this new vision and was struggling with the challenge of gaining organization buy-in and commitment. He could point out to his management team what others were doing with technology, such as American Airlines, but he was not satisfied with the responses that he was receiving to his questions regarding technology. This company president was not able to crystallize his vision and had no process for developing an effective strategic plan. He was left with the frustrating task of trying to empower his organization, but without an effective vehicle for doing so.

Conclusions

In both of these examples, there was a significant requirement for change, and the top decision maker clearly perceived a need for change. Long-term survival in both cases depended on the ability of the organizations to restructure and revitalize their operations. In each case, the president had a vision of change, but it had not been conceptualized or developed into an explicit strategy. Therefore, they were not able to explain the vision to the next layer of management, who would have to devise the required strategies for implementing the vision. The presidents of these two companies each had an intuitive feeling that they had to do something, but they were not able to determine the steps that were required to actualize their visions. They lacked a vehicle for describing their visions of the organization, other than from the traditional viewpoint of the enterprise. They were searching for a way of conceptualizing the extended enterprise in order to determine what role they were going to play. The authors have worked with many executives in business, education, and government who have felt these frustrations and have found it difficult to move their organizations toward actualizing a new vision.

In the case of the wholesaler, the president was able to address this problem by working with the top management team to form a new vision of the organization's extended enterprise—one that was predicated on consumer-sensitive marketing and win-win relationships among all members of the extended enterprise. This new vision of the organization coincided with a need to move decision making down to lower levels within the organization, thereby enabling the organization to be more flexible and responsive. The president was able to use many of the concepts discussed in this book by having his managers conduct their own linkage analysis planning sessions focused on implementing their part of the organization's new extended enterprise *retailer* vision. This enabled his managers at all levels in the organization to see the need for change as well as to assess the required tradeoffs. Bold steps were needed. And in this case, bold steps were taken. This organization is well on its way to becoming a formidable competitor in the 1990s. In the case of the travel company, its top management, at the time of writing, is still struggling with these problems and has changed management in many key areas in trying to clearly identify the changes that will be required to effectively compete in the coming leisure industry of the 1990s.

In both of the preceding examples, the top decision makers recognized that something had to be done. But how many companies and how many executives do not even perceive a need for change? In many organizations, executives are so busy constantly reacting that they haven't the time to think about anything long term. Too many organizations can only imitate or emulate their rivals. They make constant incremental adjustments but do not create real strategic advantage. The most successful organizations are those that cause meaningful change by pushing the nature of competition in the right direction—their direction.

The remainder of this chapter focuses on actualizing the vision for change that the techniques of linkage analysis planning can help you to identify. We will discuss in turn each of the steps described in the boxes on the lefthand side of the leadership chart in Figure 10-10.

Step 1: Develop an Effective Management Culture

The first step in actualizing the vision is to ensure that the organization has an effective management culture that is compatible with the innovation and change that will be required in the 1990s. Rosabeth Moss Kanter has made the following observations about change and innovation in the United States:

> It is one of the more anomalous features of American corporate life that even when a few hardy internal entrepreneurs succeed in producing innovation, officials in the company may not know what to do with it, or even know about it. Companies that are set in their ways often ignore small advances that can mushroom into larger ones.[1]

Examples of this in American business are not hard to find, nor are detailed analyses and in-depth studies of the results of it. Everyone talks about why things are not changing, but no one provides insight into how to make things move in the right direction. Explanations for this lack of corporate innovative spirit runs the gamut from short-term financial constraints to the lack of a national policy for the U.S. education system. A great many factors play a role in inhibiting change and innovation. The challenges are becoming too complex and diverse for personal leadership alone to overcome. We need to drive the spirit and feeling for innovation down to the very core of the organization. This requires a management culture that complements vision and leadership. The mere fact that the top management of an organization *desires* change is not enough. As noted in the two scenarios that began this chapter, even executive awareness and commitment to change will not alone cause it to happen. Kanter describes some reasons for this and highlights the frustration and confusion that managers at all levels feel:

The mad rush to improve performance and to pursue excellence has multiplied the number of demands on executives and managers. These demands come from every part of business and personal life, and they increasingly seem incompatible and impossible:

- Think strategically and invest in the future—but keep the numbers up today.
- Be entrepreneurial and take risks—but do not cost the business anything by failing.
- Continue to do everything you are currently doing even better—and spend more time communicating with employees, serving on teams and launching new projects.
- Know every detail of your business—but delegate more responsibility to others.
- Become passionately dedicated to "visions" and fanatically committed to carrying them out—but be flexible, responsive, and able to change direction quickly.
- Speak up, be a leader, set the direction—but be participative, listen well, cooperate.
- Throw yourself wholeheartedly into the entrepreneurial game and the long hours it takes—and stay fit.
- Succeed, succeed, succeed—and raise terrific children.

Corporations, too, face escalating and seemingly incompatible demands:

- Get "lean and mean" through restructuring—while being a great company to work for and offering employee-centered policies, such as job security.
- Encourage creativity and innovation to take you in new directions—and "stick to your knitting."
- Communicate a sense of urgency and push for faster execution, faster results—but take more time to deliberately plan for the future.
- Decentralize to delegate profit and planning responsibilities to small, autonomous business units. But centralize to capture efficiencies and combine resources in innovative ways.

By now, most major companies have launched some sort of self-improvement program—their excellence program or their quality program or their entrepreneurship and innovation program. Now they are beyond the exciting (and easy) inspirational, rhetorical, philosophical stage. They are facing tough questions such as: Who has the power to start or block innovations? Who gets the financial returns? Some companies are stumbling over the roadblocks to perfection, the backlash, the resistance, the cynicism, and the sheer fatigue of taking on so much change.[2]

Business, government, and education have too long focused on the end result of providing today's products and services instead of on the *environment* in which we create them. Drastic changes are occurring in the products and services that will be required in the future, and drastic changes will be required in the organizations that create them. Lessons can be learned from the joint American-Japanese manufacturing partnerships in American automotive manufacturing and the spirit of new young industry challengers like Walmart. The leaders of the 1990s will have to go beyond the management practices of the 1970s and 1980s. What is required to incorporate change into the fabric of business will be a rebirth in the culture of the organization—a rebirth in the definition, meaning, and enabling of the organization's culture.

Components of a Culture

What do we mean by the culture of an organization? We feel that an organization's culture has two important components; both are required:

- *Spirit and feeling.* The first component of an organization's culture is the spirit or feeling of the organization and its people. An organization that has a high level of spirit and feeling often also has a high degree of teamwork and innovative enthusiasm. In such an organization, it is relatively easy to establish buy-in and ownership of the vision and to foster a sense of commitment and urgency once an appropriate vision has been identified and articulated.

- *Structure and framework.* The second component of culture focuses on the structure and framework of the organization, helps to organize the important issues, and ensures that we focus on the relevant variables. An effective structure and framework will not, however, provide the necessary answers. The answers we are looking for result from a creative process or act. But an appropriate framework and structure can ensure that everyone has the same vision and understands their role in materializing the vision. Without such a framework, even good people will become ineffective; the dynamics of change and technology will be too great for them to overcome.

We must concentrate on both components of culture if we are to be successful in developing a work climate that fosters innovation and change. Too many organizations are focusing only on spirit and feeling and are looking only at human resource issues and promoting employee moral. Attempts to enhance spirit and feeling will not pro-

duce desired results without putting an appropriate structure and
framework into place.

Tools for Developing an Effective Culture

In order to think and act strategically, leaders need to share the process
described in this book across *all* the elements in the extended enterprise, both internal and external. Top management can use the lenses
and mindset images presented in Parts 1 and 2 to help in establishing
the culture that is required to manage the gap between vision and implementation. We might begin by reviewing with the top management
team the key messages contained in the waves of innovation. The waves
of innovation help us to examine how the technology and the environment are changing and what these changes mean in our environment.
This helps us to see how these changes affect the current and future
direction of the organization and its role in the industry. When we understand the waves of innovation, we can begin looking at how we can
exploit new experience curves.

As we have already pointed out, organizations in the 1990s will have
to cope with rapid and continual change and will need leaders who are
capable of forming visions that look 5 or more years into the future.
Figure 11-1 shows a series of rapidly evolving experience curves. We
can often best achieve strategic advantage by introducing a series of experience curves, each one building on the previous ones. In other

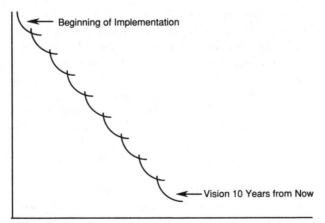

Figure 11-1. Achieving a vision requires implementing a set of
rapidly evolving experience curves with each new one building on
the others.

words, our vision should be that of a journey and not a one-time event. The vision and the strategic action plan need to be attuned to both the long-term and short-term introduction of new experience curves. The challenge becomes very complex for an organization on the receiving end of a set of rapidly succeeding experience curves. An organization on the receiving end does not perceive the total vision and can only respond to each new change and each new threat one at a time with little lead time.

The challenge for the management team in this environment of constant change and innovation is to provide everyone in the organization with the tools that are needed to implement the new experience curves that will be required. In the past, recommitment of the team to a radical change often took place only once every 5 to 10 years, or even longer. In today's world, continual change driven by innovation will be a way of life. This new world will prove frustrating unless we can prepare and enable the management team to deal with this new environment. Coping with an environment characterized by change and innovation necessitates that we empower individuals at all levels to formulate visions, predict changes, and formulate action plans for implementation. We must also give them the tools they need for mastering change rather than being driven by it.

Once we have looked at the experience curves for an industry and examined the use of technology, we can begin to understand how we can exploit it. We can then begin to examine our role in the industry and identify the changes that are occurring in industry power relationships. We must ask where are we going and what is going to happen. Such an analysis can be used to validate the experience curves we have identified. This will help us to begin building a new view of our extended enterprise. When we understand our extended enterprise and determine what role we are going to play—owner or member—then we can begin to start visualizing the electronic channels that will be required to operate effectively in the extended enterprise environment.

Once the top management team has used the tools we have been discussing to formulate a vision, they must then communicate the vision down to the next level of management. The mindsets discussed in Part 2, and especially in Chapter 8, are useful in communicating the vision. These new mindsets are what the individual managers should work with. Lower-level managers should not be concentrating on the high-level tasks of constructing the extended enterprise or on defining the role of the organization in the industry. Individual managers should focus on the key messages of the new mindsets: looking for new envelopes, expanding the size of the pie, analyzing the information component, and restructuring the channels. An effective organizational culture is indispensable in communicating the vision and the strategic action downward. A high degree of spirit and feeling helps to establish a sense of urgency and promotes buy-in and ownership of the plan. And top management must surround these mindset messages with an appropriate structure and framework so that everyone interprets the vision and the strategic action plan in an appropriate manner. Top management also gives direction with respect to setting priorities and allocating resources of money, people, and management time.

Step 2: Manage the Gaps between Vision and Day-to-Day Operations

As we saw in Chapter 1, formulating a vision and developing an effective strategic action plan often requires highly intuitive thought processes that cannot be subjected to formal analysis and proof. At some point in the planning process, we must cross over from these highly intuitive thought processes to thought processes that must be very logical, left-brain, detail oriented to ensure implementation. The gap between the vision and strategy phases of the innovation arrow and the implementation and operations phases that we introduced in Chapter 1 is again illustrated in Figure 11-2.

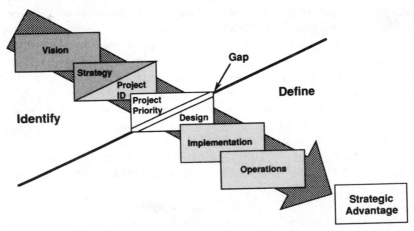

Figure 11-2. There is a gap between the vision/strategy phases and the implementation/operations phases of the innovation arrow.

As we discussed in step 1, it is an important goal to create a culture in the organization that will ensure that the unstructured, executive decision-making processes that look 5 to 7 years out are converted into more structured forms of decision making as we move down the innovation arrow. This makes it possible for middle and operational management to be able to deal with the parts of the vision that concern their own individual spheres of influence. For each individual part of the strategy, someone must now analyze it, determine the systems and procedures that are needed to implement it, determine costs, analyze benefits, conduct market analyses, and perform other essential functions that are required for implementation and for day-to-day operations.

Figure 11-3 illustrates how the tactics function in the innovation arrow is the key in bridging the gap between the vision and strategy team and the implementation and operations team. There is a similar gap between any pair of phases in the innovation arrow. Although we have been using the term *bridging the gap* to illustrate the process of moving down the innovation arrow toward implementation and day-to-day operations, the real goal should be toward *managing the gaps* and not simply jumping over them. With the decoupling, downsizing, and restructuring that is occurring in the business environment, managing the gaps will become increasingly challenging. Management must now continually focus on ensuring that the gaps between each phase are of the appropriate width. If the gaps become too wide, the various levels of management and the key functions in the organization will not work together effectively to reach a common goal. If the gaps become too small, there will be little or no distinction between the functions and responsibilities of the various levels of management. The challenge will be to manage to the appropriate width of the gaps. The gaps cannot be eliminated. They will always be there because individuals at different

Figure 11-3. Tactics bridges the gap between the vision/strategy team and the implementation/operations teams.

levels of management have different functions, time frames, personal ambitions, levels of dedication to the organization, and levels of people skills and other capabilities.

Step 3: Inspire Buy-In and Ownership of the Vision

The next step is to effectively communicate the vision to all levels of the organization and to empower individuals at all levels in the organization with the skills they need to think and act strategically. By doing this, we promote a sense of buy-in and ownership of the vision. If individual managers do not buy-in to the vision and feel that they have a real stake in making the strategic action plan happen, the organization cannot achieve its goals and objectives. Many organizations are making significant structural changes by downsizing and streamlining their organizations. Many are also pushing the decision-making process down to the tactics and implementation levels. In many cases, this is useful and necessary. However these same organizations often do not focus on training and enabling the management teams at those levels to be able to perform the required tasks and to think and act strategically. This training may be even more important than formulating the vision itself. In some organizations, very little is being done to ensure that an adequate level of focus is being applied to preparing the future leaders of the organization. Many organizations are eliminating positions that were previously used for developing future leaders, thus reducing the number of candidates for future leadership positions. Peter Drucker points out that lessons can be learned from the German *gruppe*, in which decentralized units are set up as separate companies, each having its own top management team. These subsidiaries are somewhat like the farm teams of a major-league baseball team. Within these decentralized units, the future leaders of the company get the experience they need to later assume top management positions in the main company. As many of America's organizations downsize and create smaller autonomous units, how are we going to provide new captains with the skills they need to run their ships? Each ship turns at a different speed, but we must be able to turn the fleet without creating chaos. We need a common vision. Within large organizations, the synergistic effect of all the individual functions is key to the performance of the organization as a whole. The individual captains need to have a feeling for the vision as a whole and must also have a clear understanding of their roles with respect to making the vision happen. We must then provide them with the skills they need to think and act strategically.

To do this, we must carry the linkage analysis planning process down to each level of management in the organization. Individuals at all levels can use these techniques to analyze and structure their own pieces of the organization. As managers at various levels in the organization begin to analyze the linkages that exist in their own operations, external as well as internal, they will be better able to execute their own roles in helping the organization achieve the vision. If the top management team does not provide lower level management with appropriate responsibilities and the required tools and skills, they will perceive the statement of vision and the strategic action plan only as a set of marching orders. *When the strategic action plan is perceived as a set of orders, managers will not do the necessary strategic thinking and make the required in-flight changes that are required for the organization to achieve its stated goals and objectives.*

Traditional planning techniques call for the leader to define the target and give guidelines for reaching it—go from point *A* to point *B* and avoid the land mines. But the target is often not static; it moves and changes its shape, color, and size. How can the implementation team make the necessary in-flight adjustments if they do not fully understand the vision behind the requirement for traveling to point *B* and the assumptions and tradeoffs that had to be made? If individual managers do not personally take ownership of the vision, then what is the likelihood of them having the political courage to put their hand up and tell top management that the target is moving? The organization often ends up missing the market a day late and a dollar short.

Step 4: Drive the Vision into the Day-to-Day Operations of the Organization

As we have seen, top management must have a detailed strategic action plan that lists all the steps that will be required in implementing the vision and placing it into day-to-day operation. But a top management team cannot create this detailed plan alone. Top management must formulate the vision and must establish an environment in which lower-level management develops the *detailed* strategic plans. The detailed plans must show how the organization will make the transition from people that are focusing on vision and long-range strategic plans to people whose focus is day-to-day. As we have discussed, there are fundamental differences between the thought processes that are involved at the top of the innovation arrow, where people must be creative, right-brain-oriented visionaries, and those that are involved at the bottom, where the thinking must be more

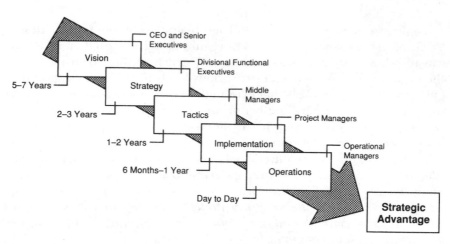

Figure 11-4. Each phase of the innovation arrow is associated with a different level of management and has a different time-frame focus.

logical, left-brain-oriented, and focused on innovative implementation. The implementors must be able to appropriately interpret the strategic plans that top management creates. The focus must be on taking plans that might appear to the implementors as "blue sky" and converting these plans into strategic action.

Figure 11-4 shows that each part of the innovation arrow is associated with a different group of individuals. Each person in the organization—top executive, divisional manager, middle manager, or operational manager—is responsible for different elements in the innovation arrow. Each function also has a different time frame associated with it and a different management orientation. The further up we go on the arrow, the further out these individuals must look, and the more important it is that the gaps that exist between the different elements of the innovation arrow be continually managed.

Vision

The formulation of the executive vision is the responsibility of the CEO and those few senior executives and functional managers who are responsible for setting policy for the organization as a whole. These executives are responsible for looking at least 5 to 7 years out to formulate the executive vision. The bottom line for the top management of the organization is to formulate a vision that will enable the organization's extended enterprise to gain substantial and sustainable strategic advantage in the marketplace. Functions that top management performs in formulating this vision include:

- Analyzing economic issues
- Identifying key market forces
- Setting a global marketing direction
- Establishing an effective corporate culture
- Designing an appropriate corporate infrastructure
- Continually positioning the organization for increased effectiveness and growth

Strategy

The strategy function in the innovation arrow is the primary responsibility of divisional and functional executives and the key staff members who are responsible for major parts of the organization. These individuals are responsible for looking 2 to 5 years into the future to develop the strategic plans that will be necessary to achieve the vision that was formulated at the top. The functions these executives perform in developing effective strategies include:

- Identifying new markets
- Creating new envelopes of products and services
- Designing new organizational structures
- Identifying and developing new technologies or new uses of technology
- Guiding research and development

Tactics

The tactics function of the innovation arrow is the responsibility of the middle management of the organization. These managers typically have a 1- to 2-year planning horizon and are responsible for developing detailed tactics that will be necessary to implement the strategic plans. The functions that middle managers typically perform in developing tactical plans include:

- Developing individual tactical plans
- Designing detailed marketing strategies
- Developing new products and services

- Managing financial resources
- Planning for efficient resource utilization

Implementation

The implementation function of the innovation arrow is the responsibility of project managers and key staff members who work for the successful completion of individual pieces of the strategic plan. These individuals may work under the supervision of top management sponsors who are interested in various functions. The implementors typically work on *individual projects* that last from six months to a year or more. The functions that are associated with the implementation of tactical plans include:

- Developing individual, detailed implementation plans
- Establishing marketing objectives
- Identifying customer requirements
- Measuring progress according to plans
- Setting professional development objectives
- Successfully completing projects

Operations

The operations function of the innovation arrow is the primary responsibility of operational managers who are involved in the day-to-day running of the organization. Operational managers normally have a day-to-day planning horizon and are responsible for handling the operating functions of the organization. These might include:

- Sales
- Advertising
- Manufacturing
- Distribution
- Administration
- Research and development

It is a primary responsibility of the top management team to ensure that assignments are made so that each level of management is focused on tasks appropriate to that level and is operating using an appropriate time frame.

Step 5: Measure and Assess Progress in All Internal and External Functions

After developing detailed plans, the organization must realize that a key responsibility of the management team is to effectively measure the progress that the organization is making in achieving the vision. If we cannot identify who is responsible for achieving a given goal or accomplishing a given task, then no one can be held accountable, and it will be impossible for the organization to assess whether it is going forward. Without adequate measurement, it is unlikely that a given goal will ever be accomplished. The day-to-day responsibility for running the organization rests with middle and operational management. We must first ensure that they understand their responsibilities and that their understanding is consistent with the vision of top management. But we must also be able to measure progress at all levels of management to see if progress is being made and that the progress is consistent with the vision. A key part of this measurement is "testing for echos." Do the efforts of middle and lower management reflect the vision that has been formulated at the top? Or are the results that are actually being achieved inconsistent with that vision?

We must also develop for each phase of the innovation arrow a *measurement system* that we can use to review the progress that each individual is making toward achieving the vision. Management at all levels must be evaluated on their ability to define, develop, and execute the activities that are defined in the strategic plans that the organization has jointly developed. Figure 11-5 shows how the bottom phases of the innovation are oriented toward the *current view* of the organization and the top phases representing *future requirements*. We must measure and assess progress toward achieving the vision differently with respect to these two viewpoints.

Current Requirements

When looking at the current organization at the lower levels of the innovation arrow, measurement systems can take a traditional focus. Key questions that we might ask of middle and lower management with respect to the current view are:

- Are the current divisions and departments executing efficiently and effectively?
- Are we maintaining market share?
- Are we providing quality products and services?

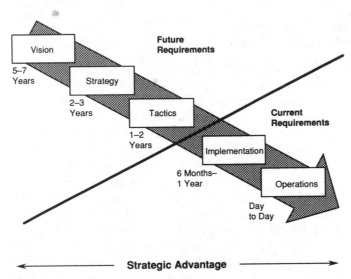

Figure 11-5. The phases of the innovation arrow can be divided between phases that focus on current requirements and phases that focus on future requirements.

- Are we meeting performance requirements?
- Are budgets and forecasts accurate?

This part of the management review process is similar to what happens today in most organizations. The nature of the questions that we ask here and the replies that can be expected will be different depending on the level of management and the importance of the operation or function to the business. The measurement systems at these levels most often take the form of numbers analyses that are objective and easy to measure.

Future Requirements

The measurement systems that are necessary in the top phases of the innovation arrow are much more difficult to define. They must be oriented to measuring the progress of reaching objectives that are 3 to 5 years and 5 to 7 years in the future. Some questions that might be appropriate at this level are:

- What are the requirements in the market over these time frames?
- What are the requirements in the organization to meet these future market changes?

- Is the management team in place or will future changes be required?
- Does the management team focus have to change?
- Do some of the capital investments for the organization change?

At the top levels of the organization, each member of the management team must be evaluated on his or her ability to articulate future requirements and to develop and execute the plans that are required for success. We must develop measurement tools that enable top management to pinpoint responsibilities and assess the actions of the management team. A key to the process is that each member of the management team must be able to explain his or her views to top management concerning product and service requirements, revenue and business performance, and education and training requirements. They must then be measured on their ability to define the present and future environment and on their understanding of what changes are necessary in order to get there. The measurement systems that are needed at the top of the innovation arrow are much more subjective than those that work in the lower-level phases.

Rather than just looking at quality, pricing, and service, the management team must be evaluated on its ability to look at the future as a place to do business, to understand the vision that top management has formulated, and to make necessary in-flight changes that are required as technology or market forces change. This way of looking at the organization is going to be a requirement for the 1990s. Most companies concentrate only in the bottom phases of the innovation chart and are looking only at current year numbers and finances rather than trying to understand future requirements.

Top management must also begin to look differently at the bottom phases in the innovation arrow because of the new capabilities of information/knowledge systems. As Peter Drucker has pointed out:

> So far most computer users still use the new technology only to do faster what they have always done before, crunch conventional numbers. But as soon as a company takes the first tentative steps from data to information, its decision processes, management structure, and even the way its work gets done begin to be transformed.[3]

Conclusion

Once we have followed the five steps described in this chapter, top management of the organization can begin to modify the structure of the organization, institute far-reaching policy changes, and begin to achieve greater degrees of teamwork. But these types of changes are not easy to achieve. As Kanter stated: "Now they are beyond the exciting (and easy) inspirational/rhetorical/philosophical stage…"[4]

Today's traditional solutions of downsizing, decentralizing, and restructuring the organization are temporary financial actions with no long-term effect. If the transformation of the organization takes place and the transformation of the management team does not, then the following paraphrase of Parkinson's law and its two corollaries will continue to have devastating effects on the organization:

> Work expands so as to fill the time available for its completion.
> - An official wants to multiply subordinates, not rivals.
> - Officials make work for each other.[5]

The important questions that top management must ask are:

- Does the management team have the ability to execute in the upper part of the innovation arrow as well as the lower section?
- Are the messages and actions consistent on both levels?
- Does everyone on the organization understand the vision?
- Have we empowered the entire management team to execute the strategic action plan?

This chapter on actualizing the vision has dealt with the complex issues of converting a vision into a strategy, a strategy into a plan, and then implementing the various steps of the plan and moving them into the day-to-day operations of the organization. We identified the different roles of various levels of management in actualizing the vision. We also discussed the need for changing the corporate culture to enable the organization to no longer simply *bridge* the gaps between the various levels of management but instead to actively *manage* the gaps. We then saw that the vision of top management will be actualized only if we develop a measurement system that can monitor progress of all members of the management team.

Our intent in this chapter was to highlight what is required for actualizing the vision. In actual practice, in-depth study, analysis, and discussion of the important topics introduced in this chapter are required for an organization to succeed in the 1990s. Creating the right culture for the organization is difficult. It will not be easy to create and maintain an appropriate "spirit and feeling" in the organization and to continually reassess and modify the "structure and framework" in order to make the vision happen.

References

1. Rosabeth Moss Kanter. *The Change Masters*. New York: Simon and Schuster, 1983.

2. Rosabeth Moss Kanter. *When Giants Learn to Dance*. New York: Simon and Schuster, 1989.

3. Peter Drucker. "The Coming of the New Organization." *Harvard Business Review*, January–February, 1988.

4. Roseabeth Moss Kanter. *When Giants Learn to Dance*. New York: Simon and Schuster, 1989.

5. C. Northcote Parkinson. *Parkinson: The Law, Complete*. New York: Ballantine, 1983.

12
Building the New Organization

Introduction

In Chapter 12 we summarize and tie together the major points covered in each of the preceding chapters. This chapter also looks at building the new organization. How must we restructure organizational relationships? What technology and what electronic channels must we use? What will the new organization look like? How can we visualize the extended enterprise and then start to construct it? What partnerships and alliances must we form? What about global competitors, niche markets, and changing power relationships? How do we expand our view beyond the extended enterprise structures of today?

The key to success in the 1990s is perceiving what is important, focusing the organization's knowledge and other resources, and energizing the organization to achieve results. To guarantee success, leaders must *live* the vision and be a part of making it happen. In the title to this book we suggested that the management team has three choices: *supremacy, survival,* or *sayonara.* Its there really any choice but the first?

In this chapter, we revisit again the leadership chart from Chapter 10. (See Figure 10-10.)

Visualizing Interrelationships Among the Strategic Forces That Affect the Organization

The box at the top of the chart, which represents the beginning of the linkage analysis planning process, summarizes the thrust of this final chapter. The functions in the boxes on the right-hand side of the leadership linkage chart are the functions associated with innovation and organizational planning:

- **Develop a view of the new organization.**
- **Foster innovation by enabling key organizational relationships.**
- **Select innovative projects that increase organizational effectiveness.**
- **Implement the vision by leveraging organizational skills and resources.**

Before we begin looking at the four steps listed above, we first discuss the nature of innovation to see why it is often so difficult to achieve.

Paradigm for Innovation—An Oxymoron

The term *paradigm* is now often seen in management literature, with the point typically being that we must search for "new management paradigms" that foster innovation and change. Why do we consider "paradigm for innovation" an oxymoron? Let us turn to Webster:

- *Paradigm.*   A pattern, example, or model.
- *Innovation.*   The act or process of innovating, something newly introduced; new method, custom.
- *Oxymoron.*   A figure of speech in which contradictory ideas or terms are combined.

To us, staying within an existing paradigm implies *evolution* and *incremental* change; true *innovation* implies *revolution* and *fundamental* change. We must step completely out of any existing paradigms. This requires a clean sheet of paper on which to begin visualizing the important linkages. Organizations that search for existing paradigms for understanding the changes that are occurring in the global marketplace may completely miss radical shifts in the environment. There are no road maps, and no existing paradigms, for achieving true innovation. Erich Seppel makes these points about the nature of change:

> Central to Kuhn's argument [Thomas S. Kuhn, The Structure of Scientific Revolutions, Chicago, IL: University of Chicago, 1962] is a

distinction between two different kinds of change: change that occurs as part of the process of "normal science" and that which occurs in periods of scientific revolution. According to Kuhn, scientific progress does not occur incrementally, one discovery building on another like so many bricks in a wall. Instead, scientists construct what Kuhn calls "paradigms," which integrate the known data and allow scientists to make predictions about the future. In other words, paradigms integrate experience and tell scientists how to approach questions and problems. Indeed, the paradigm controls what questions can be asked and what answers are legitimate....

However, there are always a certain number of anomalies that stubbornly resist being reconciled to the paradigms. These accrete and become increasingly troublesome, until the authority of the paradigm itself comes into question. Eventually, a new paradigm is promulgated which relates these anomalies to all other known observations in a new paradigm. This ensures a period of great controversy and unrest and upset; but eventually, the new paradigm is accepted and the process repeats itself.

This replacement of one paradigm by another is a scientific revolution. In such a period, the change that occurs is of the intellectual and practical structure itself—not within the framework. Hence it is a fundamentally different kind of change than occurs in normal science.[1]

Seppel goes on to apply Kuhn's concepts to what is happening today in the finance industry. He states that the various sectors of the finance industry have been built on a paradigm that includes nine elements:

- The economics of business
- The technology the industry uses
- The institutional arrangements that characterize the industry (what types of institutions meet customer needs)
- The products the industry sells
- The distribution system the industry uses
- The beliefs held by industry practitioners about how the industry operates and what works
- Regulation of the industry
- The organizational designs that typically are found throughout the industry
- The culture that typifies firms in the industry

Seppel then notes that when these elements were congruent and mutually reinforcing, the paradigm was stable and change would occur, analogously to normal science, within the structure of the paradigm. He points out that stability existed in the finance community from the 1930s until the 1970s:

> Today, however, as the discussion of change argued, there are three major anomalies which cannot be accommodated by the traditional paradigm:
>
> - technology and changes in lifestyle which have brought about
> - substitutes for traditional products and services, thereby changing the economics of the business and
> - creating new institutional arrangements
>
> These anomalies have invalidated the old paradigm; the industry has already changed. *The old paradigm has ceased to function—to be useful—and it is inconceivable that it can be reestablished.* [emphasis ours] On the other hand, a new paradigm has not gained acceptance. We are mid-passage in the business equivalent of a scientific revolution.[2]

We believe that Seppel's comments about the finance industry can be interpreted on a wider scale and can be applied to U.S. industry as a whole. This book, and especially this chapter, reflects the requirement for managing revolution—the building of a new type of organization that accommodates the identification of entirely new paradigms. The fact that *paradigm for innovation* is, in fact, a self-contradictory term, shows that we cannot continue to search for innovation and entrepreneurship by studying and focusing only on:

- Management practices
- Tradition
- Industry and government regulations
- Organizational structure and practices

Figure 12-1 illustrates how the above management focus results in bureaucracy and organizational inertia rather than the change and innovation that is required for moving into the future. We need a new way of continually viewing the forces that are continually changing the marketplace and the resulting organizational paradigms—the sandboxes we play in and the sandboxes around ours. Linkage analysis planning and the concepts presented in this book provide a means to continually visualize new industry structures and to identify new strategic alliances. Linkage analysis planning can assist management in designing an organization that is more flexible—one that does not attempt to control innovation with layers of management and one that is in constant revolution and change.

The waves of innovation and experience curves provide one method

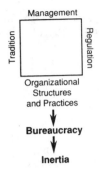

Figure 12-1. Traditional management focus. Three organizational dimensions.

for predicting and visualizing changes that are occurring. And an analysis of changing industry power relationships enables us to escape from the bonds of traditional industry thinking—from the bonds of today's and yesterday's paradigms. We can apply our new mindset of the physical component versus the information component to identify two ways in which to view the organization. With a *physical-component* perspective, we concentrate on existing organizational structures and the traditional processes of the enterprise. With an *information-component* perspective we attempt to identify the organization of the future by formulating a common shared vision, building our knowledge capability, and exercising innovative leadership. These are the factors that make the organization a dynamic, flexible entity that can differentiate itself from others by strategically planning to achieve substantial and sustainable advantage.

Chapter 12 presents a new way of thinking about the organizational structures that we will need in the 1990s. We must go beyond the old paradigms and deal with the new realities of a continually changing environment and the new rules of competition. The current paradigms of today's organizations are characterized by:

- Internal assessment of the organization in reference to quality, cost reduction, efficiency, productivity, and management control
- Restructuring the organization to reduce dependence on human resources
- Financial analysis of budgets, cash flow studies, manpower analyses, and revenue forecasts
- Statistical analysis, such as market share studies, with respect to the rest of the industry
- Strategic planning based on short term considerations and assessments

Stanley Davis, in his book *Future Perfect*, stresses this point by using an interesting play on words to contrast bureaucracies that manage "aftermath" and operate in the "past imperfect tense" with effective businesses that manage "before-math" and operate in the "future perfect" tense:

> When managers manage the consequences of events that have already happened, their organizations are doomed always to be lagging behind the needs of their business. The history of the industrial economy is strewn with companies that, once bright lights, have faded into obscurity, senescence, or death because their leaders managed in the past imperfect tense—that is, forever managing aftermath. They became bureaucracies: business that existed to run organizations. The way out of this dead end is in finding new models for managing in the new economy.... We are awaiting the ones to do it for their organization, managing the before-math, in the future perfect.[3]

It is useful to look further at Davis's ideas about businesses, organizations, and bureaucracies:

> My definition of a bureaucracy: A business, or any other institution, that exists to carry out an organization.... Remember, business and organizations are not the same thing: a business is the application of resources to create products and services to meet market needs in relation to competitors; an organization is the way in which those resources are administered. Organization is the means to accomplish the business ends. You have to know what you are going to do before you know how to do it. Organizations arise, therefore, out of societies institutions (such as government, school, church, business, and so on), not vice versa. For managers, organizations exist to carry out businesses; businesses *do not* exist to carry out an organization.... In fact I will go so far as to state Davis's law of bureaucracy: Any company giving less than two-thirds of its energies to its business and more than one-third of its energies to its organization. Where this exists, it is not merely that the company's organization is lagging behind, nor that the organizational-tail is wagging the business-dog. Something even more serious is operating.[4]

Three Organizational Dimensions

In order to create a culture that encourages innovation, we must move beyond the old, preconceived views of the organization. To help us do

Analysis of the Organization

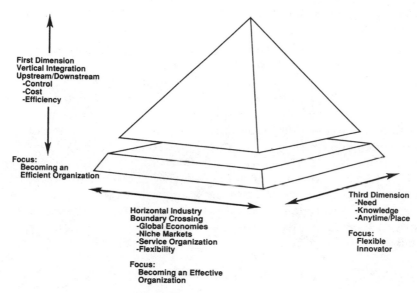

Figure 12-2. Three organizational dimensions.

this, we can characterize the organization as having three distinct dimensions, as shown in Figure 12-2. Our evolving view of the organization shows how these three dimensions have appeared.

The First Dimension: Vertical Integration

The traditional pyramid-structured organization, as depicted by Robert Anthony, allows us to concentrate on the internal structure of the organization and on those aspects of management control and decision making that are associated with this internal view. This focus was the driving force in the 1950s, 1960s, and early 1970s for enhancing an organization's efficiency.

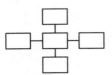

The Second Dimension: Horizontal Integration

Michael Porter made a substantial change to the Robert Anthony view with his competitive forces model. Porter shifted the emphasis from an internal/efficiency view to a view that concentrated on gaining competitive advantage by understanding and affecting the *external* forces as well as internal factors. This new direction leads to a new view of the organization that includes its suppliers, customers, and competitors—the extended enterprise. Quickly, this extended enterprise view evolved from attention on the *first dimension* of vertical integration within an industry to a new view that includes a *second dimension* of horizontal integration with industry boundary crossing. The focus here is on organizational effectiveness. This has lead to an environment where industries are beginning to converge in many sectors of the economy, especially the service sector.

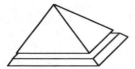

The Third Dimension: Knowledge Capability

We can now add the additional forces shown on the strategic forces model from Chapter 4. This leads us to a concept introduced by Davis of "any time, any place, no matter" to further clarify the view that we must have today of the organization:

> Those who limit their thinking to the familiar contexts of the industrial age will never be able to exploit the essential raw materials of the new economy: time, space, and matter. These basic properties have been so thoroughly transformed by science and technology that they now define the frontiers of growth. Mastering them results in real time performance, the ability to provide customized goods and services on a mass scale any time and any place.[5]

This leads us to a *third dimension* in our view of the organization where the focus is on *knowledge capability*. Knowledge workers will form the most important capital asset for organizations in the 1990s. Visualizing the inter-relationships among the strategic forces affecting the organization is a requirement for managers at all levels.

We are entering an era where electronic channel support systems are

enabling organizations to form effective alliances to attack the marketplace. We saw in previous chapters examples of organizations that have
done this. Innovative organizations, such as American Airlines and
Citibank, are combining their knowledge capabilities to create formidable trading organizations. We are now beginning to see how new technologies permit not only the converging of industries but also a converging of products and services to create new product/service mixes
that are responsive to the changing tastes and needs of the consumer.
We are in an environment where the consumer is beginning to assess
the true *acquisition cost* of products and services. Each acquisition of a
product or service has a cost that is measured not only in dollars but also
in terms of such currency as reducing anxiety, minimizing frustration,
enhancing convenience, increasing mobility, and saving time to name a
few. The average consumer today has less discretionary time than in
years past. This means that there is less time available with which to
shop and to return products for service or maintenance. Organizations
must begin to address these factors along with dollar cost if we are going to effectively meet the needs of consumers in the 1990s.

Organizational Evolution in the Three Dimensions

The ways in which businesses are evolving today parallel the three dimensions we have just described:

- *The first dimension.*   Organizations everywhere are being divided up
  into individual autonomous and semi-autonomous units, leading to
  the downsizing of corporate America. This is downsizing in the vertical dimension. The primary focus of the first dimension is on productivity, cost, and quality.

- *The second dimension.*   Market mechanisms are becoming more effective than the current tactical plans and internal controls that are
  typically used in today's organizations. This is being caused by globalization of markets, increasing use of just-in-time, quick-response
  systems, the emergence of electronic channel support systems and the
  creation of the information/knowledge worker society. The extended
  enterprise view—expansion in the second dimension—becomes critical to understanding these new external forces. The primary focus of
  the second dimension is on effectiveness and competitive advantage.

- *The third dimension.*   The dissolving of traditional industry structures is causing industries to converge. As we have seen, the traditional boundaries are blurring in such industries as manufacturing,
  banking, retail, distribution, health, and education. Government de-

regulation can be viewed as another example of the changing structure and view of both private and public sector functions. The emergence of alliances is an example of the increasing importance of knowledge capability and the third dimension. The primary focus of the third dimension is on supremacy and survival.

Analyzing the Converging Industries

As organizations confront the changes of the 1990s and begin to understand the forces depicted in the analysis of the future organization chart, the enterprise and extended enterprise structures become building blocks for developing and understanding the *converging industries*. Vertical integration, horizontal integration, and the knowledge capabilities that characterize the third dimension will cause a complete restructuring of our economy as we know it today. Downsizing and decentralization of large organizations, and the rapid growth and success of many small organizations, demonstrate the beginning of this trend. The third dimension leads us to a better understanding of the reasons that entire industries are beginning to converge. Markets in many cases will be defined as the *consumer market* instead of having the traditional customer focus. The decision by Judge Greene in reference to AT&T, which allows AT&T to begin delivering information to the home, will accelerate the shift as image and fiber-optics technology drops in cost and becomes widely available. Leading the exploitation of this technology will be education and the retail sector. The state of Indiana has already begun a fourth-grade program that provides personal computers in the home for fourth-grade children.

To understand the impact these wide-reaching changes will have on the organization, we can draw an expanded extended enterprise chart that gives a more comprehensive view of our entire economy. (See Figure 12-3.) By carefully analyzing this chart we can find many opportunities for achieving substantial and sustainable strategic advantage, as well as identifying exposures and competitive threats. In many cases, the competition for future products and services will come not from the traditional players but from new directions. The tendency will be for many organizations to shift to the center of the chart—to the pure service sector—causing even more industries to converge. The service sector is an apt target for many organizations because it is consumer oriented, is currently complacent in its use of technology, and is subject to significant impact by the information systems of the future. Examples of the converging industries phenomenon can be seen today in the following organizations:

Converging Industries
National Economy

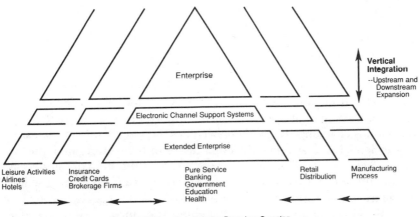

Figure 12-3. Expanded extended enterprise chart.

- General Motors, Ford, Sears, and General Electric have large financial services organizations, such as Sears with the Discover Card.

- The insurance industry is beginning to offer services traditionally offered by organizations in the banking and health industries.

- Merrill Lynch has had great success with its Cash Management Account, which offers services traditionally provided by banks.

- Business and private sector organizations have been making ventures into education.

- American Airlines, United Airlines, and Marriot are creating powerful credit card alliances.

The following are a few observations on what organizations must do with respect to the converging industries:

1. Effectively position themselves on the converging industries chart (Figure 12-3).

2. Assess the opportunities and exposures that are associated with vertical integration.

3. Understand available options for pursuing horizontal integration strategies, such as:

- Competing at the brick and mortar level (for example; buy stores, plants, equipment)
- Competing at the electronic channel support system level
- Competing at the extended enterprise level through effective alliances

4. Assess the impact of future competitive exposures.

5. Formulate and implement an effective vision for the organization.

The phenomenon of the converging industries is causing sweeping changes to the traditional roles of industries. As we mentioned earlier in this chapter, industry lines are blurring, niche opportunities are occurring, and competition is changing. What, then, becomes the role of the traditional industry leaders? Understanding the implications of the converging industries chart provides a new insight into the need to assess the strengths and weaknesses of both internal elements and the external, extended enterprise linkages. Failure to build appropriate internal systems and processes may make it impossible to expand into the extended enterprise. Such a failure may then make it impossible to meet the challenges that new competitors from the converging industries bring. The value of strategic alliances, and the management implications associated with them, start to take on a new perspective. Understanding the implications of the converging industries at all levels of the organization can make a major contribution to making the organization adaptive and flexible.

With the perspective provided by the new three-dimensional view of the forces affecting the organization, we can begin to analyze in detail each of the four steps shown on the right-hand side of the leadership linkage chart from Chapter 10 (see Figure 10-10).

Step 1: Develop a View of the New Organization

Building the "new organization" requires management to have a clear understanding of strategic market forces from the perspective of the converging industries. What will be the future direction for the organization? Will the organization vertically integrate or will it begin to cross industry boundaries? What will the competition do, and who will the new competitors be? We must analyze the waves of innovation and industry experience curves from a new viewpoint to create a vision that takes into account the impact of the converging industries. In analyzing changing industry power relationships we must use new levels of creativity and strategic thinking to truly understand and manage the changes that are occurring. For most organizations, the following factors will be key survival issues:

- Internal and external linkages
- Alliances and partnerships
- Ownership versus joint ventures versus subcontracts
- Decentralization and downsizing
- Central control
- Global markets
- Business direction

In order to bridge from the hierarchical/global view of the organization depicted in the converging industry charts, the charts of industry power relationship are extremely important. Just as we enhanced the extended enterprise charts to show the converging industries, we must also enhance the changing industry power relationships charts to include a new *linkage/network view*, as shown in Figure 12-4. This view complements the converging industry view and provides insight into what Brandt Allen describes in a presentation that he gives. One of the charts Allen uses lists "Implications of the Strategic Challenges for Organizations":[6]

- Need for faster response, flexibility to changing volume
- Looser coupling of major units

Figure 12-4. Linkage/network view.

- Ability to absorb new designs and ideas
- Integration of innovation from internal and external sources
- Fast implementation of new products
- Better control of operations (and costs)
- Coordination of external contracting

To achieve these, many organizations will have to concentrate on the linkage/network view of their organization's extended enterprise. The structures of large, information- and knowledge-based organizations will become flatter, and knowledge will tend to be concentrated primarily at the bottom of the organization instead of at the traditional top. This is because each job function in the new organization will come to have specialized knowledge associated with it. People will be carrying out few routine, repetitive tasks—the machines will be doing these. Peter Drucker points out:

> A good deal of work will be done differently in the information-based organization. Traditional departments will serve as guardians of standards, as centers for training, and the assignment of specialists; they won't be where the work gets done. That will happen largely in task-focused teams.[7]

This change is already underway in what was once the most clearly defined of all departments—research. In pharmaceuticals, in telecommunications, in paper making, the traditional sequence of research, development, manufacturing, and marketing is being replaced by *synchrony*—specialists from various functions working together as a team from inception of research to a product's establishment in the market.

Networked Management Structures

In the old hierarchical organization, information from individuals working in the different functional areas would have to flow up to a common higher-level manager and then work its way back down. Or it would have to travel to a central switching function where the various other departments come together. For example, if a sales representative wants to send customer information to a manufacturing plant in the traditional hierarchically structured organization, information would flow up the sales chain of command to a general manager and then down through manufacturing chain of command until it reached the intended party. Such a system is much too time consuming for today's environment, and also much too error prone. The intended message may never get through.

Davis points out in *Future Perfect*: "Networks will not replace or supplement hierarchies; rather the two will be encompassed within a broader conception that embraces them both."[8]

Visualizing, designing, and assembling the new organizations will require a greater emphasis on leveraging knowledge resources. Dynamic alliances will become a vehicle for achieving quick responses to market opportunities. Organizations will be linked together by a common vision and purpose. And when the common purpose has been achieved, the knowledge resources will dissolve the links and create a new vision. The trick becomes attracting, energizing, and bonding the knowledge resources to the vision.

We must continue to have a hierarchical view of many of our institutions for legalistic and competitive purposes. But the way these institutions actually operate must be much different—much more dynamic.

> **Visualizing the interrelationships of the strategic market and environmental forces requires both a hierarchical and a network perspective.**

The way the organization operates must encompass large numbers of *constantly changing functions that are linked together into dynamic networks*. Many of the functions will need to be linked to external functions outside of the traditional boundaries of the organization. The days of static, monolithic organizational structures are gone. We can again apply Michael Porter's distinction between the information component and physical component to contrast the hierarchical view of the organization with the linkage/network view. The physical component corresponds to the hierarchical, legal competitive view and the information component to the linkage/network view. We can use the linkage/network view to visualize, understand, and implement the legal, competitive, hierarchical organizational structures. The linkages inherent in the linkage/network view will enable the organization to become more effective than it is today. The linkages will bring together the new organizational structures, and the vision that is shared by all the members of the management team will be the glue that binds them. But there are no easy solutions—no paradigms.

The functions of the innovation arrow will become increasingly important as we move into the 1990s. The organization is changing, and the means to build the new organization must change as well. The converging industry hierarchical view is important in viewing the organization with respect to a legal, management control perspective, and the linkage/network view is required to focus on implementing the strategic action plan and on flattening and delayering the organization to meet the challenges of global and niche markets that require dynamic, innovative, and effective organizational structures.

As we discussed in Chapter 11, it can be difficult to manage the gaps between the phases of the innovation arrow. The appropriate width of the gaps between phases is not always easy to determine, and the proper width is difficult to maintain. As we pointed out, if the gaps are too wide, which might result from downsizing without appropriate changes in management, teamwork is difficult to achieve; if the gaps are too narrow, there tends to be no distinction between different levels of management, and further changes in management may be in order. The major thrust for management must be to:

- **Manage the gaps between the phases in the innovation arrow.**
- **Manage the linkages between external and internal elements of the extended enterprise.**

These two new management requirements will be difficult at first for management to achieve because management control and authority will dissipate in the 1990s. Examples of this can be observed in the freedom and mobility of the new knowledge workers entering the workforce and the dramatic changes taking place in the Soviet Union and in Eastern Europe. Old beliefs and traditions are no longer important; individual achievement and expression are.

Step 2: Foster Innovation by Enabling Key Organizational Relationships

From the beginning of this book, our major objectives have been to:

- Provide insight into the impact of technology on the organization.
- Present requirements for success in the changing environment of the 1990s.
- Describe a strategic planning process to assist in achieving success.

Chapter 10 described the linkage analysis planning process, and Appendixes A and B provide industry examples of how the process is being applied. In Chapter 10, our focus was on applying linkage analysis planning to the current and near-term environment. Our focus in this chapter is on a long-term view of the future that addresses the delayering of the organization, converging industries, and global and niche markets.

Our coming knowledge-based industries will require new planning techniques if they are to achieve success in the global marketplace. Because of the complexities of the future, management will have to perform strategic planning in a dynamic, ongoing manner. In order to raise the overall level of effectiveness of the organization, the management team will also have to evolve the ongoing plan, identify the organizational relationships that will be required, and implement them in a timely and effective manner. Achieving the required hierarchical and linkage/network perspectives can be viewed as a process having five phases—three phases are related to understanding the hierarchical perspective and two phases to the linkage/network perspective.

Perspective 1: Hierarchical View

In understanding the hierarchical view of the organization we begin by formulating a vision of the organization that takes an internal focus. We then expand this to a global view that enables us to clearly perceive the competitive, legal, and management control aspects of the enterprise. This provides us with a new top-down view for the 1990s.

- *Phase 1: internal vision.* In this phase, we perform an internal assessment of the major functions and requirements of the organization, both today and 5 to 7 years out. This requires that we analyze the organization's hierarchical structure to begin forming a vision of what the organization should become and what key functions, assets, and processes will be required to achieve the vision.

- *Phase 2: extended vision.* In this phase, we develop the extended enterprise view of the organization and identify the electronic channel support systems that will be required for success in this environment. We now begin to transform the hierarchical view of the organization to form an extended vision of the organization. In this phase, we must identify the key functions, assets, and processes that exist outside the enterprise that are required today and that will be required in the next 5 to 7 years. Linkages to the extended enterprise and the development of the electronic channel support systems are important in understanding how to best exploit technology in achieving the extended vision.

- *Phase 3: convergent vision.*   In Phase 3 we begin to analyze the role of the organization with respect to the converging industries, both today and in the future. In this phase, we develop a vision that identifies vertical and horizontal integration strategies and addresses the third dimension and the requirements of need, knowledge, time, and place. An understanding of tomorrow's competitors and how to compete in these new markets is crucial.

The process need not be done in the exact sequence shown above. For example, it might make sense in many situations to perform step 2 first and then go back to step 1.

Perspective 2: Linkage/Network View

In attaining a linkage/network perspective, we must expand our vision by developing a view of the new organization that provides dynamic, flexible organizational structures at the level of the implementation and operations functions of the innovation arrow. The key focus here is on the management of the gaps between the innovation arrow functions and on the management of internal and external linkages between elements in the extended enterprise. We need this view to provide insight into how we will actually implement the vision we attained by understanding the hierarchical perspective. In attaining the linkage/network perspective, we need to determine how to implement the important internal and external linkages in a network environment.

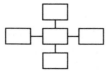

- *Phase 4: external linkage vision.*   In this phase, we again expand the vision of the organization by defining an external linkage/network view of the organization's extended enterprise. We must develop this view in order to understand the future impact of market forces and to clarify the role of the organization in the environment. Here we must analyze key internal functions and processes and identify functions outside that are complementary to our own. We must then put into place the required organizational relationships through networks of integrated functions and processes. This will allow us to provide better products and services at lower prices and in shorter periods of time.

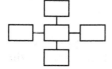

- *Phase 5: internal linkage vision.*   In the final phase, we refine our vision by developing the internal linkage/network view of the organization that focuses on internal organizational structures that will be necessary to manage the key external linkages identified in phase 4. Key to this final phase is to identify and integrate all requirements and processes into the structure of the new organization. This becomes the blueprint for building the infrastructure of the organization of the future.

Networking of functions between organizations will allow us to greatly enhance the effectiveness of the organization. The networking that exists today between organizations in providing vertical integration in the creation and delivery of products and services will become a three-dimensional activity, paralleling the three organizational dimensions we described earlier:

1. *Vertical integration.*   The first dimension is the traditional vertical networking that has occurred, both upstream and downstream, in order to enhance control, reduce costs, and increase efficiency.

2. *Horizontal integration.*   Horizontal networking of functions will occur because of the industry boundary crossing caused by converging industries.

3. *Networking for innovation.*   A third form of networking, which we call networking for innovation, reflects the third dimension of knowledge capability and Davis's "any time, any place, no-matter." Examples of this type of networking can be seen in the partnership between American Airlines and Citibank and the community holding company partnership to support education described in Appendix B.

In going through the five phases described for attaining both a hierarchical and a linkage/network perspective, the management team should reflect back on the key concepts outlined in the previous 11 chapters. Each phase should end by assessing strategies for achieving substantial and sustainable advantage that can be implemented today and over the next 5 to 7 years.

Step 3: Select Innovative Projects That Increase Organizational Effectiveness

Critical factors that will determine the organization's success is the organization's ability to select the winning projects and to make the right investments. Prioritizing and selecting opportunities for investment should be a two-step process. The first step in assessing a project's value must be to ask whether the project will add significant value to the organization. The second step consists of making financial analyses of short-term and long-term benefits. Traditional financial analyses are still vital, but in order to achieve real advantage in the new global environment, the organization will have to go further than these. The marketplace will ultimately determine who has been most effective in identifying and prioritizing the winning projects. The real test of whether an organization has truly achieved substantial and sustainable competitive advantage is to test in the financial market the value of the organization. We must ask the question:

> **Is the value of the organization greater than the sum of its parts?**

An important test of success will be to compare the stock market value of the organization with its book value. The synergism of the different parts of the business should provide a market value that is greater than the sum of the organization's individual parts. If we have chosen the right projects and built an effective extended enterprise, the integration and synergism of the internal and external functions will add significant value to the organization. If we have not done a good job, then we will continue to be subject to takeovers and leveraged buy-outs, with the selling off of different, independent parts of the organization as the means to finance these endeavors. For organizations in the public sector, such as government and education, the test of the value of the organization will be whether taxpayers support funding for the services the organization provides or whether they prefer to allow private enterprises to take over these functions.

The strength and value of the organization in the 1990s will come from leveraging the knowledge capital of the organization—the knowledge that the organization and its people have. There are two factors operating somewhat at odds with each other with respect to the knowledge capital of organizations. First, the knowledge possessed by an organization tends to increase in value over time. Second, the total number of knowledge workers in an organization will tend to decrease over time as we eliminate middle management people and because of the continuing shortage of qualified, professional people. The key to success in such an environment is to determine how the organization's knowledge capital can most effectively be used. It will no longer be possible to handle everything internally. It will be important to determine which organizational functions are best decoupled and handled by external members of the extended enterprise and which are best handled internally. Investing of the scarce knowledge resources in the most effective manner is the challenge.

It is an error to associate creativity and innovation only with invention. Technological innovation certainly depends on invention, but what is of equal importance is developing and applying invention in the most effective manner. Exploitation of technological invention involves innovation in marketing, in management, in information systems. Neglect of these important facets of innovation can be as damaging as not having the idea in the first place. We have to understand where our strengths and weaknesses are today and where they are likely to lie in the future. Then we must look to the extended enterprise for what we lack. It will become increasingly important for groups of individuals to work together interactively in supportive ways to generate not only novel solutions, but solutions that can be effectively implemented. The knowledge that is required for success in many enterprises is now becoming so vast that only groups can effectively master it. Strategic advantage will swing more and more each day to those organizations that can effectively harness groupings of knowledge workers. Networks of knowledge workers will go beyond the traditional boundaries of the organization, just as computer networks do today. Knowledge and information will transcend corporate or enterprise boundaries.

Successful implementation of networking between the traditional organization and the extended enterprise will create new levels of synergism and lead to significant increased value. We should begin prioritizing projects and choosing future investments both inside and outside the organization from this view. As we mentioned earlier, the financial markets will quickly identify the successful organizations that bring a new meaning to the phrase *leveraging of the organization's resources.*

In the new environment of the 1990s if we lose the vision and allow leadership to slip from our grasp, we will be quickly doomed. The organization of the future will no longer have large physical assets to sell in order to pay future dividends. It will not take years for market share to evaporate. New technological changes will not occur only every 10 years, or longer; they are occurring much more rapidly than this. As quickly as a business can rise, it can also fall if we allow innovative and entrepreneurial leadership to evaporate.

Step 4: Implement the Vision by Leveraging Organizational Skills and Resources

As we pointed out in the introduction to Part 3, strategy requires vision, but effective implementation requires *leadership*. Strategic advantage can usually be achieved only at the operational level, and a strategy is only as good as its implementation. We now shift our focus from building the new organization to executive leadership and the role of the visionary in the organization. What does it take to be a visionary leader? Innovation and risk taking is an important factor in innovation. The terms *manager* and *leader* were once synonymous. Abraham Zaleznik realized the need for a distinction between the two terms:

> Managers do the same things over and over again, but it takes a leader to innovate. While a good leader needs to be a manager too, a manager is not necessarily a leader.[9]

In Zaleznik's latest book, entitled *The Managerial Mystique*, he challenges the reader to reevaluate what motivates management. He asserts that, contrary to popular belief, managers and leaders are far apart in the ideas that fire them, in the practices their ideas yield, and in the way they influence the quality and effectiveness of their organizations. Zaleznik observes that too many organizations have gone overboard in their pursuit of the *beliefs* and *practices* of management. In an attempt to organize the actions of individuals, a managerial ethic has emerged that places emphasis on order, efficiency, and predictability. The emphasis in many organizations is being placed on the form and the structure of the enterprise rather than on the substance of the business. Such an emphasis tends to obscure the goals of the organization and to inhibit creativity. Too many organizations are run by people who lack leadership ability. To this, Zaleznik adds:

> This book...is a call to rediscover leadership, which may be tantamount to restoring the individual to his or her proper place as the source of vision and drive that can make an organization unique.[10]

Jack Welsh, chairman and CEO of General Electric company, stated:

> At the beginning of the decade, we saw two challenges ahead of us. One external and one internal. Externally, we faced a world economy that would be characterized by slower growth with stronger global competitors after a smaller pie.... Internally, our challenge was even bigger. We had to find a way to combine the power, resources, and reach of a big company with the hunger, the agility, the spirit, and the fire of a small one.... For one, they communicate better.... Second, small companies move faster. They know the penalties for hesitation in the marketplace. Third, in small companies, with fewer layers and less camouflage, the leaders show up very clearly on the screen. Their performance and its impact are clear to everyone. And, finally, small companies waste less. They spend less time in endless reviews and approvals and politics, and paper drills. They have fewer people; therefore they only do the important things. Their people are free to direct their energy and attention toward the marketplace rather than fighting bureaucracy. To win externally during the 80s, we believed we needed to develop these internal characteristics.[11]

Today's thinkers—people like Welsh, Zaleznik, and many others—are showing us that the conventional manager—the process caretaker—must move over and make room for the innovating entrepreneurs. An organization whose culture depends on rewarding the process caretakers is at extreme risk in a niche world characterized by rapidly accelerating change and tough global competition. In such an environment, success means not messing up. A process-caretaker mentality rewards form and predictability and discourages innovation and risk taking. The business environment of the 1990s requires leaders who can:

- Visualize the interrelationships among strategic market forces.

- Restructure and revitalize the organization to think and act strategically.

- Perform strategic planning and prioritize winning projects.

- Implement projects by leveraging organizational skills and resources.

- Innovate and take necessary risks.

- Network functions within an organization and build network alliances.

- Possess good communication skills and have a dynamic personality.

- Accept change and technology as a way of life and be pro-active in exploiting it.

- Lead their teams in making the vision happen.

Model for Success

An effective tool in assessing your own role as an innovative effective leader is to combine the phases of the innovation arrow with the ideas presented in the Innovation/Impact Model from Chapter 1 (see Figure 1-7). If we begin the planning process with a vision and then communicate that vision effectively throughout the organization, the impact on the organization of this type of planning will be great. In an organization that does not have an effective vision to harness its resources, the total organizational cost can be significantly greater than if it did harness its resources, as shown in Fig. 12-5. By combining the innovation arrow with the concepts contained in the Innovation/Impact Model, we get the model shown in Figure 12-6. From this model we can see that management leadership consists of:

- Management control
- Synergy
- Innovation
- Entrepreneurship

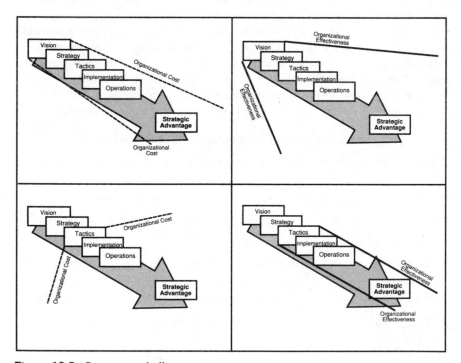

Figure 12-5. Organizational effectiveness.

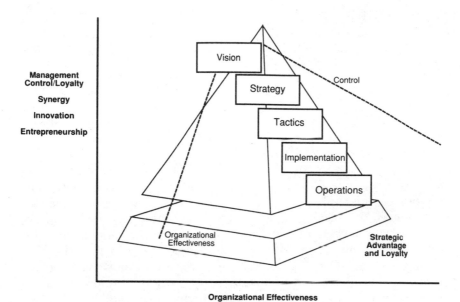

Figure 12-6. Model for assessing the blueprint for success.

The key point here is that we must ensure that we have high levels of both innovation and impact in order to effectively reach out into the extended enterprise of the future. Leadership begins with the vision, which we must then drive throughout the enterprise and into the extended enterprise. If we can accomplish this, we will be able to gain the loyalty of all members of the extended enterprise, and we will be able to gain strategic advantage in the marketplace. If our focus within the organization remains at the tactical level or lower, we will be less effective, and our chances of winning will be substantially reduced.

Formulating a National Collaborative Vision

The ideas we have presented in this book can be extended to our national economy as a whole. What is needed in the United States if we are to achieve success in the global marketplace is a *national collaborative vision.* This is a vision around which all of our institutions, in both the public and private sectors of the economy, work effectively together in networking our country into the 1990s and beyond. The ways in which we journey into the future is important to us all:

> **We create our tomorrows by what we envision tomorrow
> to be, and by what we invest or not invest in today.**

We need to build a national extended enterprise consisting of all the organizations that are critical to our success as a nation—schools, businesses, and government. (See Figure 12-7.) The test of whether such an extended enterprise is successful will again be to see if the value of the entire extended enterprise is greater than the sum of the individual parts. We issue a challenge to all the individual stakeholders in our economy: schools, individual citizens, businesses, communities, the cities. All must begin playing an active role in helping the United States to achieve greater success as an economic power. Such a national collaborative vision is important because the resulting policies establish the rules of the game. They define authority, procedures, and planning assumptions. They establish territorial and political boundaries, and, above all, delimit spheres of discretion. The more innovative a change, the less likely it fits into existing policies.

The first step in creating a national collaborative economic vision is to

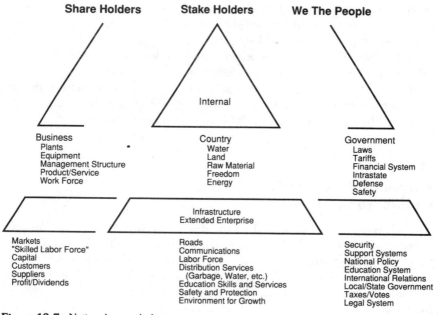

Figure 12-7. National extended enterprise.

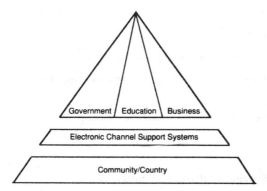

Figure 12-8. National extended enterprise model.

create an environment that makes it acceptable for individuals and organizations to present ideas and make proposals that are likely to have substantial impact on our economy. We must determine the essential elements of a linkage/network view of a national extended enterprise. We need a new model of this extended enterprise, such as that shown in Figure 12-8. America is in a scientific revolution, and leadership is required to stimulate the formulation of a vision that will enable business, government, and education to work together to address common goals. Government can supply an infrastructure and an environment that encourages growth, education can supply us with the knowledge resources that we will need, and business can use the knowledge resources provided by education and the infrastructure provided by government to create new economic wealth to fund our journey into the future.

Conclusion

The techniques of strategic thinking can be applied to a tiny department or division, to an organization, to an entire industry, or to our nation as a whole. At each of these levels we must focus on the innovation arrow. We must formulate a vision, then communicate that vision, and effectively implement it. America can continue to be strong if each of us takes the first step. Vision, leadership, and innovation are not the qualities of someone else. We are America's management team. We are the leaders and the future leaders of the United States. We will close this book by repeating the definition of leadership presented at the beginning of this book:

Innovative leadership is the ability to...

- **Formulate a vision for achieving strategic advantage**
- **Create strategies and plans for adapting and innovating in the changing environment**
- **Develop tactics for implementing the strategies and plans**
- **Implement the vision by empowering individuals with the necessary skills**

...**leading to new levels of organizational effectiveness.**

This definition then raises questions that you can ask of yourself:

- Do you have and display the ability?
- What is the new level of effectiveness that you can achieve for yourself, your family, your organization, the community, and the nation.
- Where do we stop?
- When does our responsibility end?

The first step is the toughest. Remember:

Make no assumptions.
It's a personal choice.

References

1. Erich W. Seppel. "When Change and Continuity Collide: Capitalizing on Strategic Gridlock in Financial Services." *California Management Review,* Spring, 1989.
2. *Ibid.*
3. Stanley M. Davis. *Future Perfect.* Reading, MA: Addison-Wesley, 1987.
4. *Ibid.*
5. *Ibid.*
6. Brandt Allen. "Information Technology: Four Key Decisions for Management." Presentation given in Indianapolis, Indiana, May 5, 1989.
7. Peter Drucker. "The Coming of the New Organization." *Harvard Business Review,* January–February, 1988.

8. Stanley M. Davis. *Future Perfect*. Reading, MA: Addison-Wesley, 1987.

9. Abraham Zaleznik. "Wanted. Leaders Who Can Make a Difference." *Fortune,* September 28, 1987.

10. Abraham Zaleznik. *The Managerial Mystique*. New York: Harper and Row, 1989.

11. Jack Welsh. Speech to the General Electric Annual Meeting of Shareholders. Wakesha, Wisconsin, April 27, 1988.

Linkage Analysis: Health Care Industry

Introduction

Appendix A walks through a linkage analysis planning session that the authors conducted for a hospital. In reading through this appendix, try to place yourself in the shoes of the president of the hospital board of a nonprofit, medium-sized hospital in a large city that has all types of hospitals, some larger than yours and many smaller.

Analyzing Waves and Curves

We begin with an analysis of the waves of innovation associated with the health care industry and the experience curves that predominate. We then create charts of strategic market forces that show how power relationships are changing in the health care industry. Figure A-1 shows the waves of innovation and some of the experience curve strategies that characterize the health care industry.

Identifying Power Relationships

An analysis of waves of innovation and experience curves leads to an examination of the power relationships that prevail in the health industry. Figure A-2 shows a chart of the traditional market forces that might be associated with a hospital. The health industry has undergone significant change in the last few years. A linkage analysis planning session

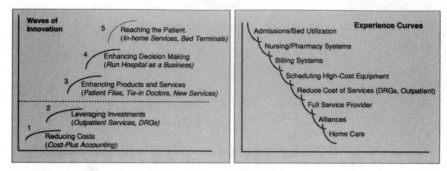

Figure A-1. Waves of innovation and experience curve strategies.

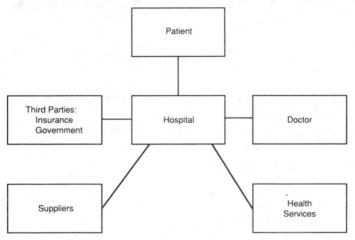

Figure A-2. Traditional market forces in the health care industry.

begins by examining the Michael Porter competitive forces model from
Chapter 2 and the expanded strategic forces model introduced in
Chapter 4. The strategic forces model is repeated in Figure A-3. We can
use the strategic forces model to begin analyzing the impact on the hospital of technology, current and future regulation, and the changes that
are occurring in the health industry as a whole. Such an analysis might
determine that the major changes are occurring in power relationships
owing to such factor as:

■ Doctors are restructuring their practices into groups and partnerships.

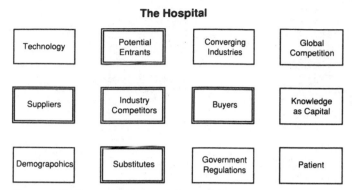

Figure A-3. Strategic forces model.

- The federal government is implementing diagnostic related groups (DRGs) to help curtail the rise in medical costs.
- Hospitals are being increasingly run by for-profit health industry organizations or large affiliated religious organizations.
- Costs are continuing to rise for medical equipment, liability insurance, labor, and medical supplies.
- The impact on the health industry due to illegal drug usage and the AIDS problem is increasing.
- The health industry is becoming highly segmented with the proliferation of clinics, prepaid medical plans, and nursing homes.

Adding to these issues, the entire health industry is in a transition period where various industries are converging. The converging industries that are playing a major role include the insurance industry and medical supply manufacturers. In addition, the hotel industry is beginning to play a role, with major hotel chains entering the nursing home business. The major medical supply manufacturers are beginning to look toward the home market for the future with self-testing procedures and self-application devices and medications.

The next step is to begin asking ourselves questions about how the environment is likely to change in the future and how the chart in Figure A-2 is likely to change with respect to strategic market forces. Many of these forces are likely to cause the chart to expand to that shown in Figure A-4. Individual hospitals are left with a shrinking revenue base and often resort to defending a piece of a shrinking pie.

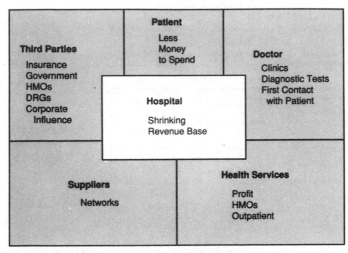

Figure A-4. Changing industry power relationships.

Visualizing the Extended Enterprise

Our analysis of the waves of innovation, experience curves, and changing industry power relationships should begin to give us a feeling for what the extended enterprise of the hospital looks like. This, in turn, should start us thinking about the electronic channel support systems that will be needed in the future for exploiting our extended enterprise view of the environment. Our vision for the hospital should now begin to materialize and should begin to focus our thinking. An example of an important aspect of the hospital's vision might be the following:

> **Increase revenue and market share by increasing the level of service the hospital provides to its customers, including doctors and patients.**

Conducting an External Linkage Analysis

Once we have charted the changing industry power relationships, we can proceed to the linkage analysis. As we discussed in Chapter 10, a linkage analysis planning session can take either an external or an internal focus. As we have stated, in most cases the process is most effective if we adopt an external focus first and then perform an internal analysis after the external linkage analysis has been completed. This is the approach we adopt here.

Level 1: The Hospital

At this level of analysis, we place at the top of the chart the question we are trying to answer and draw a box for the "hospital" in the center of the chart. Then, using the charts of changing industry power relationships as a base, we sketch in boxes around the "hospital" box that represent key external linkages. It is important to continually ask ourselves: "What is important." The techniques discussed in Parts 1 and 2 can help us focus on strategic issues. The two initial objectives of the level 1 analysis of the hospital are:

- To identify the major relationships that are related to our vision of the hospital today and tomorrow.
- To understand the positive and negative impact of the major forces on our hospital.

Figure A-5 shows the chart that might result from the level 1 linkage analysis. This chart helps us to identify the major players in the hospital's extended enterprise and to visualize potential electronic channel support systems. After we achieve agreement that we have included all the important factors in the chart, we then focus on choosing which factors are most important. As we mentioned in Chapter 10, a guideline that can be used here is to agree on the top five, and then to vote for the top one from among those. In some cases, we may not be able to choose one, but might choose two. We could then conduct further analyses on the top two factors. But try not to have more than two number-one priorities. In analyzing the level 1 chart we might try to determine who is the person most responsible for the choice of what hospital to use. We might conclude that most patients, when they are told they have to go to the hospital, respond by asking the doctor which one. Therefore, the doctor in many instances is the key to the hospital selection process. For this reason we might choose the linkage to "doctors" as the external linkage that is of most importance to achieving the vision of *increasing market share through improved service to customers*. After we achieve agreement, we can proceed to the level 2 linkage analysis.

Level 2: Doctors

In the level 2 analysis, we use the same procedure as for level 1 and explore all the existing and potential future linkages for "doctors." We

**Which External Factors Are Most Important in
Helping the Hospital Achieve Strategic Advantage?**

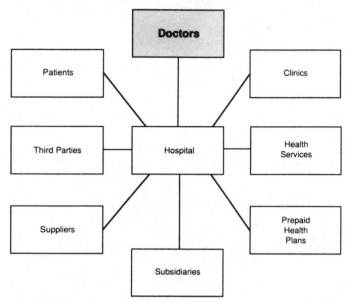

Figure A-5. Health care industry level 1 external linkage analysis: hospital.

must clearly understand all the linkages that exist between the hospital and the doctors to assist us in this evaluation. The following are a few issues that we might consider when evaluating the doctor's relationship with the hospital and the linkages that are most important:

- What are the important relationships and who has control over them?
- Who chooses the hospital the doctor uses?
- Which doctors are most important now?
- Which doctors will be most important in the future?
- Who are the customers of the doctor?
- Who in the hospital assists the doctor?
- How can we keep the doctors happy?
- What departments of the hospital does the doctor work with?
- How can we grow our "shelf space" in the doctor's mind?
- How can we increase the size of the pie?

We might draw the chart shown in Figure A-6 after answering such questions. With the doctor as the center of focus on present and future relationships, these relationships may expand or change because of converging industries or the need to grow the pie. We might at this time explore significant doctor relationships with other businesses to see if these might suggest strategic alliances that would allow us to increase the size of the envelope the hospital offers to the doctor. The boxes in Figure A-6 drawn with dashed lines represent two such relationships.

After agreeing that all the important issues are on the chart, we again try to determine which of the factors is most important. This time importance is determined by what is important to the doctor. Again, try to identify one, but no more than two, number-one priority. In this phase, we must achieve agreement on what is the most important linkage in accomplishing the strategic vision. In this case, the important aspect of the vision is to increase revenue and market share by increasing the level of service the hospital provides for doctors. In effect, we must be able to build new envelopes of products and services that we can implement quickly and can continue to sustain in the future. We might choose the "billing" function as being the most important. Because the billing and admissions functions are so closely tied together, it might make sense to group these two functions together for the level 3 analysis.

Which Factors Are Most Important with Respect to Improving the Level of Service We Provide to Doctors?

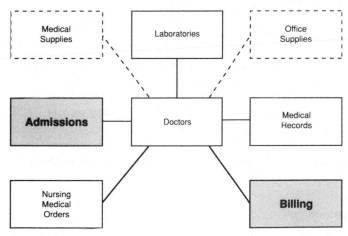

Figure A-6. Health care industry level 2 external linkage analysis: doctors.

Level 3: Billing and Admissions

Now that we have selected a particular function for detailed analysis, we might find that the linkage analysis is at a sufficient level of detail that we can begin trying to identify benefits and new application opportunities. In doing so it is important to keep the focus on the vision and on the results of the level 1 and level 2 analyses. In some cases, the level 3 analysis may not be detailed enough. If that happens, it may be necessary to do a level 4 analysis, and in some cases a level 5 analysis, and so on, to reach an appropriate stopping point. At each stage of the analysis, we must apply the following test:

Is the factor selected truly strategic? Will it lead to substantial and sustainable competitive advantage?

Documenting the Strategy

At level 3 (or level 4 or 5) of the linkage analysis process, it becomes appropriate to begin formulating a strategic plan for materializing the vision. At this point, we can draw up an action plan based on the benefits and opportunities that we have identified during the linkage analysis process. During the detailed analysis, we must also examine potential exposures that we have identified and make future plans for later implementing any additional benefits or opportunities that we may have uncovered.

Action Plan

The action plan that we develop at the final level of detail in the linkage analysis should be designed to guide the hospital in pursuing strategic advantage in the area of enhancing the billing and admissions functions. In preparing the action plan, we must list benefits or potential new opportunities for enhancing this area. We might try to define a new envelope that includes ancillary products and services for the doctor or just provide a more efficient or easier means to provide the services.

Potential Exposures

In addition to developing an action plan, we must also develop a list of potential ways in which the hospital might be threatened if we do not enhance our relationship with doctors in the areas of billing and admissions. For example, an insurance company, another hospital, or some other company in the converging industries might provide the doctor with many of the services that we can provide.

Future Enhancements

After constructing an action plan and identifying potential exposures, we look to the future and list additional benefits and opportunities that we might pursue later. Here, we might consider forming alliances with other organizations. For example, we might establish a relationship with an organization that will buy the doctor's receivables at a discount so the doctor will no longer have to spend time on collection procedures. We might also begin identifying additional services that doctors might need that are complementary to the products and services our hospital already offers. Figure A-7 shows the chart that might result from a level 3 linkage analysis of the billing and admissions function.

Conducting an Internal Linkage Analysis

After we have completed the external linkage analysis and have identified key strategic areas that must be addressed concerning our relationship with doctors, an analysis can be completed that focuses on the internal linkages within the hospital itself. In the level 1 internal linkage analysis for the hospital, we focus on how the hospital's objectives are currently being met. We trace the flow of products and services through the hospital and ask questions about efficiency, effectiveness, quality of products and services, and the locations of bottlenecks. As in the external linkage analysis, we draw a chart that shows the key internal functions for the hospital that are of the most importance from an internal perspective. (See Figure A-8.) At this stage we should try to identify internal functions that will help implement the strategic action plan documented during the external linkage analysis. Some elements of the external strategic action plan will be contingent on enhanced internal functions. Once we have identified and agreed upon the key functions, we again try to identify the most important function for further study with a level 2 linkage analysis.

That then leads to a level 3 analysis, and so on, until we have reached a sufficient level of detail. These lower level linkage analyses should focus on new and enhanced applications. The factors analyzed in the internal linkage analysis should address such things as efficiency, effectiveness, and quality of service. But the test that we must at all times

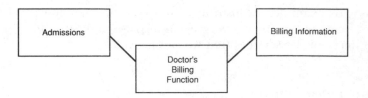

Action Plan

1. Put services into operation before the competition that will enhance the doctor-patient relationship.

2. Create services that will lock in the doctor and satisfy so many needs that it will become too difficult for the doctor to switch to some other hospital.

3. Provide billing and admissions data to the doctor through a personal computer in the doctor's office as well as a terminal at the hospital.

4. Provide billing information to third parties in the format they require.

5. Provide office accounting functions for the doctor that run on the same personal computer that is used to provide admissions data.

Exposures

1. Other hospitals may take steps to enhance the billing and admissions functions before we do and attract some of our doctors.

2. Companies in the converging industries might begin to compete with us by supplying services that we now supply.

Future Enhancements

1. Provide a larger envelope that includes ancillary products and services that the doctor needs.

2. Add new functions to old services that will significantly increase the value of those services to the doctor.

3. Identify additional new services that the doctor will find attractive.

4. Tie the doctor's personal computer into the networks of supplies companies to allow the doctor to order supplies and other products needed to run the office.

5. Provide electronic mail and other types of communication services to tie the doctor more closely to the hospital.

6. Provide access to hospital medical records.

7. Automate and digitize doctor's records and make them available anywhere a personal computer is available using suitable networks.

8. Implement a prescription and treatment conflict database.

9. Implement a diagnosis support expert system.

10. Provide medical treatment updates and other enhanced doctor networking and consulting services.

Figure A-7. Health care industry level 3 external linkage analysis: doctor's billing function.

**Which Internal Functions Are Most Important in
Helping the Hospital Achieve Strategic Advantage?**

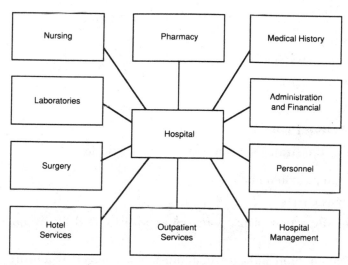

Figure A-8. Health care industry level 1 internal linkage analysis: hospital.

apply to each factor is whether that factor will lead to substantial and sustainable strategic advantage. The following are a few examples of internal systems that we might identify as critical during the internal linkage analysis of the hospital:

- A patient information database that includes medical history, results of laboratory tests, and financial information
- A network that allows all departments in the hospital to communicate with one another quickly and easily
- A system that provides the capability for transmitting medical images and other types of information from one place to another
- A system for scheduling laboratory tests and other types of patient services

Summarizing the Results

The linkage analysis of the hospital ends by documenting the vision and the strategic action plan following the guidelines discussed in Chapter 10.

The Vision

The documentation of the vision should include charts and other documentation that shows:

1. Waves of innovation
2. Experience curve strategies
3. The extended enterprise

The Strategic Action Plan

Documentation of the strategic action plan should include:

1. An overall strategy statement
2. Linkage analysis charts
3. Summaries of the action plans, potential exposures, and future enhancements
4. Critical implementation linkages that must be managed to ensure success
5. Assignments of managers or work groups to each item in the action plan

Electronic Channel Support Systems

The documentation that results from the linkage analysis planning session should include information about the channel flows of the hospital and potential electronic channel support systems that will be required to achieve strategic advantage in the extended enterprise environment. The linkage charts that document the final level of detail must include information about how channel flows can be improved in order to improve products and services. It is important to identify the constriction points that exist today in the channel flows because these often point to new opportunities for achieving strategic advantage.

Conclusion

The health care industry is undergoing a significant degree of technological change and industry restructuring. The rate of change is accelerating because of government involvement, increasing costs, skill shortages, medical advancements, the implications of illegal drugs, the AIDS problem, and the convergence of other industries into the health arena. With the addition of hotel chains to the health care industry, we will begin to see a rapid evolution of the structure and membership of the hospital's and the doctor's extended enterprises. To succeed, a hospital will have to be able to effectively harness the thinking skills of its staff in order to address internal hospital systems and also the evolving extended enterprise. For some this will represent a new challenge to the hospital's management and leadership. However, the challenge must be met because our health care system, like education, is key to our future.

Linkage Analysis: Education

Introduction

Appendix B shows how the techniques of linkage analysis planning have been applied to areas in which the environment has traditionally been thought to be very different from the business environment. Here, we see how linkage analysis planning has been applied to the creation and operation of community-based partnerships between business and education and to life planning by high school seniors. We attempt to show how in the future we will be able to extend electronic channel support systems into businesses, classrooms, and the home in order to substantially improve the educational process for all our citizens.

The children that we are educating today will become the labor force of tomorrow; they will create a United States that many of us will not see. These children are going to carry a message into the future. What will the message be? It is the opinion of the authors that the need to formulate a new vision for our educational system is one of the paramount challenges facing the United States today. The impact on the United States of changing demographics dictates that we must more effectively leverage our knowledge resources. As stated by Richard J. Haayen, retired chairman of the board, Allstate Insurance: "[M]aybe most important is the realization that we can give the next generation no better gift than the greatest possible chance to succeed."[1]

Between now and the year 2000, the population, and therefore the work force, will increase in number more slowly than at any time since the Depression years—less than half as fast, for instance, as during the 1950s. Contrast that projection with a conservative estimate of an average 2.9 percent annual growth in the GNP over the same period, and it is apparent that the labor shortage could have grave consequences for the American economy. The result will be social changes as fundamental as the changes that occurred as we shifted from farms to factories. These fundamental changes will require that tomorrow's workers be equipped with new knowledge, new skills, and new attitudes. The danger is that our educational system will continue to play catch up and will not formulate a vision based on where our economy will be in 10 or 15 years.

The high school class of 2000, which started school a few years ago, will encounter an extremely demanding job market when it graduates. Marvin J. Cetron, author of *Schools of the Future*, says:

> Less than 6 percent of workers will find a place on the assembly lines that once gave high school graduates a good income; the rest will have been replaced by robots. Instead, service jobs will form nearly 90 percent of the economy. A decade ago, about 77 percent of jobs involved at least some time spent in generating, processing, retrieving, or distributing information. By the year 2000 that figure will be 95 percent, and that information processing will be heavily computerized.[2]

Our new knowledge workers will need more than a passing familiarity with information processing technology. Gone are the days when employees were expected to perform only routine tasks. In service industries today, workers are being asked to make complex, on-the-spot judgments regarding customer satisfaction. In manufacturing, they are being asked to contribute ideas through quality circles and other participatory programs. The result is a great and growing need for workers who can think creatively and respond intelligently to changing situations—people who can spot opportunities and make the right choices. Those will be the qualities most prized in the work force of the future. Yet, in many ways today's schools are not oriented toward developing those attributes.

It is clear that what we need is an educational vision for the *Information* Age that is as powerful as the vision Adam Smith developed for the *Industrial* Age and the vision Thomas Jefferson had for *government*:

Our vision of the *education* system must coincide with our vision of the *economic* system and with our vision of *democracy*.

Analyzing Waves of Innovation

We saw in Chapter 2 that innovation and the technology that we employ tend to evolve in a series of successive waves, with each wave building on its predecessor. Our analysis of education in the United States begins by examining the waves of innovation that characterize our educational system.

First Wave: Little Red Schoolhouse

Figure B-1 shows the waves through which most of our schools have already passed with respect to our knowledge delivery systems. Education in the United States began in the first wave when the country was characterized as an agricultural-based economy. The knowledge delivery systems of the time typically consisted of the "little red schoolhouse" with students of all grade levels occupying the same classroom.

Second Wave: Neighborhood Schools

Our educational system crossed over to the second wave as the United States entered the era of the industrial revolution, and we began the move from the farm to the city. At this time, many of the little red school houses were replaced by larger neighborhood schools as a

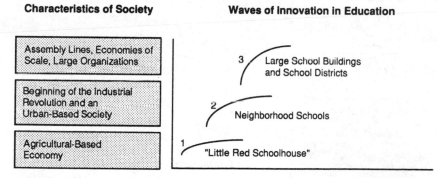

Figure B-1. Waves of innovation in education have tended to progress in parallel with changes in the characteristics of our society.

greater percentage of Americans began to live in an urban environment.

Third Wave: Large Buildings and Districts

We entered the third wave of our knowledge distribution systems—the wave most school systems are on at the present time—as our industrial economy matured and became characterized by mass production, economies of scale, and large organizational structures. In our urban environments, the relatively small neighborhood schools gave way to large school buildings and large school districts, especially in our secondary schools.

Fourth Wave: Restructuring of Education

Now that our economy is making the transition from an industrial society to one that is knowledge based, our schools must undergo a parallel restructuring. The fourth and fifth waves of innovation that we can project for our knowledge distribution system are shown in Figure B-2. The fourth wave is necessary now that our economy is making the tran-

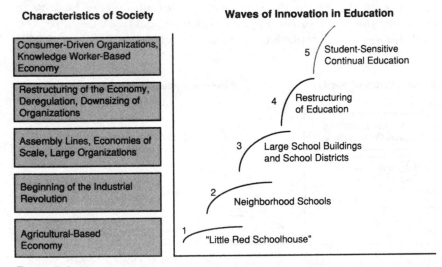

Figure B-2. New waves of innovation in education must keep pace with the changes that are occurring in our society.

sition from an industrial economy to a knowledge-based economy. Our business and government organizations are involved in a massive restructuring, in which organizations are downsizing, streamlining, and forming strategic alliances. The fourth wave in our knowledge distribution systems should parallel this restructuring and focus on increasing the effectiveness of the teacher and the student. We must recognize that the student is also a knowledge worker. As we will see later in this appendix, strategic alliances are as important to our school systems as they are to any other of society's institutions.

Fifth Wave: Student-Sensitive Continual Education

With the advances of technology that are occurring in today's environment, it is desirable that the fourth wave be a short-lived transitional wave. A fifth wave is quickly coming, in which we will be able to use affordable computer and communication technology to create a highly individualized, student-sensitive educational system in which citizens will be able to develop their knowledge and skills through continual education. Such a system will be required to meet the needs of the knowledge-worker-based society into which we are quickly evolving.

Identifying Experience Curves

An analysis of the waves of innovation can help to show us how our school systems are changing and how they should begin to evolve in the future. Chapter 3 showed that the next step in formulating a vision is to focus on experience curves. Figure B-3 shows the experience curves that characterize our educational systems today and some new experience curves that may predominate in the future. Some innovative school systems are beginning to exploit the personal computer experience curve and are achieving good results. However, much learning is still required to exploit the computer technology that is available and affordable. Many new experience curves will be built from our experience with personal computers as we begin to use advanced computer and communication technology to create highly individualized, highly

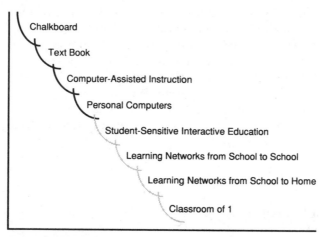

Figure B-3. Experience curves in the education.

interactive, and highly visual knowledge acquisition systems. The experience curves that predominate in the computer and communications industry must begin to play a much more important role in restructuring our educational system in order to provide for continual education in the school, the home, and the workplace. The structural enhancements that we need to apply to our educational system are the same ones that we have already discussed regarding achieving substantial and sustainable strategic advantage in the service sector of our economy.

Documenting Power Relationships

Chapter 4 discussed ways in which changes in industry power relationships are causing organizations to reassess their relationships with the strategic forces in the environment. In order to formulate a new vision of U.S. education, we must take into account a number of powerful strategic forces. These include advances in technology, levels of available funding, public support, and collaborative arrangements between schools and other institutions within the community, including business. In light of the waves of innovation through which our educational system is passing and the experience curves that characterize our knowledge distribution systems, we can identify the strategic forces that are having the greatest impact on our school systems. Some of these are shown in Figure B-4.

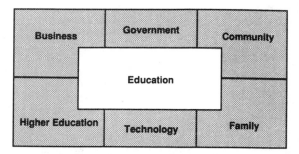

Figure B-4. Changing power relationships in education.

Visualizing the Extended School System

As described in Chapter 5, business has traditionally viewed the enterprise using the classical management triangle; it is possible to view our existing school systems using this same paradigm. The classical view of the school system shows the superintendent at the top, principals and administrators in the middle, and teachers and support staff at the bottom, as shown in Figure B-5. However, just as this classical view of *business* no longer applies in today's environment, this classical view of the *school system* is also outmoded. The internal organizational structures are often no longer viewed as just hierarchical. What is even more important, the new economic realities demand that school systems, as well as our other institutions, define themselves in the context of an *extended enterprise*, as shown in Figure B-6.

An important part of strategic thinking as it applies to our educational system is to form in our minds a new view of the school system. The view should consider the linkages that exist with important organizations that have traditionally been regarded as external to the educa-

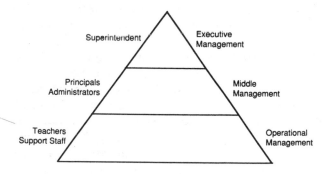

Figure B-5. Classical view of the school system.

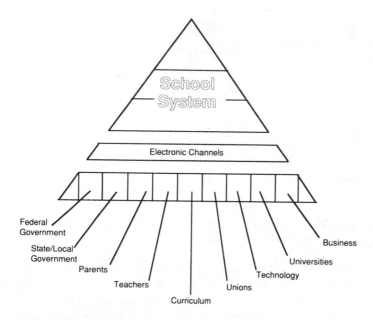

Figure B-6. Extended enterprise view of the school system—the extended school system.

tional system. In formulating a strategic vision, members of the community must bring together the environmental information, expectations, and joint goals and then use these to formulate a shared vision. Perceiving the school system as an extended enterprise will require a clear understanding of both internal and external linkages among all elements of the extended school system. Long-term success for our education system will be determined by how well community partnerships can identify the critical elements and how well they are able to collectively manage and use them.

The current knowledge distribution system in the United States is characterized by significant structural rigidity that is consistent with its historical paradigms. Today's education process is linear and sequential, with students proceeding in an orderly fashion from grade to grade. It operates with yesterday's requirements and solutions and, like large business and government organizations, tends to resist change. The diminishing competitiveness of education, just like that within the business community, has made many business leaders take an active interest in the competitiveness of their main supplier—America's education system is the main supplier of our knowledge workers. The shortcomings of our education system have made many of our businesses take an aggressive role, out of survival; some estimates show that business may annually spend over $100 billion providing basic remedial education and training.

A key message in Chapter 4 is that *strategic alliances and partnerships* will be of increasing importance in the rapidly changing business environment. Alliances and partnerships will be required to enhance the effectiveness of our educational system as well—partnerships that share ideas, human and financial resources, understanding, and responsibility. These partnerships must formulate a shared vision that combines the perspective of educators, business leaders, government officials, community groups, and parents. Many groups have major roles to play in education, including government, education itself, business, and the community.

The Role of Government

Government has the role of providing the necessary services and infrastructure to promote our economy's growth and to increase our standard of living. Government can play a major role in enhancing the effectiveness of our schools by providing an environment and infrastructure that will:

- Provide the necessary legislation and funding
- Provide insights regarding the economic situation and a give us a broad view of educational needs
- Enable and encourage community partnerships by reducing the need for centralized directives and eliminating excessive and redundant administrative requirements

The Role of Education

Education has the responsibility for providing society with the knowledge resource that society requires—the citizens that become the actual producers. Education can play a major role in formulating a vision for our education system by:

- Seeking and promoting a spirit of partnership in the community
- Viewing the educational environment in the context of an extended enterprise
- Playing an active role in sharing resources, skills, and facilities with other partners in the community
- Viewing the student, business, government, and the community as a whole as its customers

The Role of Business

Business has the responsibility for using the infrastructure, knowledge resources, and physical resources to create economic wealth to fund our society. Business can play important roles in the restructuring of our educational system by:

- Determining future global, economic, and technology direction
- Identifying changing business and social needs
- Providing methodologies, techniques, and skills for planning and analysis
- Defining changes in student requirements and skill needs associated with the shift to knowledge workers in our knowledge-based society
- Viewing education as a key supplier

The Role of the Community

Individual members of the community must realize that it is our participation in government, education, and business and our commitment to the community that make our country work. Community groups can play a major role by:

- Encouraging community leaders to be involved
- Fostering an environment of community partnership and pride
- Assuming responsibilities and duties relating to family and community functions

Once the vision has been formulated, the partnership must effectively communicate that vision to all members of the community and create a strategic action plan to empower all the relevant groups to implement the vision. The partners must not disappear after the concept stage; they must stay and make sure that the work gets done. To succeed in this environment, priorities must be set at the national, state, and local levels. Each community will have to form its own partnership with the explicit mission of building the vision and developing the strategic action plan that will meet its own needs. This is not a one-time event but rather a long and continuous journey.

Electronic Channel Support Systems

Communication theory studies suggest that a teacher may be able to effectively communicate and share knowledge with only one-third of his or her students at any given time, leaving the other two-thirds to either struggle or be bored. One reason for this is that the two-thirds of the class did not have appropriate examples presented to them. They may come from the other side of the elephant and view the teacher's concepts slightly differently. Other studies of different classroom environments around the country have shown that as little as 7 minutes out of a 55-minute classroom period is actually spent teaching. A great deal of time is spent in the classroom performing non-value-added *administrative* functions instead of value-added *teaching* tasks. We need to ask ourselves what new tools can we provide to the teaching community to enhance their effectiveness?

Chapter 6 showed that the major tools that organizations have to implement and exploit the extended enterprise are electronic channel support systems. The beginnings of the electronic channel support systems that will someday revolutionize our educational system can already be seen in many of the forward-looking school systems in our country. Our vision of education in the United States is to use technology to provide individual students with student-sensitive access to knowledge. Students will use powerful workstations both at home and in the school. Individual school computers will then be connected with community, state, and national computer networks. These networks will allow computers and workstations owned by businesses in the community and by individuals in the home to connect to them for the purposes of two-way communication and information sharing. Such networks will be of great value in enhancing the effectiveness of our educational system and will allow the various partnerships between the classroom, the home, government, and business to operate effectively. Such electronic channel support systems will be extremely important to the future of education in America. They could be deployed relatively quickly if the necessary funds and expertise were made available.

The challenge is to drop the old baggage as quickly as possible and to use appropriate technology in our education system. The use of sophisticated electronic channel support systems to support the extended school system will permit us to completely redefine the term *student*. The United States can no longer afford to limit itself to a K-12 through higher education mentality. We must begin to include the entire labor force in a continual learning process so that businesses and individual workers will also benefit from the extended school system that sophisticated computer- and communication-based educational tools will help to create. Such workstations and networks are not just a dream. The technology is available now. Electronic channel support systems can and will increase the number of teaching moments that each student experiences. Electronic channel support systems will allow us to provide

student-sensitive, interactive education, both inside and outside the classroom. We will someday use this technology in our schools; the only question
is when. Will our educational system wait until the Japanese, the French, or
the Germans show us the benefits of such advanced technology?

> **"The real classroom is not four walls;
> it is the mind of the student."**

The Information Component
of Education

The chapters in Part 2 discussed ways of converting a vision into effective strategies. One of the new mindsets that is important for success in
the business environment is to recognize the importance of the information component of products and services and to wrap those products
and services in new envelopes. This mindset can be of equal value in
improving the quality of our educational system. We might characterize
the physical component of the education "product" as the concepts or
bits of knowledge that a teacher wishes to communicate or share with
his or her students. We can then characterize the information component of teaching as all those tools, examples, and techniques that the
teacher uses to communicate each concept. (See Figure B-7.)

The teacher uses the information components of teaching to create an envelope for each concept being taught with different examples and messages
for each student. This concept is no different from how advertisers market
products. They develop different selling and marketing messages for each
group of buyers. Expert teachers differentiate themselves from their peers
by creating unique envelopes for the concepts they teach. If we reflect back
on the teachers we have had, those who stand out in our memories are those
who were able to reach out to us and effectively "market their product." We
need to implement new experience curves that will enhance the teacher's "information component." This subtle shift to concentrate on both the "product" and the "information component" of education changes the role of the
teacher. A teacher should no longer only instruct the student but must market and persuade the student in the most effective manner. Technology can
be effectively used to enhance both the "product" and the "information component."

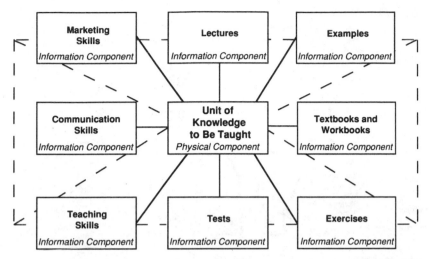

Figure B-7. The information component of teaching can be characterized as all those tools and techniques that a teacher uses to communicate a concept.

External and Internal Linkage Analyses

The chapters in Part 3 discussed techniques that can be used to convert a vision into reality through linkage analysis planning. We can apply these same strategic planning techniques to our education system in order to redefine the role that the school systems will play in the community. In order to effectively conduct strategic planning for a school system, a group should be assembled that includes members from all the important segments that we identified previously—education, business, the community, and government. This group can then use the techniques of linkage analysis planning to determine what are those elements that are most important to the success of the school system and to develop a strategic action plan for implementing the vision that the group formulates. Both external and internal analyses are important. In an external analysis, we define the school system's role in the community and determine the important linkages that exist with external organizations. In an internal analyses, we try to understand the critical linkages that exist within the school system itself. As we discussed in Chapter 10, it is generally most effective to conduct an external analysis of the school system before conducting the internal analysis.

Figure B-8. The view from outside the schoolhouse.

Place yourself in the shoes of a community leader as we walk through a linkage analysis planning session for a school system. It is important to realize that each of the individuals in the group tends to have a different view of the elephant. (See Figure B-8.)

Conducting an External Linkage Analysis

In analyzing the external view of the school system, the group should include school boards, individual schools, higher education, unions, business, parents, taxpayers, community groups, and state, local, and federal government. Because of these differing perspectives, it is essential for these groups to visualize the school system in a similar manner. The external linkage session can help us determine how each group can assist education in achieving necessary benefits and in focusing all members to think and act strategically.

Level 1: Educational Needs of the Community

In developing a model of the school system that takes into account the school system's extended enterprise, we begin by identifying and understanding the key educational needs of the community. Only then can we perform a more detailed analysis. We write at the top of the chart the question we are trying to answer and then place the "educational needs of the community" in a box in the center. Members of the group will express opinions concerning the educational needs of the community, and discussions will result. We then begin placing around the central box all those elements that we agree are important in answering the question at the top. With the key leaders in the community being catalysts for this process, we might draw a chart similar to Figure B-9. The objective of drawing this chart is to provide a common framework so that community leaders can visualize the key linkages that are important

What External Factors in the Extended School System Will Have the Most Impact on the Educational Needs of the Community?

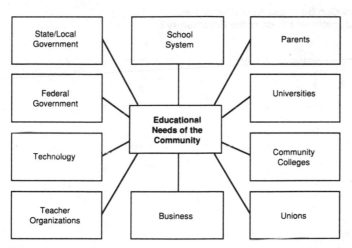

Figure B-9. Level 1 external linkage chart: educational needs of the community.

when viewing the extended school system today and also 5 to 7 years in the future.

Level 2: Business

We then attempt to gain a consensus on what is the most important element on the chart in meeting the educational needs of the community. We then further analyze that element. For example, if we achieve a consensus that the cooperation of business is the most important factor, we start a new chart with "business" in the center. We again write at the top the specific question that we are trying to answer about business. We then conduct a detailed analysis of the "business" element of the extended school system using the same techniques as for the level 1 chart. At this point, we identify business requirements, available resources to share, responsibilities, and expectations. We discuss the same issues from the school system's side and try to discover the school system's requirements, resources, responsibilities, needs, and expectations. Figure B-10 shows a chart that might result from such an analysis.

Level 3: Business Partnerships

Once we have identified the major linkages between business and education, we again must decide which are the most important to pursue. We can then conduct a level 3 analysis of the most important element

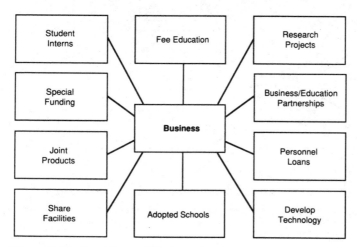

Figure B-10. Level 2 external linkage chart: business.

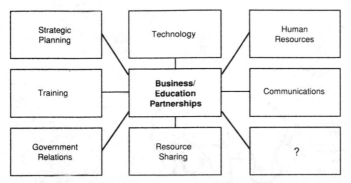

How Can Business/Education Partnerships Best Help to Meet the Educational Needs of the Community?

Figure B-11. Level 3 external linkage chart: business/education partnerships.

on the level 2 chart. In our example, we have selected "business partnerships." The objective of the planning session is now to identify the specific ways in which the business/education partnership can raise the level of effectiveness of the extended school system. The real challenge is to ensure that the linkages we have identified will provide substantial and sustainable benefits for all. A possible level 3 chart for the "education/business partnership" element is shown in Figure B-11. We can continue the analysis to whatever level of detail we feel appropriate, sometimes going to level 4 or 5. At the final level, we shift our focus to documenting action plans, identifying exposures, and outlining additional follow-up activities, as discussed in Chapter 10.

Conducting an Internal Linkage Analysis

After the external linkage analysis has been completed, each involved group should have the necessary perspective to analyze its own organization from an internal perspective. During the internal analysis, each group attempts to identify the key elements of its own extended enterprise. As an example of an internal linkage analysis, we will use the school system itself, including teachers, students, faculties, and so on.

The elephant analogy again comes to mind with respect to an internal view of the school system. (See Figure B-12.) Principals, teachers, administrators, and students all have a different view of the school system. The challenge is to create a shared vision, through which the various

Figure B-12. The view from inside the schoolhouse.

members can begin to view the school system in a similar manner. The first step is to identify the key functions that we feel are critical to the school system. The chart will be different for each school system, but a possible one is shown in Figure B-13. Once we reach consensus on the level 1 chart, we step back and look 5 to 7 years out and see if any of the linkages shown in the chart are likely to change or whether new ones will be added. We must thoroughly explore the implications of the changes that will be occurring and must determine what the impact will be on the rest of the school system. Changing technologies, demographics, business conditions, global competition, and government regulations will tend to cause changes in priorities. As with the external linkage analysis, we can conduct level 2, level 3, and even more detailed analyses as appropriate.

Summarizing the Results

The final phase of the linkage analysis planning session is to document the results. This documentation should include the following elements:

Which Internal Functions Are Most Important to the Extended School System in Meeting the Educational Needs of the Community?

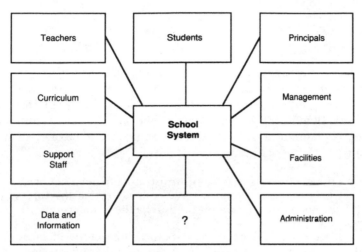

Figure B-13. Level 1 internal linkage chart: school system.

- *Documentation of the vision.* This should include documentation of the waves of innovation, experience curves, and our view of the extended school system.

- *Strategic action plan.* Documentation of the strategic action plan must include an overall strategy statement, linkage charts for both the external and internal linkage analyses, summaries of the action plans, potential exposures, and future enhancements listed on the lowest-level linkage charts, documentation of the critical implementation linkages that must be managed to ensure success, and assignments of individual managers and/or work groups to each action item in the strategic action plan.

- *Electronic channel support systems.* Documentation of potential electronic channels allows us to identify potential electronic channel support systems that will be required to effectively implement the vision.

A key element of the strategic action plan is to make assignments for detailed studies. Two comments are appropriate for this phase of the process. The first is that you should not start too many projects; the extended school system may not be capable of managing or implementing them because of limitations of resources and time. Second, community leaders must stay actively involved through the implementation stages. Leaving the process before the work is done will doom the plan.

Comments on Linkage Analysis Planning

One example of how linkage analysis planning has been successfully used in performing strategic planning for school systems is provided by Dr. Jean McGrew, superintendent of Glenbrook High School District 255 in northern Illinois. McGrew made the following comments about a linkage analysis planning session conducted at a conference of K-12 superintendents:

> This was an initial effort for school administrators to get a better insight as to what our goals should be. We concluded that the forces that supported and impeded schools tend to be the same groups, depending on the issue.
>
> It complicates the ability of schools to form long-term alliances. The next step was pinpointing the economic and other factors, such as financing, that affect a school's operation. Other issues, such as an area's unemployment rates, admission requirements for local colleges, and business requirements were considered. After identifying about 20 problem areas, the school administrators developed prioritized action plans to deal with these problems, taking into consideration the community "supporters" and inhibitors that had been identified earlier.
>
> Linkage Analysis means recognizing that expanded communication (of information) can also be used as a tool to "grow" an organization, improve its relationships, and make it more effective over the long run. One of the assumptions of linkage analysis is the sharing of information. This allows us to start our problem solving on a common set of assumptions based on shared knowledge. To some at the AASA session, it was an eye-opening exercise, allowing them to verbalize long-held intuitive concerns. To others, it was just an interesting way of looking at a complicated problem. But I think it heightened everybody's view of the importance of preparing for the future.[3]

Formulating and Sustaining Community Partnerships

When formulating community-based education partnerships, whether it be at the state or the local level, the involved parties must consider, and effectively answer, the following questions:

1. Is the partnership perceived by the group as a one-time event or as a continuous journey?

2. How can the key community leaders continue to stay involved and responsible for the vision, the strategy, and their effective implementation?

3. How can the partnership ensure that its investment of time, resources, people, and money lead to achieving substantial and sustainable advantage?

4. How can the partnership remain flexible and responsive and use time as an ally?

5. How can the partnership encourage the support of existing organizations and not be perceived as duplicating, threatening, or controlling them?

6. Who is going to build and manage the comprehensive plan for actualizing the vision of the partnership?

7. How can the partnership achieve timely funding and assignment of resources to projects without getting entwined in the normally slow-moving government funding process?

8. How can the partnership measure the impact of its investment and continue to have a major say in where resources are invested?

9. What other challenges could the partnership tackle, such as drugs, economic development, and adult literacy?

10. If the partnership is at the state level, how does it assist local communities in forming their own partnerships?

The Community Holding Company

One approach that is being used by a number of communities throughout the country to address the above issues is to establish nonprofit corporations, or *community holding companies*, to administer partnerships on either the state or local level. Such holding companies have established *project offices* for the purposes of administering partnerships between the school, business, government, and the community. Many of these holding companies have been privately funded. In such organizations, key business, government, school-system, and community leaders have cooperated in forming organizations of great flexibility. In a typical holding company, the day-to-day, core project office operations staff is privately funded or supported by volunteers from the community. Each specific project identified for implementation is then funded individually, with funding coming from all available sources, including government, education, business, and existing school system operating budgets. The holding company is not meant to compete with existing organizations but rather to work with them. It also may serve as a funnel through which the contributions of business and other organizations can be coordinated using a comprehensive plan.

> **The holding company provides the structure that enables the community to implement the project office process to achieve a community shared vision.**

Figure B-14 illustrates a possible structure for the community holding company. The following are descriptions of each level in the pyramid:

- *Advisory committee.* At the top level is an advisory committee that is composed of leaders from all parts of the community. It is the job of this committee, in collaboration with the operating committee, to obtain and provide funding, to define the vision and communicate it throughout the community, and to promote buy-in and ownership of the vision.

- *Operating committee.* The operating committee is charged with developing strategies, allocating resources, and measuring performance and results. It is their job to ensure that the investments that the hold

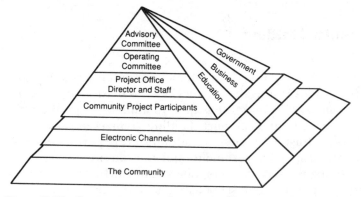

Figure B-14. Community partnership project office organization.

ing company makes lead to substantial and sustainable advantage for the partnership. The operating committee should be made up of leaders from education, government, business, the community, and professional organizations.

- *The project office.* The project office is responsible for the day-to-day operation of the holding company. The key objectives of the project office are to develop comprehensive plans within assigned areas and to manage all aspects of specific projects, including definition, estimating, assigning of resources, implementation, and measurement. The project office staff maintains program and project databases for the purposes of sharing and distributing project results. The project office also works with various education, government, business, and community groups to implement projects and to help shape project proposals for consideration by the operating committee.

- *Community members.* Various individuals, groups, and professional organizations in the community serve as resources that the project office staff calls upon to implement the projects that it is charged with implementing. These community members also serve as advisers to all three of the above groups. To a very great extent, the success or failure of the project office approach depends heavily on the participation and active support of the community.

As community leaders become familiar with the strategic planning process and better understand the changes that are occurring, they will realize that in addition to prioritizing the key linkages that are important to the community, they must also focus attention on managing the links between the various elements on the linkage charts. For example, from the school system's perspective, a change in business requirements may alter the curriculum, which will have an impact on students, teachers, information requirements, and, possibly, facilities and administrative systems. A shift in student enrollment up or down could have a serious impact on budgets, facilities, and teachers. Understanding near-term changes and predicting long-term changes to the external and internal linkage charts will enable community organizations to become proactive. Management of the links will become as important as picking the right functions. The very survival of many communities will be determined by their ability to manage the links both internally and externally on a community basis. The interdependencies of community organizations will only increase in the future. The community holding company can become the catalyst to start the formation of a collaborative vision among the community groups.

Life Planning

Another innovative application of linkage analysis planning has been documented by Superintendent Milton C. Roeder of Kim School District, Kim, Colorado. Superintendent Roeder had nine high school seniors define in their own terms the key linkages that are required to become successful adults. One of the charts that resulted from this analysis is reproduced in Figure B-15. It became clear in this case that it was not as useful in this context to ask the question: "Which box is most important." Indeed, we might ask: "Which boxes are not important?" The answer is obviously that all the boxes, and many more, are critical to the development of a student into a well-rounded adult and citizen of the community.

What is interesting about this student's chart is that it leads to a vision of what is sometimes called the "nuclear family" or the "nuclear community." With today's demographics, and the increasingly common household in which both spouses work outside the home, or in which there is only one parent, we might ask how we can achieve the required results? We feel that the answer lies in each individual in the community rethinking his or her role as a member of an *extended family*. It is clear today that in many cases, parents and the educational system alone cannot do all that is required and that the rest of the community, including

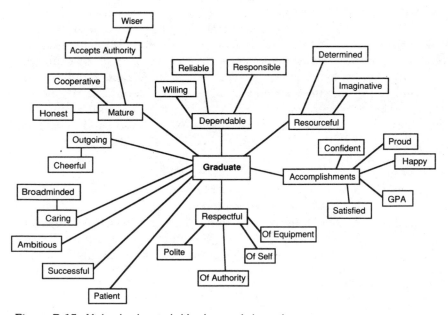

Figure B-15. High school senior's life planning linkage chart.

our senior citizens, must play a more active and collaborative role in growing the next generation of citizens.

Conclusion

Community-based strategic planning can provide a vehicle through which education, business, government, and the community can cooperate to build a framework for common understanding and sharing of goals. The planning process should begin with a conceptualization of both the needs and the vision of the community. This includes understanding the key linkages within the school system itself as well as understanding the key linkages between organizations in the extended school system. To ensure success, leaders must focus on the management of these linkages. This must be a formal process initiated by leaders of the partnership. The overall goal must always be:

To raise the overall level of effectiveness of the community.

Strategic planning for the extended school system should become a circular process, as shown in Figure B-16. Education must continue to iden-

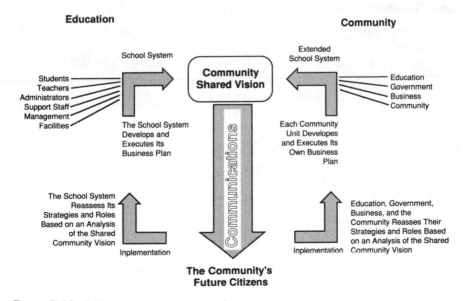

Figure B-16. Achieving a community shared vision.

Figure B-17. Managing the linkages—creating the shared vision to the future. (*From Labor Force 2000.*)

tify and develop the vision of the school system and empower its members, including teachers, students, administrators, and support personnel, to understand and implement the vision. To form a community shared vision, education and its partners in the community, including government, community organizations, and business, must work together in a spirit of community commitment to formulate, communicate, and implement the shared vision.

References

1. *Labor Force 2000, Corporate America Responds.* Allstate Forum on Public Issues, 1989.
2. Marvin J. Cetron. *Schools of the Future.* New York: McGraw Hill, 1985.
3. Dr. Jean McGrew. "The Future and America's Schools." American Association of School Administrators (AASA) seminar.

Index